The Charlotte Cookbook

30th Anniversary Edition

Published by
The Junior League of Charlotte, Inc.
1999

The Junior League of Charlotte serves up a hearty selection of delicious recipes and festive menus in this 30th anniversary edition of The Charlotte Cookbook. Entertaining is made easy using these classic recipes that are sure to delight your family and friends. From cozy family suppers to elaborate dinner parties, we hope this cookbook will inspire you to fill your table and treat your palate with flavorful new creations.

From those cooks who submitted their "personal favorites" to the many who have purchased this collection of recipes, all have contributed to the numerous worthwhile community projects initiated and supported by the Junior League. Founded in Charlotte nearly 75 years ago, this organization of women has provided countless volunteer hours and financial support. As The Charlotte Cookbook celebrates its culinary history, we also celebrate our mission to make a difference by reaching out to others.

Over 800 recipes have been tested and edited for this book. The cookbook committee has tried every recipe and in some cases slight variations have been made.

In 1942 the Junior League of Charlotte published its first cookbook "Old North State Cookbook", and in 1964 its second "Cooking Mother's Goose". The Committee has borrowed from both these books the recipes they considered most outstanding. Recipes from "Cooking Mother's Goose" are marked with an asterisk *; those from "Old North State Cookbook" are so designated.

Charlotte, The Queen City, is the namesake of the Queen Charlotte of England, the wife of King George III. Named in 1768, the city is the seat of Mecklenburg County, so-called in honor of Queen Charlotte's birthplace, Mecklenburg Strelitz, Germany.

ISBN #0-9613214-0-7

JUNIOR LEAGUE OF CHARLOTTE, INC.
CHARLOTTE, NORTH CAROLINA
COPYRIGHT 1969

THIRD EDITION
FIRST PRINTING, 1969, 7,000 COPIES
SECOND PRINTING, 1970, 7,000 COPIES
THIRD PRINTING, 1971, 7,000 COPIES
FOURTH PRINTING, 1972, 10,000 COPIES
FIFTH PRINTING, 1974, 10,000 COPIES
SIXTH PRINTING, 1976, 10,000 COPIES
SEVENTH PRINTING, 1977, 10,000 COPIES
EIGHTH PRINTING, 1979, 10,000 COPIES
NINTH PRINTING, 1981, 10,000 COPIES
TENTH PRINTING, 1984, 10,000 COPIES
ELEVENTH PRINTING, 1999, 10,000 COPIES

**Printed in The United States of America
by Jostens Printing Company
Winston-Salem, North Carolina**

Table of Contents

Foreword

BY CATHERINE BATES

Drawings

BY EDWARD H. SPRINGS, A.I.D.

Courtesy of

Edward H. Springs Interiors, Inc.

1236 East Morehead

Charlotte, N. C.

The Junior League of Charlotte, Inc.

1332 Maryland Avenue

Homes and Menus

* Indicates Recipe Included

Brunch For Houseguests

Home of Mr. and Mrs. William Erwin Jones

Grapefruit Supreme*
Broiled Squab a' la Country Ham
Sautéed Fresh Sherried Mushrooms
Hot Buttered Grits
Crab and Tomato Deluxe*
Cheese Biscuits
"Cold Duck" in Chilled Champagne Glasses
Hot Coffee

Summer Luncheon On The Terrace

Home of Mr. and Mrs. Dennis Myers

Cheese Souffle*
Grapefruit and Avocado Salad*
with
Celery Seed Dressing*
Melba Toast
Brownie Cup Cakes*
Iced Coffee

Informal Luncheon

Home of Mr. and Mrs. McAlister Carson

Creamed Chicken in Patty Shells*
Spinach Souffle*
Molded Individual Fruit Salads with Sweet Salad Dressing*
Hot Rolls
Pound Cake or Cookies*
Coffee or Tea

Bridge Luncheon

Home of Mr. and Mrs. Thomas Cummings

Seafood Casserole*
Florida Garden Salad with Whipped Cream Dressing*
Hot Popovers — Butter
Sherry Pie*
Iced Tea with Mint

Buffet Supper For 12

Home of Mr. and Mrs. John J. Hanes

Chicken Country Captain*
Steamed Rice with Parsley
Fresh Asparagus or French Green Beans
Lettuce-Endive-Artichoke Salad with Piquante Dressing*
Croissants
Miniature Lemon Chess Tarts*
Demi-Tasse

Dessert Shower

Home of Mr. and Mrs. Samuel R. Sloan

Spring Flower Dessert*
Fresh Fruit dipped in Confectioners Sugar
Mints   Nuts
Tropical Punch*

Refreshments After A Meeting

Home of Mr. and Mrs. Charles L. Wickham, Jr.

Cheese Crisps*
Chocolate Crispies*   "Rock" Cookies*
Salted Pecans
Russian Tea*

Afternoon Tea

at

Springfield

Home of Mr. and Mrs. Eli B. Springs

Chicken and Almond Filling in Puff Shells*

Cheese and Chutney Sandwiches*

Marguerites*

Mints   Nuts

Russian Tea*

Cocktail Buffet

Home of Mr. and Mrs. H. F. Kincey

Pyramids of Fresh Ocean Shrimp   Asparagus Wrapped in Ham

Roast Strip of Beef   Chicken Salad Balls

Seafood Valencienne Rice   Avocado Pears

Chicken Liver Wrapped in Bacon

Pineapple and Chicken Liver with Bacon

Bouchees Varies Au Fromage   Ham Biscuits

Hot Bouchees Quiche Lorraine*

Party Bread of White, Whole Wheat, and Pumpernickel

White Seedless Grapes

Petits Fours

White Chocolate   Peppermint Mints

Coffee

Formal Dinner

Home of Mr. and Mrs. Roddey Dowd

Filets de Poisson a' la Bretonne*
Wine: Meursault — Pierre Matrot 1960

• • •

Sauté de Boeuf a' la Parisienne*
Wine: Pommard — Prince de Merode 1961
Green Beans   Wild Rice
Romaine Lettuce with Oil and Vinegar

• • •

Mousse a l'Orange*
Demi-Tasse

Stag Dinner

Home of Mr. and Mrs. O. D. Baxter

Shrimp and Crabmeat Cocktail

• • •

Doves in White Wine with Grapes*
Wild Rice Casserole*
Spinach Souffle*
Marinated Hearts of Palm Salad

• • •

Cherries Jubilee*
Coffee

Informal Dinner

Home of Mr. and Mrs. Rufus Safford

Crabmeat Sycamore*
Wine: Domestic White

• • •

Coq au Vin*
Wine: Red Burgundy
Mixed Green Salad   French Bread

• • •

Chilled Orange Souffle
Coffee

Anniversary Dinner

(For Small Group)
Home of Mr. and Mrs. John L. Dabbs III

Curried Chicken* in Rice Ring
Finely Chopped Hardboiled Eggs   Chutney   Crushed Peanuts
Fresh Fruit in Season—   Honeydew and Cantaloupe Balls
Green Grapes topped with Blueberries
or
Grapefruit Sections and Avocado
or
Grapefruit and Orange Sections,
Sliced Apples, Bananas, Grapes
French Salad Dressing*
Hard Rolls
* * *

Grasshopper Pie*
Iced Tea   Coffee

Midnight Buffet For New Year's Eve

Home of Mr. and Mrs. Amos Bumgardner, Jr.

Brisling Sardine Canapes*

Caviar Canapes*   Ham and Olive Canapes*

• • •

Goose and Wild Rice Casserole*

Baked Potato Mold with Peas and Onions*

Crabmeat Souffle*

Tomato Aspic Molds*   Crescent Rolls

Burgundy

• • •

Mother's Pots de Creme*

Demi-Tasse

Christmas Dinner

Home of Mr. and Mrs. James J. Harris

Oyster Stew*

• • •

Turkey with Pecan Dressing

Rice and Gravy

Carrot Souffle Ring with Stewed Corn*

Creamed Mushrooms with Chestnuts

Whole Cranberry Sauce

Hot Rolls

• • •

Maple Mousse with White Grapes*

Coffee

Luncheon Around The Pool

Home of Mr. and Mrs. John Scott Cramer

Gazpacho Soup*

Salmon Mousse*

Marinated Bean Salad*　　　　　Spiced Peaches

Poppy Seed Rolls

White Grapes Divine*

Iced Tea

Back Yard Picnic

Home of Mr. and Mrs. C. E. Williams, Jr.

Fried Chicken*
Corned Beef Potato Salad*
Quick Cornish Sandwiches*
Deviled Eggs*   Potato Chips
Pickles and Olives   Carrot and Celery Sticks

• • •

Easy Pound Cake*   Cornflake-Oatmeal Cookies*
Fresh Fruit in Season
Iced Tea Supreme*   Lemonade

(A good formula for a picnic: "Always include something hardy, something crisp, something toothsome, something to drink, and something to surprise!")

Informal Patio Party

Home of Mr. and Mrs. Donald O. Evans

Fresh Fruit Daiquiris
Cheese and Nut Mold

• • •

Marinated Beef Kababs*
Chilled Bean Salad*   Party Slaw
Hot Buttered Rolls

• • •

Creme de Menthe Parfaits
Clove Flavored Iced Tea

19

Debutante Supper Party

Home of Mr. and Mrs. Philip Small

Sliced Filet Mignon*

Fresh Corn Pudding*

Assorted Salad Greens

Thousand Island, Roquefort*, and French* Dressings

Thinly Sliced French Bread

Watermelon Filled with Fresh Fruits

(Strawberries, Grapes, Watermelon, Cantaloupe

and Honeydew Balls)

Fresh Peach Custard Mousse*

Iced Tea

Teen Age Party

Home of Mr. and Mrs. Alex R. Josephs

Spaghetti*
Tossed Salad with French Dressing*
Hot Buttered French Bread

• • •

Strawberry Parfaits and/or Blonde Brownies*
Iced Tea or Russian Tea*

• • •

Hot Buttered Popcorn

Birthday Party For Six-Year-Olds

Home of Mr. and Mrs. Hall M. Johnston, Jr.

"Casey Jones Celebrates"

Decorations: Red and white checkered tablecloth

Lunch in brown paper bags with child's name written on outside

Red bandanna napkins

Favors: Engineers' hats

Toy plastic trains with suckers tied to them

Menu: "Cattleburgers" (Sloppy Joes)

French Fry Logs

Carrot and Celery Stick Rails

Tank Car Milkshakes

• • •

Choo Choo Train Cake*

Dixie Cups

(Vanilla. Remove lids and decorate top with chocolate sauce, making a railroad crossing sign.)

Appetizers

Canapes

CAVIAR CANAPE

30 large rounds of bread
3 hard boiled eggs, grated
1 large jar caviar (black or red)

Few drops evaporated milk
Large package cream cheese
Mayonnaise

Allow cream cheese to soften at room temperature. Mash cheese with fork and thin with a little evaporated milk and mayonnaise to spreading consistency. Spread on rounds of bread. Decorate around edge of canape with grated egg, and fill inside with caviar. (These can be made in the morning and placed in sealed box with damp cheesecloth in refrigerator.)

MRS. AMOS BUMGARDNER, JR.

CRABMEAT CANAPES

Fresh crabmeat (boned)
Mayonnaise
Grated onion

Ritz crackers
Grated cheese

Mix the crab with a little mayonnaise (I added a small amount of grated onion) and pile on crackers. Top with grated sharp cheese and place under broiler until it melts. Serve warm with tomato juice cocktail. (Crackers re-crisp after coming out of oven.)

MRS. LARRY ROGER

EGG CANAPE

6 rounds of Holland Rusk
2 3-ounce packages cream cheese, softened
3 hard boiled eggs, cut in half

1 tube anchovy paste
6 thick slices tomato
½ cup mayonnaise
2 tablespoons milk

Spread rounds of Holland Rusk with anchovy paste (optional). Place large slice of tomato on each and half an egg on the tomato. In electric mixer beat cream cheese, mayonnaise and milk until mixture is consistency of cake icing. (Might have to add a few more drops of milk.) For variation, add roquefort cheese. Ice each canape with the cream cheese mixture. Rounds of toasted bread can be used instead of Rusks. This makes a good first course. Serves 6.

MRS. FRANCIS O. CLARKSON, JR.

HAM AND OLIVE CANAPES

1 small jar green olives stuffed with pimento

1 jar ground Smithfield ham spread
Mayonnaise

Thin ham spread with a little mayonnaise and mix well. Spread on fresh rectangles of bread (trimmed) and garnish with olive slices. Use sandwich loaf sized bread.

MRS. AMOS BUMGARDNER, JR.

LIVER PATÉ CANAPE

1 jar liver paté
1 jar button mushrooms (halved)
Very thin slices of sweet onion

Very thin slices of canned pimento
Rectangles of bread
Chopped parsley

Thin paté with mayonnaise. Spread on bread. Put thin slice of pimento in center of bread surrounded by several slices of onion. Place a mushroom half at each end. Garnish with parsley.

MRS. AMOS BUMGARDNER, JR.

RIPE OLIVE CANAPE

4½ ounces chopped ripe olives
¼ cup chopped green onion
¾ cup sharp cheese, grated

4 tablespoons mayonnaise
Salt to taste
½ teaspoon curry powder

Mix above ingredients and put on toast rounds. Heat in 350° oven until bubbly.

MRS. MICHAEL BACCICH

BRISTLING SARDINE CANAPE

1 large package cream cheese
Few drops evaporated milk
Sandwich relish

1 can Bristling sardines
Diamond-shaped pieces of bread
Paprika

Spread bread slices with cream cheese mixture softened with a little milk; then spread on a little sandwich relish. Top with a sardine and trim with parsley. Dust with paprika.

MRS. AMOS BUMGARDNER, JR.

ANCHOVY PUFFS

½ cup butter
1 3-ounce package cream cheese
1 cup flour

1 tube anchovy paste
½ cup chopped pecans

Soften butter and cheese and blend well. Add flour. Chill. Roll very thin and cut with small biscuit cutter. Spread each round with anchovy paste. Sprinkle a few chopped pecans on top. Fold over, making a puff. Bake in hot oven (400°) for about 10 minutes. Serve hot. Makes about 45.

MRS. HALL M. JOHNSTON, JR.

HOT BACON HORS D'OEUVRES

10 strips of bacon
½ cup evaporated milk
4 tablespoons catsup
2 tablespoons Worcestershire

Dash of Accent
Dash of pepper
Cornflakes

Cut bacon strips into fourths. Combine remaining ingredients except cornflakes. Dip each piece of bacon in the milk mixture. Roll in the crushed, fine cornflake crumbs. (Crush in blender.) Bake at 375° on cookie sheet until crisp and brown, about 20 minutes. Drain well and serve hot. Makes about 40 pieces.

MRS. JOHN BRABSON

BACON-WRAPPED OLIVES

Cut bacon strips in half lengthwise and across. Wrap olive and secure with a toothpick. Cook in deep amount of bacon grease until bacon is done (about 10 minutes over medium heat). Drain and serve warm.

MRS. WALTER SUMMERVILLE

BACON WRAP-UPS

10 slices bread	1 can cream of mushroom soup
15 slices bacon	33 wooden toothpicks

Take crusts off bread. Cut bread in 3 strips. Generously spread undiluted soup on each strip. (It will not take a whole can). Cut bacon in half. Place half piece of bacon under bread strip (not the soup-spread side). Wrap up as tight as you can and insert toothpick to hold in place. Place all wrapped pieces on cookie sheet that has sides to catch the grease. Bake at 300° for one hour. Can be made a day ahead. Makes 33. Men love them.

MRS. TERRY YOUNG

BUTTER PUFFS

12 pieces bread	2 egg yolks
2 3-ounce packages cream cheese	Paprika to taste
½ stick margarine	

Cream cheese, margarine and yolks together until fluffy. With a biscuit cutter or bottle cap about the size of a 50¢ piece, cut out rounds from bread without crusts. Spread mixture on rounds and lightly sprinkle with paprika. Place under broiler for a few minutes, until bubbly and turning brown. Makes 40 to 50.

MRS. BRUCE RINEHART

HOT CHEESE PUFFS

2 jars Old English cheese spread	1½ sticks margarine
	1 egg

Have ingredients at room temperature. Whip until creamy. Trim crusts from bread. Spread slices of bread with the mixture; cut into 4 squares. Place on cookie sheet in refrigerator for 24 hours or overnight. Bake in preheated 350° oven for 10 minutes. Serves 10 as appetizers.

MRS. DOUGLAS BOOTH

HOT OLIVE CHEESE PUFFS

2 cups sharp cheese, grated	1 teaspoon paprika
6 tablespoons soft margarine	48 stuffed olives (large ones)
1 cup flour, sifted	drained and dry
½ teaspoon salt	

Blend cheese with butter; stir in flour, salt, and paprika and mix well. Wrap small amount of cheese dough around each drained and dried olive. Make sure each olive is covered well. Place on ungreased cookie sheet and bake in 400° oven for 10 or 15 minutes, until golden brown. These may be frozen before cooking.

MRS. ROBERT COXEY
MRS. HUGH CAMPBELL

CHEESE RICE KRISPIE ROUNDS

2 cups sharp cheese, grated
1 stick butter
1 stick margarine

2 cups flour
2 cups Rice Krispie cereal

Mix grated cheese, butter and margarine well. Add flour and mix well. Fold in Rice Krispies. Shape into small balls. Place on greased cookie sheet. Flatten each with a fork and top with pecan. Bake at 375° for 10 minutes or until golden brown around edges.

MRS. R. S. PLONK
MRS. GENE MCGARITY
MRS. CHARLES WICKHAM

BAKER'S CHEESE STRAWS

2 packages Flako pie crust mix
1 pound sharp New York state
    cheese

Cayenne pepper

Empty pie crust mix in mixing bowl. Grate cheese on top. Allow to reach room temperature. Sprinkle liberally with pepper. Knead and knead and knead! Put through cookie press (or roll out as pie crust on floured board and cut in strips). Place on ungreased cookie sheet and cook at 375° about 8 minutes.

MRS. HARLEY GASTON

CHICKEN AND ALMONDS IN PUFF SHELLS

1 cup chopped cooked chicken
½ cup finely chopped celery
¼ cup copped blanched almonds

Enough mayonnaise to moisten
Salt, pepper and lemon juice
to taste

Mix above ingredients together and fill cream puff shells.

CREAM PUFF SHELLS

½ cup boiling water
¼ cup butter

½ cup flour
2 unbeaten eggs

Melt butter in water. Add flour all at once and stir vigorously. When a ball forms in the center of the pan, remove from heat and cool for 5 minutes. Add 1 egg and mix in mix-master or beat thoroughly by hand. Add second egg and repeat beating. Drop 1 teaspoon at a time, 2 inches apart, on a buttered cookie sheet. Bake at 375° until brown or until all beads of moisture have disappeared (about 25 minutes). Take one shell out and test it. If it doesn't fall, the puffs are done. When cool, fill with mixture.

MRS. ELI SPRINGS

HOT CHEESE ROUNDS

8-ounce package cheese
(Old English or Velveeta)
1 egg, well beaten
½ teaspoon Worcestershire

1 teaspoon grated onion
Salt and red pepper to taste
10 pieces of bread

Blend desired type of cheese with egg. Mix with seasonings. With medium-sized round cutter, cut out bread circles (no crusts). Spread cheese mixture on rounds and place on cookie sheet. Place under broiler for a few minutes, until they puff up and turn slightly brown. Good for afternoon teas. Makes about 30.

MRS. BRUCE RINEHART

BARBECUED CHICKEN WINGS

2 to 3 pounds chicken wings,
cut up (throw away the tips)
1 cup soy sauce
3 teaspoons sugar or
¼ cup pineapple syrup
¼ cup white wine

2 cloves mashed garlic or
sprinkle wings generously
with garlic powder
¼ cup Mazola oil
1 teaspoon Accent
1 teaspoon (level) ground ginger

Marinate for 16 hours. Bake at 325° for 1½ to 2 hours. Sauce may be saved in refrigerator and used again.

MRS. W. B. BRADFORD

CLAMS WALLACE

2 dozen cherry stone clams
1 medium onion, minced
¼ teaspoon tarragon

½ cup white vermouth
6 strips bacon

Open clams, saving the largest shells. Cut bacon into 2-inch pieces. Mince onion and add tarragon and vermouth. Let stand for 1 hour. Preheat oven to 500°. Place one clam in a shell, add 1 teaspoon of the onion-vermouth mixture, and cover with a piece of bacon. Place on a baking sheet and put in oven about 6 inches from top. Cook until bacon is done and serve at once.

MRS. WALLACE GIBBS, JR.

BROILED CLAMS

Fresh clams (6 per person)
Garlic salt, minced parsley,
and/or grated onion

Bacon
Butter
Freshly ground black pepper

Open fresh clams. Plan to have 5 or 6 per person. Sprinkle garlic salt, parsley, or onion on top. Cut small piece of bacon and place on top of this. Dot with butter. Sprinkle pepper over all. Broil until bacon is done.

MRS. J. WALTER BARR

STUFFED DATES

4 ounces cream cheese
2 teaspoons frozen orange juice concentrate
½ teaspoon orange extract or
1 tablespoon grated orange peel

⅔ cup chopped pecans
1 pound package of dates

Let cheese soften, blend in juice, extract or peel, and add nuts. This amount will fill 70 to 75 dates (approximately the number in a 1-pound package) using half a demitasse spoonful in each date. Chill, then roll in powdered sugar. Keep in refrigerator.

MRS. JULIAN CLARKSON

MELON AND PROSCIUTTO

Cut a chilled small melon (cantaloupe or honeydew) into thin crescent-shaped slices. Remove seeds, pulp, and rind. Arrange on a plate with very thin slices of Prosciutto (raw smoked Italian ham). Any good aged ham will do, but slice it very thinly.

The same may be served as an hors d'oeuvre by cutting the melon into cubes about 1-inch in size, wrapping in chipped beef slices and spearing with a toothpick.

MRS. CARLISLE ADAMS

ONION STICKS

1 package Lipton onion soup
¼ pound butter

Slices of white bread with crusts cut off

Mix soup and butter together and spread on bread slices. Put in oven for 10 minutes at 325°. Cut into strips. Serve hot.

MRS. LAWRENCE REGER

PEANUT BUTTER ROLL-UPS

Spread thin bread with peanut butter, roll and wrap with thin small pieces of bacon. Place in oven to toast under broiler until bacon is crisp.

MRS. DOUGLAS BOOTH

SAUSAGE-CHEESE BISCUIT

1 pound lean hot sausage
3 cups Bisquick

10 ounces Kraft Sharp Cracker-barrel Cheese, grated

Mix Bisquick according to directions. Break up sausage, soften to room temperature. Add Bisquick and cheese. With hands, work until well blended. Pinch off little balls. Put on cookie sheet. Bake in center of oven at 375° for 15 minutes. Watch to keep bottom from burning. (*May be frozen*, put in plastic bags. Cook at 300° for 10 minutes while frozen.) Makes 150 balls.

MRS. ROBERT CHERRY
MRS. GABE C. HILL

Dips

ANCHOVY DIP

2 large packages cream cheese
1 tube anchovy paste

½ small onion, grated
Worcestershire to taste

Soften cream cheese with equal parts milk and mayonnaise to dip consistency. Add Worcestershire sauce and salt to taste. Blend well. Serves 6 to 8.

MRS. JOHN TILLETT, JR.

BLACK BEAN DIP

1 can black bean soup
½ cup sour cream
½ teaspoon dry mustard

1½ teaspoons lemon juice
4 tablespoons cooked bacon, crumbled

Mix, refrigerate and serve.

MRS. WYLIE ARNOLD

BROCCOLI DIP (HOT)

4 packages frozen broccoli florets, (cooked, drained and chopped fine)
1 pound cheddar cheese (cubed) or shredded)
3 to 4 cans cheddar cheese soup (as is)

2 large cans mushroms, stems and pieces (drained and cut fine)
2 large cans pimento (drained and cut fine)
⅔ cup sherry

Combine all chopped and drained ingredients (can mix in blender). Heat on low heat in top of double boiler until cheese is completely melted. Serve from chafing dish, using crackers or toast points. Makes about 3 quarts and fills a large chafing dish with a little extra. Any left over makes a good soup with a little milk added to thin it.

MRS. LYN BOND, JR.

CLAM DIP

1 8-ounce package cream cheese
1 can minced clams
1 tablespoon grated onion (optional)

Tabasco
Worcestershire

Use liquid from clams to soften cream cheese to desired consistency. Use Worcestershire and Tabasco to season to taste. Serve with Fritos. Enough for 8 people.

MRS. ROBERT R. COXEY
MRS. JOHN STEDMAN

CRAB MEAT DIP I

1 cup mayonnaise
½ cup sour cream
1 tablespoon parsley flakes
1 tablespoon sherry

1 teaspoon lemon juice
Salt and pepper to taste
1 6½-ounce can crab meat, well
  picked over

Combine all the above. Chill at least 2 hours. Good with raw vegetables or toast rounds.

CRAB MEAT DIP II

4 tablespoons onion, chopped fine
1 tablespoon butter (add and stir
  until melted)

8-ounce package Philadelphia
  cream cheese
½ pound fresh crab meat, boned
  and flaked

In double boiler cook until clear the onion, butter and cream cheese. Add crab meat. Season with Worcestershire sauce to taste. Blend well. Serve on toast for dinner or in a chafing dish with Melba toast for cocktails.

MRS. JOHN R. CAMPBELL

INTRIGUING DIP

1 pint sour cream
1 small package (or 2/3 large
  package) cream cheese
¼ pound blue cheese
1 tablespoon wine vinegar
1 tablespoon horseradish

2 teaspoons salt
2 tablespoons onion juice
1½ teaspoons dry mustard
1 teaspoon paprika
½ teaspoon pepper

Cream softened cheeses with sour cream. Combine with other ingredients, mixing thoroughly in mixer. Serve as dip with raw cauliflower, carrots, celery or potato chips. Keeps well.

MRS. RICHARD GILLESPIE

RANDON WOODS DIP

1 can anchovy fillets
1 small onion, grated
1 small package cream cheese

1 tablespoon Worcestershire
2 tablespoons lemon juice

Mix well and serve heaped in bowl. Use Melba toast or crackers.

MRS. HARLEY GASTON, JR.

EASY SHRIMP DIP

1 can small shrimp
4 tablespoons mayonnaise

3 tablespoons cream style
  horseradish

Drain and chop shrimp (a pastry blender is helpful for this), add mayonnaise and horseradish and mix well. Add more or less mayonnaise and horseradish according to how runny and "hot" you want it to be. Delicious with Triscuits. Serves 6 to 8 people.

MRS. HOWARD C. BISSELL

CHILI CON QUESO

2-pound box Velveeta cheese
1 onion, chopped
½ of a #2 can tomatoes, drained

3 or 4 Jalapenos chili peppers
¼ teaspoon chili powder
¼ teaspoon cumin powder

Sauté onion. Melt cheese in double boiler and add onions, tomatoes, powders and cut-up peppers. Serve hot in a chafing dish with Fritos. (Chili peppers are very hot — use less if desired).

MRS. JOSEPH DULANEY

LOBSTER CHUNKS WITH GREEN GODDESS DRESSING

4 1-pound frozen lobster tails
1 clove garlic, minced
½ teaspoon salt
½ teaspoon dry mustard
1 teaspoon Worcestershire
3 tablespoons tarragon wine vinegar

2 tablespoons anchovy paste
3 tablespoons grated onion
⅓ cup chopped parsley
1 cup mayonnaise
½ cup sour cream
⅛ teaspoon pepper

DRESSING

Combine all above ingredients, except lobster, the day before serving. Allow to season, covered, in refrigerator until serving time.

LOBSTER

Cook the day it is to be used. Drop tails in boiling salted water and cook 3 minutes per pound, based on weight of largest tail. Cool and cut into bite size chunks. Use dressing as dip. Serves approximately 20.

This also makes delicious salad for lunch. Serve over lobster in lettuce cups or over mixed greens topped with croutons.

MRS. A. S. BUMGARDNER, JR.*

MARINATED SHRIMP

2 pounds cooked, peeled, veined shrimp
2 medium Bermuda onions, sliced thin and divided into rings
1 cup olive oil
2 cups vinegar
½ bottle Worcestershire

1 teaspoon French's mustard
Salt and pepper to taste (1 teaspoon salt and ½ teaspoon pepper)
2 cloves garlic, crushed
1 teaspoon paprika
2 small onions, diced

Arrange shrimp and sliced onion rings alternately in a serving bowl. Combine the remaining ingredients and mix well. Let stand for a few minutes, strain, and pour over shrimp. Allow to marinate in refrigerator for 24 hours. Serves 8 to 10. (This can be used as an hors d'oeuvre on crackers or toothpicks, or as a salad on lettuce.)

MRS. RICHARD AUSTIN JONES*

OYSTER APPETIZER

24 select oysters
Salt and pepper

½ cup flour
5 tablespoons butter

SAUCE

2 tablespoons melted butter
¼ cup fresh lemon juice
½ cup A-1 steak sauce
2 tablespoons Worcestershire

½ cup sherry or Madeira
2 tablespoons flour
3 tablespoons water

Salt and pepper oysters and dredge in flour. Melt butter on griddle and grill oysters until crisp and brown on all sides. Sprinkle butter (or cooking oil) on oysters while grilling. It browns and crisps them. Heat, but do not boil, the following sauce ingredients: Butter, lemon juice, A-1 sauce, Worcestershire sauce, and sherry or Madeira. Blend the flour and water and stir in to thicken. Re-heat sauce and correct seasoning to taste—more A-1 if too thin or more sherry if too thick and highly seasoned. Pour sauce over oysters. Serve from chafing dish with toothpicks. Makes 24 servings.

MRS. ERNEST H. BARRY*

PICKLED SHRIMP

1 can undiluted tomato soup
¾ cup vinegar
1½ cup salad oil
1 teaspoon salt
½ teaspoon red pepper
1 teaspoon onion juice
½ teaspoon paprika
⅓ cup sugar

1 tablespoon Worcestershire
1 teaspoon dry mustard
2 teaspoons lemon juice
Thinly sliced lemons
4 pounds cooked shrimp
2 onions (thinly sliced)
1 tablespoon bay leaves

Mix all ingredients in electric mixer except shrimp, lemons, onions and bay leaves. Put layers of shrimp, lemons, onions and bay leaves into a bowl. Pour sauce over this, and let stand in refrigerator for 24 hours. When shrimp have been eaten, the sauce can be used over and over to make more pickled shrimp. Serves 8.

FRANCES WADDILL

SAUSAGE HORS D'OEUVRE FOR 20

2 pounds sausage
½ pint sour cream

1 bottle Major Grey's Chutney
½ cup sherry

Make sausage into little balls and cook. (Can be stored in freezer until ready to use.) Mix sour cream, chutney, and sherry. Put in chafing dish. Put sausage balls in mixture. Serve with toothpicks. (If you have any left over, serve it on rice.)

MRS. GEORGE LILES

SWEDISH MEAT BALLS

3 pounds lean ground chuck or round steak (ground twice)
4 slices white bread, crusts removed
1½ cups milk

3 whole eggs, beaten
Dash of thyme, allspice, garlic salt
2 tablespoons catsup (more if needed)
Salt and pepper to taste

Tear bread in pieces and soak bread well in milk. Slightly wring out bread. Mix all ingredients thoroughly. Should be a little moist. Make small meatballs. Fry in a little shortening until well done. Put in sauce and simmer for 1½ hours, covered. Can serve from a chafing dish using toothpicks to spear meat balls. Serves 15 to 20.

SAUCE

1 package dried onion soup mix
1 can beef consomme
1 large can crushed pineapple

1 cup seedless raisins
Juice of 1 lemon
2 or 3 tablespoons molasses

Mix well.

MRS. VERNER STANLEY, JR.

Spreads

CHEESE BALL

2 ounces cream cheese
4 ounces bleu cheese
4 ounces grated sharp cheese
⅛ teaspoon garlic powder

1 teaspoon Worcestershire
⅓ cup chopped parsley
⅓ cup chopped pecans

Mix all ingredients except parsley and pecans. Shape into a ball and roll in parsley and nut mixture. Serve with crackers or Melba rounds. Makes small ball, about 2½ inches in diameter.

MRS. ROBERT R. COXEY

MILD CHEESE BALL

1 package Old English cheese, small jar
1 package Velveeta cheese, small package
1 package cream cheese, 3 oz. size
1/3 teaspoon garlic powder
1 tablespoon Worcestershire sauce
paprika
chili powder

Buy the three cheeses approximately the same size. When cheeses are at room temperature, mix in beater until well blended. Add garlic powder and Worcestershire mixing until smooth. Form into ball with hands. Put paprika and chili powder in wax paper and roll ball in it until evenly covered. Make a day ahead. Chill. Serves approximately 8.

MRS. TERRY YOUNG

PARTY CHEESE BALL

1/2 cup chopped walnuts
3 to 5 ounces blue cheese
8-ounce package cream cheese
1/4 teaspoon garlic salt
1 tablespoon chopped green pepper
1 tablespoon chopped pimento

Toast walnuts in 350° oven until golden, about 8 to 10 minutes. Blend cheeses and add other ingredients. Chill until firm and shape into a ball. Roll in toasted nuts. Chill until serving time.

MRS. DONALD A. GRAHAM

HAM BALL

2 4½-ounce cans deviled ham
3 tablespoons chopped stuffed green olives
1 teaspoon prepared mustard
Tabasco sauce to taste
1 3-ounce package cream cheese, softened
2 teaspoons milk

Blend deviled ham, olives, mustard and Tabasco. Form ball on serving dish; chill. Combine cream cheese and milk; frost ball with mixture. Chill. Remove from refrigerator 15 minutes before serving. Trim with parsley. Enjoy with assorted crackers.

MRS. C. FREDERICK CLARK, JR.

ROQUEFORT CHEESE BALL

8 ounces roquefort cheese
8 ounces cream cheese
1/2 cup butter
2 tablespoons lemon juice
1 cup chopped ripe olives
1 tablespoon minced green onion

Mix softened cheeses with lemon juice in mixer on low speed. Add butter and mix. Add olives and onions. Make into roll or mound. Cover with paprika or parsley. Chill.

MRS. J. C. PURNELL

CHICKEN LIVER PATE I

½ pound chicken livers
½ cup soft butter
½ teaspoon salt
Dash of cayenne, cloves, black
pepper

1 teaspoon dry mustard
½ teaspoon Worcestershire
½ teaspoon grated nutmeg
2 teaspoons lemon juice
1 teaspoon onion juice

If livers are frozen, defrost before cooking. Pour boiling water over, drain, cover with fresh boiling water, and simmer for 20 minutes. Drain, put through meat grinder, food mill, or blender. Cream butter, then rest of ingredients and blend well. If you need more salt, add onion salt. and black pepper. If you wish to use as a dip, do not chill. If used as pate, put in a container and chill, but stir several times during chilling to keep butter from separating. Remove from refrigerator 30 minutes before serving. Serve with crackers or Melba toast.

MRS. BREVARD S. MYERS

CHICKEN LIVER PATE II

¼ cup chopped onion
¼ cup butter
1½ pounds chicken livers
2 hard-cooked egg yolks, sieved
½ cup soft butter
½ cup heavy cream

½ cup cognac
¼ teaspon nutmeg
Salt and pepper to taste
½ cup chopped chives
Parsley

In large skillet, saute onions in butter until tender but not brown. Add liver and cook over low heat until tender. Puree mixture in blender. Add remaining ingredients (except chives and parsley) to blender and blend until smooth. Fold in chives and chill until serving time. Garnish with parsley and serve with crisp crackers as an hors d'oeuvre.

MRS. EDWARD J. WANNAMAKER, JR.

HOPIE'S GOOSE LIVER PATE

1 pound liverwurst
2 tablespoons onion (grated)
1 can consomme
1 envelope plain gelatin

6 tablespoons sherry
Red pepper and Worcestershire to
taste

Soak gelatin in ¼ cup of the consomme. Heat remaining consomme and dissolve gelatin in it. Add 2 or 3 tablespoons of the hot consomme, seasonings and some sherry to liverwurst and onion mixture. Pour a little consomme into well-greased mold and allow to set in refrigerator. Pile liverwurst on the set consomme, keeping space on all sides. Add remaining sherry to remaining consomme. Pour around liverwurst and allow to set. Serves 18 to 20.

MRS. JAMES MCNEELY

SALMON ROLL

1 small can salmon, drained
1 small package cream cheese
2 tablespoons lemon juice

2 tablespoons grated onion
½ teaspoon liquid smoke
Salt and pepper

Mix and chill. Roll in chopped nuts and/or parsley. Serve with crackers or toast.

MRS. HERBERT H. BROWNE, JR.

SHRIMP BUTTER

2 pounds uncooked shrimp
¼ cup crab boil (see below)
½ pound butter

1 cup sherry
Tabasco

CRAB BOIL

1 teaspoon whole peppercorns
2 bay leaves
1 medium onion (cut in chunks)
1 teaspoon salt

4 celery tops
1 teaspoon salt
½ teaspoon red pepper

Make a court bouillon, using 5 cups of water and the crab boil, and boil briskly for 10 minutes. Strain and reserve. Peel the shrimp and put into court bouillon. Bring to a boil and cook for 5 minutes. Allow the shrimp to cool enough to handle. Cut each shrimp into several pieces.

Melt butter in sherry. Put shrimp in a blender and gradually add the butter-sherry mixture while blending at medium speed. When all the butter and sherry has been added, blend at high speed until thoroughly pureed. Add about ¼ teaspoon of Tabasco and more salt if needed. Finish blending at high speed. Pour mixture into a mold and refrigerate for several hours, overnight if possible. To serve, unmold by putting mold in hot water. Serve as a spread with crackers.

MR. WALLACE D. GIBBS, JR.

CREAM CHEESE SPREAD

4 large packages Philadelphia
  cream cheese

1 bottle chili sauce
Sesame seeds

Brown sesame seeds in oven. Smooth 4 blocks of cream cheese together to form square mold. Pour chili sauce over mold. Sprinkle with browned sesame seeds. Spread on crackers.

MRS. JACQUES BROURMAN

PIMIENTO CHEESE SPREAD

1 pound sharp New York state
  cheese, grated
1 stick margarine
2 cans pimiento, drained and cut
  fine

2 tablespoons Durkee's dressing
¼ to ½ cup mayonnaise
Few drops Tabasco
Dash of salt

Bring cheese and oleo to room temperature. Mix all ingredients together. Good as sandwich spread. Makes 1 quart.

MRS. NAT G. SPEIR

PINEAPPLE CHEESE SPREAD

1 fresh pineapple	3 or 4 teaspoons Worcestershire
2 pounds grated sharp cheese	Few drops hot sauce (Tabasco)
1 large package cream cheese	1 small grated onion
(softened)	½ cup mayonnaise

Mix all ingredients (except pineapple) together and refrigerate. Day of use: soften cheese for 3 or 4 hours at room temperature. Slice pineapple lengthwise into 2 pieces, leaving all of green top on one piece. Using that piece, scoop out pineapple and fill with cheese. Score cheese like a pineapple. Use cloves and green cherries for decoration. Cheese will acquire some of the pineapple flavor.

MRS. JOHN DABBS

MOCK CHICKEN SALAD SANDWICH SPREAD

1 cup nuts, chopped fine	1 small onion, grated
1 hard boiled egg, chopped fine	1 pint mayonnaise
1 small bottle of olives, drained and chopped fine	

Mix dry ingredients well. Blend in mayonnaise. This will keep well refrigerated. Makes enough spread for 1 loaf of bread.

MRS. WALTER SCOTT, JR.

COLD CRAB MEAT SPREAD

1 pound crab meat	2 to 3 teaspoons prepared
6 shakes red pepper	mustard
1 medium onion, chopped	4 tablespoons mayonnaise

Pick over crab meat thoroughly. Mix with other ingredients until well blended. Serve in mound with crackers. Makes enough for 25 to 30 canapes. Leftovers can be heated with buttered bread crumbs on top for quick deviled crab. Also can be used for crab meat salad.

MRS. JOHN TILLETT, JR.

SHRIMP SPREAD

1 3-ounce package cream cheese	Juice of 1 button garlic
Dash Worcestershire	2 tablespoons Miracle Whip
1 teaspoon prepared mustard	1 can shrimp (or 1 cup fresh)
1 teaspoon curry powder	1 tablespoon pickle relish
Dash of red pepper	2 tablespoons chili sauce

Cream cheese and season with Worcestershire, mustard, pepper, curry powder, garlic juice and Miracle Whip. Add cut-up shrimp. Blend well. Add relish and chili sauce. (For dip, use 8-ounce package cream cheese and more mayonnaise.)

MRS. JAMES PURNELL

Sandwiches

CHEESE AND CHUTNEY SANDWICHES

1 cup grated sharp cheddar
  cheese
Major Grey's Chutney (finely
  chopped) to taste

Thin slices of fresh, fine-grained
  bread
Parsley

Mix cheese with chutney. The spread should be spicy and smooth enough to spread. Cut each sandwich three times to make finger-sized sandwiches. Press a small piece of parsley in the center of each. Makes approximatly 12 to 15 finger sandwiches.

MRS. ELI SPRINGS

BETSY'S HOT CORNED BEEF SANDWICHES

1 can (12 ounces) corned beef
1 stick butter, melted
½ cup sweet pickle relish
½ cup chopped celery
1 onion, finely chopped

1 tablespoon Worcestershire
1 teaspoon chili powder
8 hamburger buns
Aluminum foil

Mix first seven ingredients in skillet. Cook about 15 minutes, until celery and onion are soft. Place in 8 hamburger buns. Wrap in foil. Heat in 350° oven for 20 minutes. Makes 8 sandwiches.

MRS. ERVIN JACKSON, JR.

QUICK CORNISH SANDWICH

1 7-ounce can tuna, drained and
  flaked (or may substitute
  deviled ham)
1 cup shredded cheddar cheese
¼ cup chopped celery

1 tablespoon chopped parsley
⅓ cup sour cream
1 8-ounce package refrigerator
  biscuits
1 tablespoon butter, melted

In a bowl, combine tuna, cheese, celery, parsley and sour cream. Pat or roll each biscuit into a 3x4-inch oval; place half of biscuits on greased baking sheet. Place 1/3 cup of tuna mixture on each biscuit. Top with remaining biscuits; seal edges with fork. Brush tops with butter and let stand for 15 minutes. Bake in preheated oven at 400° for 15 to 18 minutes, or until golden. Serves 4 to 6.

MRS. C. E. WILLIAMS, JR.

HOT CRAB SANDWICHES

1 carton crab meat (you may use
  canned)
Equal amount grated New York
  state cheese

1 teaspoon grated onion
Enough mayonnaise to hold
  together

Mix all ingredients together. Spread about ½-inch thick on halves of toasted hamburger rolls, or spread on Melba toast for hors d'oeuvres. Top with paprika. Place under broiler until golden brown and bubbly. Serves about 8.

MRS. A. G. ODELL, JR.*

CUCUMBER ROUNDS

Cucumbers
Vinegar
Ice Water

Bread
Mayonnaise
Paprika

Use amounts desired. Peel the cucumbers and slice thin. Soak cucumbers in vinegar mixed with ice water (Use about 1 tablespoon of vinegar for each cucumber.) Drain well and pat dry. Cut out circles of soft bread with biscuit cutter. Spread bread lightly with mayonnaise and place slice of cucumber on each round. Top with dash of paprika. Garnish with sprigs of parsley for color. Make the sandwiches as close to serving time as possible.

MRS. CHARLES L. WICKHAM, JR.

LUNCHEON CRAB SANDWICH

2 tablespoons mayonnaise
1 3-ounce package cream cheese
2 teaspoons Worcestershire

½ teaspoon seasoned salt
6½ ounces crab meat

Mix above ingredients. Spread on half of a semi-toasted hamburger bun and top with slice of tomato, then a slice of cheese. Cook at 350° for 15 minutes. Serves 4.

MRS. ELLEN G. GOODE

RIPE OLIVE SANDWICHES

3 small packages cream cheese
1 small can ripe olives, chopped
1 small onion, grated
1 cup broken nut meats

Salt and pepper to taste
Dash of red pepper
1 teaspoon lemon juice
½ cup Miracle Whip salad
dressing

Mix above together adding salad dressing last. Makes about 12 sandwiches. Good for dip or crackers.

MRS. JOHN STEDMAN

SPEDINI ALIA ROMANA

1 long loaf of French bread
1 stick butter
¼ cup chopped onion
2 to 3 tablespoons mustard

1 tablespoon poppy seeds
¼ pound sliced Swiss cheese
¼ pound sliced American cheese
4 or 5 slices bacon, cut in half

Trim most of the crust from the top and sides of the bread, and slash almost to the bottom at one-inch intervals. Saute the onion in the butter until wilted, then mix with the mustard and poppy seeds and spread beween the slashes of the bread. Insert the slices of cheese between the slashes and arrange the bacon over the top of the stuffed loaf.

Bake in a 350° oven until bacon is crisp and cheese is melted. Serves 4. (Serve with spiced tomato juice, a green salad, and bowl of fresh fruit cut in bite size pieces, sprinkled with lemon juice.)

MRS. DOUGLAS BOOTH

SANDWICHES

TOMATO SANDWICH FILLING

1 large package cream cheese
2 finely chopped tomatoes
1 tablespoon onion, grated

4 slices bacon, fried and crumbled
Worcestershire, few drops
Salt and pepper to taste

Blend well. Enough for 12 finger sandwiches.

MRS. ROBERT LYNN

VEGETABLE SANDWICHES

4 firm tomatoes
2 small onions
2 small cucumbers
1 green pepper
2 grated carrots

1 tablespoon gelatin
3 tablespoons juice (from
  vegetables)
1 cup mayonnaise
½ teaspoon salt

Grind tomatoes, onions, cucumbers and peppers, saving 3 tablespoons of juice. Drain remaining juice lightly. Soak gelatin in 3 tablespoons juice and put gelatin over hot water, stirring until dissolved. Combine vegetables, grated carrots, and gelatin mixture well. Add mayonnaise and salt. Store in refrigerator overnight. Spread on bread, making open-face or regular sandwiches. Makes about 1½ pints.

MRS. WILLIAM A. NICHOLS
MRS. CORSON ROSE

Soups

CHILLED CURRY AVOCADO SOUP

2 tablespoons butter
1 teaspoon curry powder
2 cups water
1 package chicken noodle
  soup mix

1 cup whole milk or light cream
1 avocado, peeled and seed
  removed
Bit of fresh ground nutmeg

Melt butter, stir in curry, and simmer over low heat for a minute. Add water, bring to a boil and add soup mix. Cover and cook 7 minutes. Stir in milk. Reheat, but do not boil. Pour into blender with half of avocado. Blend for 3 minutes. Add rest of avocado, chopped, and chill all day. Add sprinkle of nutmeg and serve. Serves 6.

MRS. JOHN TILLETT, JR.

COUNTRY CHICKEN CHOWDER

1 onion, chopped (½ cup)
2 tablespoons butter
2 cans condensed chicken noodle
  soup
1 soup can water

1 can cream style corn
1 small can evaporated milk
¼ teaspoon pepper
2 tablespoons chopped parsley

Sauté onion in butter until soft. Add remaining ingredients, except parsley. Heat to boil. Serve topped with parsley. Serves about 8.

MRS. GABE HILL

BERTHA'S CLAM CHOWDER

1 7-ounce can minced clams,
  drained
2 tablespoons butter
1 small can tomato juice
1 small can tomato paste
2 medium potatoes (diced or
  grated)

1 medium onion, chopped fine
1 teaspoon Worcestershire sauce
Dash of Tabasco
Black pepper
Salt

Combine all ingredients other than clams. Cook for one hour. Add clams, cook 15 minutes. Serves 4.

MRS. JOHN ALEXANDER STEWMAN III

CORN SOUP

½ cup celery, chopped
½ cup onion, chopped
1 tablespoon butter
1 beef bouillon cube
½ cup water

2 cups milk
1 1-pound can cream style corn
(or corn from 6 ears, if fresh
corn desired)

Sauté, but do not brown, celery and onion in butter. Simmer bouillon cube in ½-cup water. Add to celery and onions and cook until onions are done. Add milk and corn to mixture and simmer 15 minutes. Season to taste. Serves 6.

MRS. JOHN BRABSON

CREAM CRAB MEAT SOUP

1 can Chalet Suzanne Romain
Soup
1 can mushroom soup
1 pint half and half cream

1 8-ounce can King Crab Meat
Sherry to taste
Salt and pepper to taste

Mix and dissolve together soups and cream in double boiler. At the last, add a can of King Crab Meat and sherry. Serves 4 to 6.

MRS. JOHN PENDER

COLD CUCUMBER SOUP

1 large cucumber, peeled
1 can cream of chicken soup
½ cup milk

1 carton sour cream
1 or 2 teaspoons celery salt

Put cucumber in Waring Blender and blend. Add other ingredients and blend. Chill thoroughly. Serves 4 to 6, depending upon size of cup or dish used.

MRS. CORSON ROSE

GAZPACHO

4 cups chicken bouillon (canned
or cubes)
Handful of herbs (parsley,
chives, basil)
2 cloves of garlic, minced
¼ cup olive oil
1 lemon, juiced

1 mild onion, cut in very thin
rings
1 green pepper, cut in very thin
rings
2 fresh tomatoes, chopped
Salt, pepper, paprika

Mix in pitcher or bowl. Refrigerate overnight. Before serving, add cup of sliced unpeeled cucumber. Serve chilled.

MRS. HENRY PIERCE

ONION SOUP

12 onions, thinly sliced
14 cups beef bouillon (canned,
undiluted)
4 tablespoons butter
2 teaspoons Worcestershire

¼ teaspoon Tabasco
1 teaspoon Kitchen Bouquet
6 tablespoons Parmesan cheese
Salt and pepper to taste
6 1-inch slices French bread

Sauté onions in butter in large saucepan until golden brown, about 15 minutes. Add bouillon, sauces, cheese, pepper and salt. Bring to a boil, reduce heat, cover and simmer for about 4 hours. Toast French bread on both sides in 350° oven until brown. Put bread on soup, top with more grated Parmesan and broil until bubbly. Makes 6 to 8 large servings.

MRS. VERNER E. STANLEY

OYSTER STEW

7 freshly opened oysters (or 1 small carton canned oysters)
¼ cup clam liquor (bottled juice) or ¼ cup liquid from canned oysters

1 teaspoon Worcestershire sauce
Paprika to taste
Celery salt to taste
1 cup milk
4 teaspoons butter

In deep pan bring to boil Worcestershire, paprika, celery salt, and 1 teaspoon of butter. Add oysters and clam liquor and cook until oysters curl (about 5 minutes). Add milk and heat thoroughly, but do not boil. Pour in bowl, top with paprika and remaining butter. Serves 1 or 2.

MRS. PAUL B. GUTHERY

SAUSAGE-BEAN CHOWDER

1 pound bulk pork sausage
2 cans (16-ounces) kidney beans
1 can (1-pound 13-ounces) tomatoes, broken up
1 quart water
1 large onion, chopped
1 bay leaf

1½ teaspoons seasoned salt
½ teaspoon garlic salt
½ teaspoon thyme
⅛ teaspoon pepper
1 cup diced potatoes
½ green pepper, chopped

In a skillet, cook sausage until brown and pour off grease. In a large kettle combine beans, tomatoes, water, onion, bay leaf seasoned salt, garlic salt, thyme, and pepper. Add sausage and simmer, covered, for one hour. Add potatoes and green pepper. Cook, covered, 15-20 minutes until potatoes are tender. Remove bay leaf. Makes 8 generous servings.

MRS. W. R. PITTS

SEA BREEZE SOUP

3 cans cream of celery soup
3¾ cups water
1½ cups flaked, boned crabmeat (fresh or canned)
3 tablespoons thinly sliced green onion

1½ medium tomatoes (cut in cubes)
¾ teaspoons grated lemon rind

Blend soup and water. Stir in crab, tomato, lemon rind and onion. Place in refrigerator for at least 4 hours. Serve in chilled bowls. Serves 6-8.

MRS. JOHN BRABSON

SHRIMP BISQUE

1 pound shrimp
4 tablespoons flour (heaping)
4 tablespoons butter
1 quart milk
1 teaspoon Worcestershire

1 teaspoon Tabasco
3 twists lemon peel
½ cup sherry
Dash of nutmeg
Salt to taste

Cook shrimp in boiling, salted water. Remove veins. Run shrimp through coarse food grinder. Make rich sauce in double boiler with milk, butter and flour and seasonings. Add shrimp and wine, just long enough to get hot. Delicious, rich soup—perfect for luncheon. Serves 4.

MRS. WYLIE ARNOLD

SPLIT PEA SOUP

1 16 ounce package dried green
  split peas
2 small ham hocks or bone

1 or 2 bay leaves
1 lemon
Hard boiled eggs

Soak peas overnight. Drain. Cook ham hocks, or bone from baked ham, in enough water to cover until meat falls off (about 1 to 1½ hours). Take bones out to cool. Add the ham stock to split peas. Add bay leaves and lemon cut in half, simmer until peas are very soft. Add cut-up meat from bones and simmer a while longer. Take out leaves and lemon and *don't* strain, but mash peas and meat. Serve hot with a thin slice of lemon, or garnish with chopped hard boiled eggs. A very hearty winter soup. Serves 8-10.

MRS. WYLIE ARNOLD

COLD CHIVE TOMATO SOUP

2 cans tomato soup
2 tablespoons chopped chives
3 cups milk
1 cup cream
1 tablespoon chopped basil

2 teaspoons soy sauce
2 tablespoons lime juice
1 tablespoon celery salt
Black pepper to taste

Mix ingredients. Heat. Chill. Garnish with chopped chives. (Can be served hot.) Serves 6.

MRS. CARLISLE ADAMS

CREAM OF TOMATO SOUP

6 cups cut-up fresh tomatoes
  (canned may be substitued)
½ cup chopped celery
¼ cup chopped onion
2 teaspoons white sugar
4 tablespoons butter

4 tablespoons flour
2 cups milk
2 cups half and half
1 teaspoon salt
⅛ teaspoon paprika

Cover and simmer for 15 minutes, tomatoes, celery, onion and sugar. In a double boiler, melt butter and add flour, stirring well. Scald and add milk and half and half, stirring constantly into strained tomato mixture. Season with salt and paprika. Place soup over hot water and heat before serving. Serve with whipped cream, parsley or croutons. Serves 6.

MRS. JOE LINEBERGER

GARDEN TOMATO SOUP

4 large tomatoes
1 cup canned chicken broth
4 small spring onions, thinly sliced
1 small cucumber, sliced
½ cup diced green pepper

1 cup canned tomato juice
Juice of 1 lemon
2 teaspoons sugar
1 tablespoon seasoned salt
¼ teaspoon seasoned pepper

Day before, or early day of serving, peel tomatoes and cut in chunks. In large saucepan, simmer onions, cucumber, green pepper and tomatoes in chicken broth for 5 minutes. Add tomato juice, lemon juice, sugar, salt and pepper. Simmer, covered, for 10 minutes. Transfer to a large bowl and refrigerate. Serve this cold soup in bowls as a "start off" or as refreshing luncheon main dish with French bread. Makes 10 appetizers or 6 luncheon servings.

MRS. ALEX R. JOSEPHS

TURKEY-BONE SOUP

Bones of one turkey or chicken
2 stalks celery
1 medium onion, sliced thick
¼ bell pepper, cut in pieces
6 pepper corns

1 teaspoon paprika
1 teaspoon Worcestershire sauce
Salt to taste
2 quarts water

Combine all in large pan. Bring to *slow* boil for 2 to 3 hours. Strain and use chicken stock as desired.

MRS. JOHN ALEXANDER STEWMAN III

VEGETABLE SOUP

1 pound stew beef
Soup bone or roast bone
2 stalks celery, cut up
2 small onions, sliced
2 medium potatoes, diced
1 package frozen mixed vegetables

1 28-ounce can tomatoes
1 package Lipton's Onion Soup mix
1 10¾-ounce can roast beef gravy
Salt to taste
Dash of sugar
Worcestershire sauce to taste

Cook meat and bone in 4 cups of salted water in pressure cooker until tender, about one hour. Cool meat and stock in refrigerator until fat solidifies. Remove fat and bones. Cook celery, onions and potatoes in stock under pressure about 5 minutes. Add sugar, onion soup mix and gravy and simmer in open pot. Taste, and add more salt if needed and dash of Worcestershire. It can be served at once or frozen. Serves 8.

MRS. GEORGE K. SELDEN, JR.

VEGETABLE SOUP WITH MIDGET MEAT BALLS

3 tablespoons margarine
5 carrots, sliced
2 medium onions, chopped
1 cup celery, diced
½ cup chopped parsley
1 cup corn
½ cup green pepper, chopped

2 cups canned tomatoes
4 cups hot water
2 beef bouillon cubes
2 teaspoons salt
¼ teaspoon pepper
1 small bay leaf
½ teaspoon basil

Dissolve bouillon cubes in hot water in large saucepan and add all ingredients to it. Simmer for 30 minutes, but do not boil. Drop in midget meat balls and simmer another 15 minutes. Serves 6.

MIDGET MEAT BALLS

½ pound ground beef
¼ cup dry bread crumbs
¼ to ½ cup milk
1 egg
½ teaspoon salt

⅛ teaspoon pepper
½ teaspoon nutmeg
2 tablespoons minced onion
½ clove garlic, chopped

Combine ingredients and mix thoroughly. Shape into very tiny balls. Brown quickly on all sides in small amount of fat in heavy skillet. Add meat balls to soup. Add grease to soup if desired.

MRS. TERRY YOUNG

REESA'S VEGETABLE SOUP

1 soup bone or 2 pounds short
  ribs
1 large can tomato juice
2 small cans of tomatoes
4 stalks of celery, chopped
1 green pepper, chopped
½ pound fresh green beans

1 large onion, chopped
4 diced carrots
1 package frozen okra
3 cubed potatoes
1 package frozen mixed
  vegetables
Seasonings

Cook meat in tomato juice and tomatoes until almost done. Add celery, pepper, beans, onion, carrots and potatoes. When almost done add frozen vegetables and okra. A dash of seasoned salt, Accent, black pepper and salt can be added at any time. A half teaspoon of sugar eliminates the acid taste. Simmer all day.

MRS. J. W. DUPREE, JR.*

VICHYSSOISE

3 cups potatoes (diced)
3½ cups sliced onion
1½ quarts water

3 beef bouillon cubes
1½ cups heavy cream
Fresh chives (to taste)

Simmer 30-40 minutes (until very soft) 3 cups diced potatoes and 3½ cups sliced onion in 1½ quarts water. Within 10 minutes after simmering, add 3 broken beef bouillon cubes. When soft, transfer to blender (may take 4 transfers) and blend on high speed 10-15 seconds, then slowly stir in 1 to 1½ cups heavy cream (depending on desired thickness). Chill and garnish with fresh chives. Serves 8.

MRS. WILLIAM MARCHANT

QUICK VICHYSSOISE

1 can Campbell's frozen potato soup
¼ soup can of whole milk

½ cup sour cream
2 tablespoons chopped chives
Salt to taste

Blend, adding chives after other ingredients are well blended. Chill well. Serves 4.

MRS. JOHN TILLETT, JR.

Breads

Breads

BISCUITS

1 cup self-rising flour
½ teaspoon sugar (optional)
1 heaping tablespoon shortening

Plain milk (or buttermilk)
  approx. ⅓ cup

Cut shortening into flour and sugar. Make a well in the mixture and fill with milk. Use just enough to moisten. Mix. Fold on cloth 3 times. Roll out and cut. Bake 10 minutes in 450° oven on greased cookie sheet. Makes 8.

MISS CRAIG MASON

ALVENA'S BISCUITS

2 cups plain flour
½ teaspoon salt
1 teaspoon sugar
2 teaspoon baking powder

¼ teaspoon baking soda
3 tablespoon shortening
⅔ cup buttermilk
  (approximately)

Sift all dry ingredients together. Cut shortening into dry ingredients. Add enough buttermilk to moisten. Mix with hands. Roll out and fold once. Roll again and cut desired size biscuits. Bake at 375° for 15-20 minutes on an ungreased cookie sheet. Makes about 24 medium sized biscuits.

MRS. VERNER STANLEY, JR.

APRICOT TEA BREAD

½ cup dried apricots
1 large orange
½ cup seedless raisins
½ cup chopped nuts
2 cups flour
1 teaspoon baking soda

2 teaspoons baking powder
1 cup sugar
1 egg
2 tablespoons butter, melted
1 teaspoon vanilla

Cover apricots with cold water and let stand for half an hour. Drain. Squeeze juice from orange, saving peel. Add enough boiling water to juice to make 1 cup. Put peel, fruits and nuts through medium blade of grinder. Sift together: flour, soda, baking powder, and sugar. Add nuts, fruits, juice, egg, melted butter and vanilla, mixing well. Bake in a greased loaf pan at 350° for 50 minutes. Serve hot and buttered or cold.

MRS. WALTER SCOTT, JR.

BANANA BREAD

1 stick butter
1 cup sugar
2 eggs
2 cups flour
½ teaspoon soda

½ teaspoon salt
1 teaspoon baking powder
1 cup mashed bananas (very ripe — about 3)
1 cup pecans

Cream butter and sugar. Add eggs. Sift dry ingredients together. Add mashed bananas to first mixture, then flour and nuts. Bake in greased loaf pan at 350° about 1 hour.

MRS. GEORGE IVEY, JR.

MEXICAN CORN BREAD

1 cup buttermilk
1½ cups self-rising corn meal
3 eggs, beaten
½ cup oil
1 cup creamed corn
½ large green pepper, finely chopped

1 small hot red pepper, finely chopped (optional)
1 cup sharp cheddar cheese (grated)

Combine ingredients except cheese and pour half of batter in 8-inch square greased pan. Cover with grated cheese and pour remaining batter over it. (Use more if desired). Bake in preheated 400° oven for 35-45 minutes, until golden.

MRS. VERNER STANLEY, JR.

DATE NUT BREAD

1 package dates, chopped
2 cups boiling water
2 teaspoons soda
2 tablespoons Crisco
2 cups sugar

2 eggs, beaten
4 cups flour
1 teaspoon salt
1 cup chopped nuts
2 teaspoons vanilla

Pour hot water over chopped dates. Add soda. Let cool. Cream Crisco and sugar. Add eggs and beat. Stir in date mixture; stir in sifted flour and salt. Add nuts and vanilla and mix well. Bake in tube pan or 3 medium-sized loaf pans at 350° for 1 to 1¼ hours. Cool in pan slightly before turning out. Good sliced thin and served warm or cold with butter and/or cream cheese.

MRS. TERRY YOUNG

HERB CHEESE BREAD

2 cups warm water (105°-115° F)
2 packages active dry yeast
2 tablespoons sugar
2 teaspoons salt

2 tablespoons soft butter
½ cup (heaping) grated Parmesan cheese
1½ tablespoons dried oregano
4¼ cups sifted plain flour

Sprinkle yeast over water in a large bowl. Let stand a few minutes, then stir to dissolve. Add sugar, salt, butter, cheese, oregano, and 3 cups flour. Beat at a low speed until blended. At medium speed, beat until smooth (2 minutes). Scrape bowl and beaters. With a wooden spoon, gradually beat in the rest of flour. Then cover bowl with a sheet of waxed paper and a towel. Let rise in a warm place free from drafts for 45 minutes, or until double in bulk.

Preheat oven to 375°. Lightly grease 1½ or 2-quart casserole. Stir down batter and beat vigorously 25 times. Turn into baking dish and sprinkle with a little cheese. Bake 55 minutes, until brown. Serve slightly warm.

MRS. VERNER STANLEY, JR.

MOTHER'S BREAD AND ROLLS

6 cups flour
1 teaspoon salt
½ cup sugar
3 eggs

½ cup shortening
1 package dry yeast
2 cups lukewarm water

Sift and measure flour, salt and sugar. Sift all together. Make a hole in flour and add eggs, shortening, and blend all together. Dissolve 1 package yeast in 2 cups warm water, add to mixture and mix. Place dough in greased bowl, covered with plate, and set in refrigerator for at least 6 hours (longer is better).

Grease pans well with margarine. (Makes 2 large loaves). Let dough rise, in pans, 3 hours at room temperature before baking. Bake in preheated 325° oven for 45 minutes. (To make rolls: grease biscuit pan and let rolls rise 2 to 2½ hours. Bake at 425° for 10 to 15 minutes.)

MRS. DOUGLAS BOOTH

PUMPKIN TEA BREAD

3 cups flour
3 cups sugar
2 cups pumpkin (#303 can)
3 eggs
1 cup oil
1 teaspoon nutmeg

1 teaspoon ground cloves
1 teaspoon cinnamon
1 teaspoon baking soda
1 teaspoon baking powder
½ teaspoon salt

Add measured amount of sugar to oil. Mix well. Add pumpkin and eggs. In a separate bowl, mix spices and flour well. Add to liquid mixture. Pour into ungreased angel food cake pan. Bake at 350° for about 1 hour and 15 minutes, or until knife comes out clean. (Optional additions: 1 cup nuts and 2/3 cup raisins)

MRS. HOWARD C. BISSELL
MRS. DOUGLAS BOOTH

SALLY LUNN BREAD

1 quart flour (4 cups)
3 large eggs
1 cup shortening and butter mixed
1 cup tepid milk

3 tablespoons sugar
2 teaspoons salt
1 yeast cake (or equivalent) dissolved in ½ cup lukewarm water

Separate the eggs and beat. Add the sugar and salt to the flour. Melt the shortening and pour into the beaten yolks. Add milk, yeast, shortening, flour and stiffly beaten egg whites. Beat thoroughly and set aside in warm place until risen to double in size (about 3 hours), then beat, beat, beat. Pour into greased tube pan and let rise again (1½ to 2 hours). Bake in moderate oven about 45 minutes and serve with melted butter. (Moderate oven: Start at 325° and when half done, increase to 375°.)

OLD NORTH STATE COOKBOOK

JANE'S SOUR CREAM COFFEE CAKE

2 sticks margarine or butter
1½ cups sugar
2 eggs
1 8 oz. carton sour cream
2 cups sifted flour
1½ teaspoons baking powder

½ teaspoon baking soda
1 teaspoon vanilla
2 teaspoons cinnamon
¾ cup pecans, chopped
2 tablespoons sugar

Cream butter and sugar. Add eggs and mix well. Add flour and sour cream, alternately. Add baking powder, soda and vanilla. Mix well. Grease and flour a tube pan. Pour in half of batter. Mix together cinnamon, sugar and nuts. Sprinkle over first half of batter. Pour the remaining batter over sugar mixture. Bake at 350° for 50 minutes. Cool on rack in pan for 15 minutes before removing from pan.

MRS. WALTER SCOTT, JR.

PECAN COFFEE CAKE

2 cans Pillsbury crescent rolls
3 tablespoons butter
½ cup sugar

1 to 2 teaspoons cinnamon
¼ cup chopped pecans

TOPPING

2 tablespoons honey
¼ cup confectioner's sugar
2 tablespoons butter

1 teaspoon vanilla
Pecan halves

Unroll crescents and separate into 16 triangles. Spread each with butter. Sprinkle with sugar-cinnamon-nut mixture and roll each up toward point. Place point side down in 2 layers (8 to a layer) in 9x5-inch greased loaf pan. Bake at 375° for 35 to 40 minutes. Remove at once and drizzle with topping. For topping: Bring all ingredients to a boil, stirring constantly. (Note: Do not make until time to bake; dough will not rise if made ahead). Makes 16.

CORN CAKES

1 cup corn meal
½ teaspon salt
1 teaspoon baking powder
⅛ teaspon sugar

2 eggs
1⅓ cups milk
⅓ cup oil

Mix well and cook on hot griddle. Batter will be thin. Serve for breakfast with syrup.

MRS. MARSHALL WARE

CORN MEAL GRIDDLE CAKES

2 cups corn meal (water ground
  if possible)
1½ cups flour
2½ teaspoons salt
2 tablespoons sugar
5 teaspoons baking powder

3 cups milk
3 eggs, beaten
¾ cup lard (or oil) and butter,
  melted together
1 teaspoon vanilla
2 tablespoons syrup

Mix dry ingredients. Beat eggs well, add milk, and combine with dry ingredients. Add syrup, vanilla, and melted shortening. (You can prepare batter the day before and add baking powder before cooking.)

MRS. R. E. JONES, JR.

MARGUERITES

2 eggs
1 cup brown sugar
½ cup flour

½ teaspoon salt
1 cup chopped pecans
¼ teaspoon baking powder

Slightly beat 2 eggs. Add next ingredients in the order listed. Mix well and fill small buttered muffin tins 2/3 full. Place half a pecan on each. Bake at 350° until mixture begins to leave sides, usually 8 to 12 minutes. Serve hot or cold. Store in a tin box. Makes 12 muffins. Especially nice served at coffees or teas.

MRS. ELI B. SPRINGS

WHOLE-WHEAT MUFFINS

1½ cups whole wheat flour
½ cup flour
¼ cup sugar
1 cup milk
1 egg

1 teaspoon salt
3 tablespoons melted butter
3 teaspoons baking powder

Combine dry ingredients and sift together. Add milk, egg, and butter. Bake in 375° oven for 20 to 25 minutes. Makes 12.

MRS. ROBIN JOHNSON

MORAVIAN SUGAR CAKE

1 package dry granulated yeast
½ cup lukewarm water
1 cup hot mashed potatoes
  (unseasoned)
1 cup white sugar (granulated)
4 tablespoons soft butter

½ cup shortening
1 teaspoon salt
2 eggs, beaten
Flour (amount needed)
Butter and brown sugar

Allow yeast to soak in ½ cup lukewarm water. To the hot mashed potatoes add sugar, butter, shortening and salt. When potatoes cool to just warm, add yeast mixture and 1 cup of potato water (water from boiled potatoes). Set aside and allow to rise for 2 hours in warm place, until spongy. Add 2 beaten eggs and sufficient flour to make a soft dough. Allow this to rise until double in bulk. Punch down on lightly floured board. Spread in greased flat baking pan. When "light", make holes with fingers and fill with pieces of butter and plenty of brown sugar. (Use as much as possible.) Dust with cinnamon. Bake at 375° for 20 minutes. Cut in squares.

MRS. MORRIS NEWELL

BUTTER HORNS

1 cake yeast
½ cup sugar
1 cup lukewarm water
1 teaspoon salt (scant)

3 eggs, beaten
½ cup melted butter
5 cups flour

Dissolve yeast and sugar in water. Add eggs and butter. Add flour and salt to form a stiff dough—adding more if needed—½-cup each time. Knead until smooth. Place in greased bowl until double in size (about 3 hours). Divide into 6 parts. Roll each into a circle. Cut into 6 pie-shaped parts. Brush with soft butter. Roll up into crescent horns (or fold over rolls). Place on buttered pans. Refrigerate. Bake the next day, after letting rise for 3 hours. Bake at 450° for 10 to 15 minutes. Makes 3 to 4 dozen, depending on size.

MRS. THOMAS MASSEY

CHOCOLATE MUFFINS

1 cup sugar
Less than ½ stick butter
⅓ cup water
1 good teaspoon baking powder
Dash of salt

1 cup flour
1 egg
1½ squares bitter chocolate
1 teaspoon vanilla

Cream butter; then add sugar and cream together well. Add one egg to above mixture and beat well. Put flour, baking powder, and salt in flour sifter. Sift the dry ingredients into the creamed mixture alternately with water. (Always start with flour mixture.) Last add the bitter chocolate, which has been melted, and 1 teaspoon vanilla. Preheat oven to 400° and bake 12 minutes. Do not open oven to check muffins until they have baked 10 minutes. Good served at luncheons.

MRS. RICHARD D. GILLESPIE*

PINEAPPLE MUFFINS

1 cup flour
2¼ teaspoons baking powder
¾ teaspoon salt
¼ teaspoon cinnamon
¾ cup instant Ralston

⅓ cup brown sugar, packed firmly
1 egg
⅓ cup oil (or melted shortening)
1 cup crushed pineapple, not drained

Sift together dry ingredients. Add Ralston and brown sugar. Beat egg and oil and pineapple. Add this to dry ingredients all at once. Stir only until flour is moistened. Bake in 12 large greased muffin cups for 20 to 25 minutes at 400°. Can be frozen.

MRS. JOHN RODDEY

SAUSAGE-SPICE CAKE MUFFINS

1 box spice cake mix

1 pound sausage

Fry sausage and drain thoroughly. Mix cake according to directions on box. Add sausage to cake mix and bake in muffin tins at 375° for 15 to 20 minutes. Makes 2 to 3 dozen muffins. Delicious with fruit salads, seafood or chicken salad.

MRS. ALFRED H. MURRELL

HOT MUFFIN TEA CAKE

2 cups sugar
4 eggs
1 stick margarine
1 cup milk

2½ cups flour
2 teaspoons vanilla
2½ teaspoons baking powder
¼ teaspoon salt

Sift flour with baking powder and salt. Beat eggs, add sugar, and beat well. Add flour mixture; then add hot milk and vanilla in which butter has been melted. Beat well. Pour in greased muffin tins. Bake for 20 minutes at 350°. Makes 3 dozen.

MRS. JAMES M. TROTTER

TEA MUFFINS

½ cup margarine or butter
1 cup light brown sugar
1 egg
1 cup sweet milk

½ teaspoon soda
2 scant cups all-purpose flour
½ cup nuts, chopped fine

Soften shortening and mix with sugar. Add egg. Add soda to the milk. Alternately add milk and flour to other mixture. Add nuts. Refrigerate at least 1 hour before baking. Bake for 20 minutes in 375° oven in small muffin tins. Can be kept in refrigerator more than a week. Delicious served with hot spiced tea. Makes about 24.

VIRGINIA GRIFFIN

WAFFLES

2 eggs	1 tablespoon sugar
2 cups plain flour	¼ cup melted butter
2 cups milk	2 heaping tablespoons Royal
½ teaspoon salt	Baking Powder

Beat eggs. Add remaining ingredients and beat together. Make waffles. With leftover batter, add milk and bake as muffins. Makes about 16 squares.

MRS. J. W. BARR

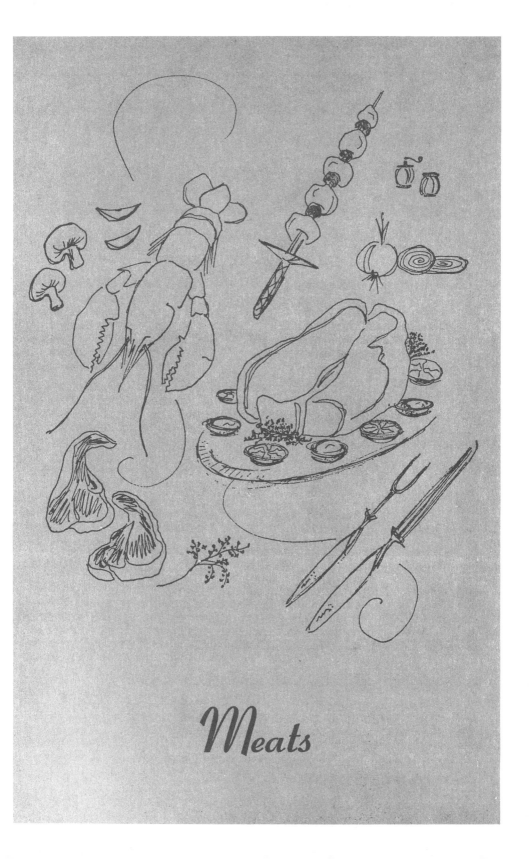

Meats

Beef

BOEUF AU VIN ROUGE

1 4-pound chuck or round roast
(boned and tied)
1 cup chopped onion
2 chopped carrots
6 pepper corns
1 cup Burgundy wine
1 tablespoon maple syrup

1 garlic clove, mashed
1 can beef broth
1 small can tomato paste
1 teaspoon anchovy paste
¼ teaspoon savory leaf
Salt and pepper to taste

Brown meat in Dutch oven in a little oil. Add onions and garlic, and cook about 3 minutes more. Add all other ingredients and allow to cook very slowly for about 4 hours with lid on. Reserve the juice for serving as gravy over meat. Serves 6 to 8.

MRS. H. M. JOHNSTON, JR.

COMPANY STEW

2 pounds boneless stew meat
6 to 10 strips of bacon
6 to 8 small onions
¾ pound fresh mushrooms, sliced
2 cups red wine

1 teaspoon thyme
1 clove garlic, crushed
1 bay leaf
Salt to taste

Cook bacon in water for 10 minutes, then fry. In this fat, brown the beef. When meat is brown, remove it and pour off any grease. Pour the wine into the pan and scrape the bottom with spatula. Add the seasonings to the wine, pour it over the meat, and cook in a covered dish at 325° for 2 hours. The liquid should barely cover the meat; if more is needed, use bouillon.

Cook onions in water until done; save the liquid. Sauté mushrooms and save the butter.

When meat is done, combine the liquid with that of the onions and mushrooms. Thicken with flour, and put it back over the meat. Add the onions and mushrooms at serving time. This can be made the day before if desired. Serve over cooked rice. Serves 4 to 6.

MRS. JOHN HILLHOUSE, JR.

63

CHE-ME-GO

2 pounds beef (chuck or shoulder)
1 cup soy sauce
6 tablespoons lemon juice

2 teaspoons dry mustard
2 teaspoons Accent or meat tenderizer

Marinate meat for 24 hours, turning once or twice. Then charcoal for a delightful flavor. Serves 4 to 6.

MRS. ROBERT CHERRY

BAKED CORNED BEEF HASH

2 cups chopped corned beef hash (canned)
2 tablespoons finely chopped onion

⅓ cup sour cream
Salt and pepper to taste

Combine all ingredients and bake in shallow greased casserole at 350° for 25 to 30 minutes or until top is well browned. Serves 4.

MRS. MARK P. JOHNSON

FRENCH POT ROAST

3 to 6-pound bottom round roast
⅔ cup finely chopped carrots
½ cup finely chopped onion
½ cup finely chopped celery

¼ pound fresh mushrooms, sliced
½ cup tomato puree
½ cup consomme
¼ cup water

Dredge roast in flour, salt and pepper. Brown quickly in hot fat. Place the vegetables around the roast in a large skillet with lid. Mix together tomato puree, consomme, and water. Pour over meat and vegetables. Cover and cook slowly for 4 to 5 hours, until tender. If you desire gravy, remove meat, strain gravy (being sure to get as much of the vegetables through as possible). Thicken broth with a little flour, salt, and pepper. Return meat to gravy. Serves 6 to 8.

MRS. WALTER SUMMERVILLE, JR.

BEEF BRISKET

3 pounds beef brisket
3 tablespoons catsup
2 tablespoons A-1 sauce
1 tablespoon Worcestershire

2 teaspoons minced onion
1 teaspoon instant coffee
¾ cup water

Place roast in iron skillet and brown on all sides. Mix the catsup, A-1, Worcestershire, onion, and instant coffee into a paste and cover the meat. Add the water to the bottom of the pan. Cover the pan with a tight-fitting lid. Cook in 300° oven for 3 hours. Baste occasionally, so it makes its own thick gravy. Slice on the diagonal grain. Serves 6 to 8.

MRS. WALTER SUMMERVILLE, JR.*

BEEF AND MUSHROOMS

1 3-ounce can sliced mushrooms
1 tablespoon butter
1 4-ounce can beef gravy
½ cup red wine

2 teaspoons A-1 steak sauce
Dash of Tabasco
3 to 4 cups cooked beef chunks
Rice, cooked

Saute mushrooms in butter. Add other ingredients and simmer about 5 minutes. Serve on rice. Serves 4.

MRS. ELLEN G. GOODE

SIRLOIN BEEF WITH SAUCE

9 tablespoons bourbon
6 tablespoons soy sauce
2 tablespoons garlic vinegar
2 tablespoons Mazola oil
½ teaspoon salt

½ teaspoon Accent
½ teaspoon freshly ground
pepper
3 to 4 pounds thick sirloin steak

Mix all the ingredients except meat. Cover steak with sauce, marinating it all day. Cook or grill steak, as desired. Serve with remaining heated sauce. Serves 4 to 6.

MRS. ROBERT BRADSHAW

BEEF STROGANOFF

2 pounds round steak, cut in thin
strips
2 tablespoons flour
1 teaspoon salt
Dash of pepper
2 onions, chopped fine
½ pound chopped mushrooms
1 clove garlic

4 tablespoons butter
1 can beef bouillon
1 teaspoon paprika
1 tablespoon Worcestershire
Salt and pepper to taste
2 cups sour cream
2 cups uncooked rice

Cut meat into thin strips. Dredge in flour, salt and pepper. Sauté onions, mushrooms, and garlic in butter. Add meat and brown lightly. Add bouillon and simmer meat until tender (several hours). Add Worcestershire and paprika. Add a little water during cooking to keep meat tender. Before serving, add sour cream. Cook rice according to directions on box. Serve Stroganoff over hot rice. Serves 6 to 8.

MRS. JOHN P. MAYNARD

SHERRIED STROGANOFF

3 pounds beef tenderloin
2 onions, chopped fine
2 large cans mushrooms
½ cup sherry
½ teaspoon pepper

3 teaspoons salt
3 to 4 cartons sour cream
2 boxes Uncle Ben's wild and
white rice mix, cooked

Cut meat in bite-sized strips and brown quickly in butter so juice won't run out. Sauté onions and mushrooms in butter. Add sherry, seasonings, and then the sour cream. Pour over the meat and keep warm in chafing dish. Serve over rice. Serves 10 to 12.

MRS. PERRIN Q. HENDERSON

TOMATO BEEF STROGANOFF

1 large onion
1 can mushrooms
1 bay leaf
1 pound top round beef cubes
1 clove garlic

1 tablespoon Worcestershire
Salt and pepper to taste
1 small can tomato paste
1 pint sour cream
Rice, cooked

Brown onions and mushrooms in butter and set aside. Brown beef cubes with bay leaf, garlic, Worcestershire, salt and pepper. Combine all these ingredients in the top of a double boiler, and add the tomato paste and half the sour cream. Cook, covered, for 2 to 3 hours. Just before serving, add the other half-pint of sour cream. Serve over rice. Serves 4 to 6.

MRS. J. O. ERWIN

MARINATED SHISH KABAB

5 cubes per person sirloin steak,
very lean, cut in 1½-inch cubes
2 small fresh potatoes,
parboiled, per skewer
3-4 whole buttered mushrooms
per skewer
2 small onions per skewer
3-4 pieces green pepper per skewer

3-4 pieces firm ripe tomatoes,
quartered, or whole Tiny Tims,
per skewer
2 small pieces corn on cob,
parboiled, per skewer
1 small can crunchy water
chestnuts
Melted butter
6-8 individual sized skewers

Marinate steak cubes in beef marinade. Have your coals in the grill hot—to the ash-grey stage before you begin cooking. Cut vegetables evenly and neatly for equal doneness and attractiveness. Grease skewers ahead of time and rub with a piece of garlic to ease in spearing and to add flavor. Alternate meat and vegetables on skewers as desired. Top skewer with a water chestnut to help hold them firm. Broil kababs about 5 to 6 inches above coals, turning often. Baste meat during cooking with the remaining marinade. Baste vegetables with the melted butter. Cook about 6 or 7 minutes to each side. Remove ingredients from skewer with a fork, gently.

While you are cooking this you can also spear "Brown 'n Serve" rolls, brush with butter, and warm. This is an easy way for the hostess to serve them and is in keeping with the atmosphere. Serves 6.

BEEF MARINADE

½ cup salad oil
⅓ cup vinegar
⅓ cup chopped onion
1 teaspoon salt

Dash of pepper
2 tablespoons Worcestershire
Juice of 1 lemon

Mix all ingredients and marinate your meat for 6 hours.

MRS. DONALD EVANS

CHINESE PEPPER STEAK

1 to 1½ pounds round steak (cut in thin 1-inch strips)
Oil for browning
1 small onion, chopped
½ cup diced celery
¼ teaspoon pepper
1 teaspoon salt
½ teaspoon sugar
1½ cups water
2 beef bouillon cubes
1 large green pepper, cut in thin strips
1 tablespoon cornstarch
1 tablespoon soy sauce
Rice, cooked
Chinese noodles

Brown onion, celery, and steak in hot oil. Add salt, pepper, sugar, water and bouillon cubes. Cover, reduce heat, and simmer one hour. Add green pepper and cook 15 minutes longer. Blend cornstarch and a little water until smooth. Add soy sauce and stir until thickened. Serve over hot rice with Chinese noodles. Serves 4.

MRS. CARL HORN, JR.

COUNTRY STYLE STEAK

1½ pounds round steak
Salt and pepper to taste
Flour to dredge steak
3 tablespoons fat for browning
1 tablespoon flour
1 cup water
1 tablespoon onion flakes (optional)

Dredge steak in flour seasoned with salt and pepper. After it is browned on both sides, remove from pan and add 1 tablespoon flour to pan drippings. Slowly stir in water to form a gravy. Add onion flakes. Return meat and cover; simmer for 1½ to 2 hours. Serves 4 to 6.

MRS. WALTER SUMMERVILLE, JR.

GREEN PEPPER STEAK

1 pound boneless round steak (sliced very thin)
¼ cup soy sauce
½ teaspoon ground ginger
1 small clove garlic, crushed
2 tablespoons salad oil or bacon drippings
2 green peppers, seeded and cut in thin strips
2 #303 cans tomatoes
1 tablespoon cornstarch
Rice, cooked

Place steak in bowl and cover with marinade of soy sauce, ginger and garlic. Cover and let stand for at least 30 minutes. Remove meat and drain. Save marinade. Quickly brown meat in heated oil (electric skillet perfect). Add peppers and tomatoes. Cover and simmer about 5 minutes. Blend cornstarch with marinade; stir into beef-pepper-tomato mixture, and cook, stirring constantly, until sauce is thickened. Serve with rice. Serves 4. (325 calories per serving).

MRS. ERVIN JACKSON, JR.

FILET MIGNON

3 to 3½ pounds filet mignon
½ teaspoon salt
¼ teaspoon pepper
¼ teaspoon garlic salt

1 tablespoon sugar
1 teaspoon meat tenderizer
Dash of hickory smoked salt
Pieces of thinly sliced fat

Rub meat with each of the above ingredients in the order in which they are listed. Rub well, getting into all the pores of the meat. Let stand for 15 minutes. Lay pieces of fat over the filet. Cook in 350° oven for 35 minutes or until desired doneness. Serves 8.

MRS. PHILIP SMALL

SAUTÉ DE BOEUF A LA PARISIENNE

(Beef Sauté with Cream and Mushroom Sauce)

SAUCE

1 pound sliced fresh mushrooms
6 tablespoons butter
6 tablespoons minced green onions
½ teaspoon salt and pinch of pepper
½ cup Madeira (or dry white vermouth)

1½ cups canned beef bouillon
2 cups whipping cream
2 tablespoons cornstarch (blend with 2 tablespoons of the cream)

Sauté the mushrooms until lightly brown (4 to 5 minutes). Add onion, cook a minute longer and add seasoning. Set this aside. In another skillet, pour wine and bouillon in and rapidly boil it down until there is about 1/3 cup of liquid remaining. Beat in the cream, then the cornstarch mixture. Simmer a minute, then add sautéed mushrooms and simmer a little more. Sauce should be lightly thickened.

BEEF SAUTÉ

5 pounds fillet of beef
4 tablespoons butter

2 tablespoons cooking oil

Remove fat from fillet and cut into pieces 2 inches wide and ½-inch thick. Put butter and oil in skillet and sauté a few pieces of beef at a time for 2 or 3 minutes. The beef should be brown on the outside, but the inside should be red.

When all beef has been sautéed, season with salt and pepper and drain excess fat from pan. Pour the cream and mushroom sauce over the beef. As sauce is basted over the beef, add 4 tablespoons butter and mix until butter melts and is absorbed. Place in casserole or serving dish and garnish with parsley. Serves 12.

MRS. RODDEY DOWD

LONDON BROIL

3 pounds top round steak
4 teaspoons Adolph's meat
tenderizer
2 tablespoons sugar
4 tablespoons sherry

4 tablespoons soy sauce
2 tablespoons honey
2 teaspoons salt
2 teaspoons Accent

Pierce meat all over with the above ingredients, having been mixed well. Marinate six hours. Broil on grill. Serves 6.

MRS. NOEL LEE DUNN

SOUTH GEORGIA FLAMING STEAK

2½-inch flat-bone sirloin steak
2 cloves garlic, mashed
4 tablespoons wine vinegar
2 ounces olive oil

Freshly ground black pepper to
taste
Allspice to taste
Salt

Remove bone from steak. Roll flat, using heavy string, and skew with long handled skewer through the flat plane. Marinate for at least 6 hours at room temperature in the above ingredients.

Build a charcoal fire at least 6 inches deep and 12 to 15 inches around. A short time before all coals have turned white and are ready, remove the skewed steak from the marinade and coat it with table salt. The steak should literally be coated, using a regular cardboard salt container instead of a table shaker.

When coated, place steak *directly* on the coals—no grill. Cook 15 minutes, turn, and cook another 15 minutes for medium rare. Don't let the flames scare you, as this steak will char to a crust on the very outside only. Slice on the diagonal after removing skewer. Liberally serves 6.

MR. ALSTON RAMSAY

CHILI I

1 small onion, chopped
1 pound hamburger meat
1 can tomato soup
1 can red kidney beans with liquid

2 or 3 teaspoons chili powder
1 tablespoon flour
1 cup water
Salt and pepper to taste

Brown chopped onion in 1 or 2 tablespoons bacon grease. Crumble meat in with onion and brown. When brown, add soup, beans, and chili-flour mixture (chili powder and 1 tablespoon flour mixed in 1 cup water). Cover and simmer 45 minutes to 1 hour, stirring occasionally. Serves 6.

MRS. EVERETT WOHLBRUCK

CHILI II

1 pound ground chuck
1 tablespoon bacon drippings
1 medium onion, finely chopped
  or 4 tablespoons instant onion
Salt and pepper to taste
1 tablespoon Worcestershire

1 tablespoon chili powder
1 cup grated cheddar cheese
1 10-ounce can tomato soup
1 #2 can kidney beans
Rice, cooked
Cheese, grated

Brown meat, onion and drippings in skillet. Drain. Add seasonings to meat. Add soup and beans. Mix well. Simmer, uncovered, for 20 to 30 minutes. Serve in individual bowls, or over hot rice or Fritos. Top with grated cheese. Serves 4 to 6.

MRS. JOHN DABBS III

HAMBURGERS DELUXE

6 hamburger patties
6 hamburger buns
2 tablespoons butter

Worcestershire to taste
Bourbon to taste

Prepare hamburger patties as you normally would. Toast buns. Melt butter in saucepan. Skim butter or purify it. Add Worcestershire and bourbon to taste. Dip buns in sauce. Place hamburgers on buns and have a feast. Good for a quick snack. Serves 6.

MRS. BRUCE H. RINEHART

HAMBURGER SUPREME

1 can Golden Mushroom Soup
2 teaspoons Worcestershire
1 teaspoon horseradish
1½ pounds lean ground beef
1 egg, slightly beaten

¼ cup fine dry bread crumbs
¼ cup chopped onion
½ teaspoon salt
Dash of pepper

Blend first three ingredients. Combine ¼ cup of this mixture with remaining ingredients and shape into patties; brown in skillet, pour off excess fat. Stir in remaining soup mixture and add about ½ cup water. Cover and cook over low heat for 20 minutes. Serves 6.

MRS. WALTER SUMMERVILLE, JR.

SLOPPY JOES

2 pounds ground chuck
½ cup celery, chopped fine
1 medium onion, chopped fine
½ medium green pepper, chopped
  fine
2 teaspoons vinegar
2 teaspoons dry mustard

2 teaspoons white sugar
1 family size bottle catsup
1 teaspoon Worcestershire
Salt and pepper to taste
½ cup green olives, chopped fine
  (optional)

Brown meat, celery, and onions until lightly browned in large heavy skillet. Pour off grease. Add remaining ingredients to meat and simmer slowly for 1 to 1½ hours. Serve on heated buns. Serves 10.

MRS. TERRY YOUNG

PORCUPINE MEAT BALLS

1 pound ground beef
⅓ cup uncooked rice
¼ cup chopped onion
¼ cup water
1 teaspoon salt

Pepper to taste
1 large can condensed tomato
   soup or 2½ cups tomato juice
½ teaspoon chili powder
½ cup water

Combine meat, rice, onion, ¼ cup water and seasonings in large bowl. (I find it easier to mix with my hands.) Shape into 15 1-inch balls. Blend soup, chili powder and water in electric skillet or large, heavy skillet. and bring to a boil. Add meat balls. Cover and barely simmer for 45 minutes to an hour, basting as often as possible. (This could be cooked in a 350° oven, covered, for about 1 hour.) The rice pops through, looking like porcupines, which children love. Serves 4 to 5.

MRS. BRUCE RINEHART

SWEDISH MEAT BALLS

1 pound beef
½ pound lean fresh pork
½ pound salt pork
1 cup fine bread crumbs
1 medium onion, minced
1 egg
¼ teaspoon marjoram
¼ teaspoon basil

1½ teaspoons salt
1½ teaspoons black pepper
½ cup thin cream
3 tablespoons butter
1½ cups hot water
2 bouillon cubes
¾ cup sour cream
3 tablespoons flour

Have butcher grind beef and pork together twice. Combine meat, crumbs, onion, egg, herbs, salt, pepper and then cream. Mix thoroughly and shape into balls about the size of walnuts. Brown on all sides in butter and place balls in casserole as they brown. After all are in casserole, add flour to butter in pan. Stir well and add 2 bouillon cubes which have been dissolved in hot water. Mix and boil 3 minutes. Stir in sour cream. Pour over meat balls or reheat in oven. Serves 6.

MRS. JAMES O. COBB, JR.*

BARBECUED MEAT LOAF

1½ pounds ground beef
1 cup soft breadcrumbs or 1
   cup uncooked rolled oats
½ cup milk
2 beaten eggs
½ cup tomato sauce or juice
1½ teaspoons salt

½ cup finely chopped onion
¼ cup finely chopped green
   pepper
1 tablespoon Worcestershire
1 teaspoon prepared mustard
2 strips bacon
Bottled barbecue sauce

Moisten bread crumbs in milk. Combine all ingredients except bacon and barbecue sauce. Mix thoroughly with hands. Mold into shape in baking dish. Lay bacon strips on top. Pour barbecue sauce over all. With hands smear top and sides of loaf, covering it well. (You will need about ¾ cup of barbecue sauce.) Bake at 350° for 1 hour. If desired, add more barbecue sauce during last half hour. Serves 4 to 6.

MRS. WILLIAM A. WHITE, JR.

OATMEAL MEAT LOAF

1½ pounds ground beef
(chuck or hamburger)
¼ cup minced onion
1 cup uncooked oats
2 teaspoons salt

¼ teaspoon pepper
1 teaspoon prepared mustard
¼ cup catsup
1 egg, beaten
1 cup water or milk

Mix beef, onion, oats, salt, pepper, mustard, & catsup well. Add beaten egg and milk and mix thoroughly. Use hand or electric beater for blending. Form in loaf shape and place on open pan, or pack in loaf pan 9x5 inches. Bake in 350° oven for 1 hour or until meat is brown and cooked Serves 6.

MRS. NED R. CORZINE

ONION BEEF LOAF

1½ pounds ground beef
1 8-ounce can tomato sauce
1 egg, well beaten
1½ teaspoons salt

¼ teaspoon pepper
¼ teaspoon garlic powder
1 3½-ounce can French fried
onion rings, crumbled

Combine the above ingredients together and shape into a loaf. Put in baking dish and bake at 300° for 45 to 50 minutes. Pour off drippings. Place cooked carrots and whole new potatoes around the loaf and continue cooking about 15 more minutes, or until meat is thoroughly done and the vegetables are hot. (If you don't want to add carrots and potatoes, cook the meat about 1 hour.) Serves 4.

MRS. RICHARD BILGER

SWEDISH MEAT LOAF WITH PICKLE SAUCE

1½ cups soft bread crumbs
½ cup milk
½ cup catsup
2 eggs, beaten
1 tablespoon Worcestershire

¼ teaspoon pepper
2 teaspoons salt
2 pounds ground beef
½ cup onion, finely chopped
½ cup dill pickles, finely chopped

Combine all ingredients together, mixing well with electric mixer or hands. Bake in 9 x 5 x 3 pan in 350° oven for about 1 hour. Serve hot, with sauce. Serves 8.

SOUR CREAM PICKLE SAUCE

½ pint sour cream
½ cup chopped dill pickles, drained
¼ cup dill pickle juice

¼ cup mayonnaise
1 tablespoon flour

Mix all ingredients well. Heat slowly until thickened, stirring constantly. Serve hot (or cold) on meat loaf. Makes 1¾ cups.

MRS. CHARLES WARNER

SAVORY BEEF LOAF

3½ pounds lean ground beef
6 to 8 saltines, rolled fine
4 tablespoons milk
3 eggs
4 teaspoons salt

1 teaspoon black pepper
¼ teaspoon red pepper
1 teaspoon savory herbs
Dash of nutmeg
2 slices uncooked bacon

Mix beef with cracker crumbs. Add milk, eggs, and seasonings. Shape into two rolls, wrap bacon around them. Place in greased pan. Bake in moderate oven (350°) for 1 hour or more. Baste with its own juices while cooking. Delicious when served cold (sliced thin) as well as hot. Serves 8 to 10.

MRS. WALTER SCOTT, JR.

LASAGNA I

1 pound mild sausage
1 pound ground beef
1 envelope Chef Boyardee Spaghetti Sauce Mix
2 8-ounce cans tomato sauce
1 6-ounce can tomato paste
1½ cups water

2 tablespoons grated Parmesan cheese
½ pound Lasagna noodles
1 pound cottage cheese
2 tablespoons chopped parsley
1 8-ounce package sliced Mozzarella cheese

In large skillet, brown sausage, add beef and brown. Drain off fat. Blend next 4 ingredients to make sauce. Add sauce and Parmesan cheese to meats and simmer for 10 minutes. Cook and drain noodles. Cover bottom of casserole with sauce, then layer noodles, cottage cheese, parsley, and sauce. Repeat layers. Bake at 350° for 20 minutes, or until hot. Serves 6.

MRS. BONN GILBERT, JR.

LASAGNA II

1 8-ounce package Lasagna noodles, cooked as directed
1 #2½ can Italian style peeled tomatoes, mashed
2 6-ounce cans tomato paste
1 teaspoon salt
1½ teaspoons oregano
¼ teaspoon pepper
1 teaspoon onion salt
¼ cup salad oil

1 cup minced onions
2 cloves garlic, minced fine
1 pound ground chuck
1 teaspoon salt
¾ pound ricotta or cottage cheese
½ pound Mozzarella cheese, sliced thin
¾ cup Parmesan cheese, grated

Simmer tomatoes, tomato paste, salt, oregano, pepper and onion salt in uncovered saucepan. Put oil in skillet. When hot, saute finely minced onion and garlic until lightly browned. Add ground meat and salt to onion mixture and cook until it is crumbly and the red color is gone. Add to tomato sauce. Simmer 2 to 2½ hours, until thickened.

Cover bottom of baking dish (12x8x2) with 1/3 of the sauce. Place half the Lasagna crisscross over the sauce. Cover noodles with half the ricotta (or cottage) cheese, half the Mozzarella cheese and one-third of Parmesan cheese. Repeat these layers and end with meat mixture on top. Add the remaining Parmesan cheese. Bake at 350° for 30 to 40 minutes, or until bubbly. Let stand 15 minutes before serving. Serves 6 to 8.

MRS. E. O. AYSCUE, JR.

SPAGHETTI SAUCE I

1 large onion, chopped
1 bell pepper, chopped
3 tablespoons olive oil
1 pound ground beef
2 small cans tomatoes
1 can tomato paste
2 bay leaves
Salt to taste

Pepper to taste
Tabasco sauce to taste
Worcestershire to taste
Garlic powder to taste
Dash of red pepper
1 small can sliced mushrooms
1 small can pitted black olives
Spaghetti, cooked

Sauté onion and bell pepper in olive oil. Add ground beef and cook until brown. Add tomatoes, tomato paste, bay leaves, salt, pepper. Tabasco, Worcestershire, garlic powder, and red pepper. Simmer for 1 or 2 hours. Add mushrooms and olives before serving. Serve over cooked spaghetti, and sprinkle with Parmesan cheese. (After spaghetti is cooked and drained, add a tablespoon of butter and mix well. This keeps it from sticking together.) Serves 4.

MRS. ALEX R. JOSEPHS

SPAGHETTI SAUCE II

1 cup tomatoes
4 cups tomato puree or
  tomato sauce
1 pound ground beef
1 cup chopped onion
½ cup olive oil
½ cup butter
2 garlic cloves, crushed
6 bay leaves (remove at serving
  time)

½ teaspoon chopped parsley
2 tablespoons chopped green
  pepper
2 teaspoons oregano
½ teaspoon allspice
¼ teaspoon red pepper
1 teaspoon salt
Dash of pepper
Spaghetti

Sauté onion in oil and butter 10 minutes; add garlic and bay leaves; cover and simmer 10 minutes more. Add beef and sauté 10 minutes, stirring constantly. Add remaining ingredients, bring to a boil; reduce heat and simmer for 1 hour. (This is better if made early in the day and allowed to sit all day before serving.) Serve hot over spaghetti. Serves 6.

MRS. PHILIP G. CONNER

MOTHER'S SPAGHETTI CASSEROLE

6 strips bacon
2 medium onions
1 pound ground round steak
1 pound American cheese, grated
2 #303 (medium-size) cans
  tomatoes

2 teaspoons salt
½ teaspoon red pepper
1 box spaghetti

Put strips of bacon in deep frying pan and fry until crisp. Remove and drain. Chop onion fine and sauté until brown. Add ground beef, stirring, and cook until brown. Add tomatoes (heat to start boiling) salt, and pepper. Mash tomatoes in mixture so there are no big pieces. Simmer about 45 minutes. Break bacon in small pieces and add a little before removing mixture. When mixture is done, put in a casserole—a layer of cooked noodles, a layer of grated cheese, a layer of sauce. Repeat, ending with a layer of cheese. Put in preheated 450° oven and cook until cheese is browned. Can be fixed ahead and frozen. Serves 6 to 8.

MRS. W. WELLS VAN PELT

HAMBURGER PIE

1 medium onion, chopped
1 pound ground beef
Salt and pepper to taste
1 #2 can (or ½-pound cooked) green beans
1 can tomato soup
5 medium potatoes, cooked
½ cup warm milk
1 egg, beaten

Brown onion lightly in small amount of fat. Add meat and seasonings and brown. Add drained, cooked beans and soup. Pour into greased casserole. Mash potatoes, and add milk, egg, and seasonings to potatoes. Spoon them in mounds over meat mixture. Bake in 350° oven for 30 minutes. Serves 6.

MRS. JAMES S. WILCOX, JR.

PIZZA HAMBURGER PIE

1 pound ground chuck
1½ teaspoons salt
¼ teaspoon pepper
1 teaspoon horseradish
1 teaspoon Worcestershire
½ teaspoon dried basil
1 8 oz. can tomato sauce
½ teaspoon dried oregano
1 teaspoon dry mustard
2 tablespoons minced onion
2 tablespoons parsley
1 cup sharp cheese, grated
1 cup Mozzarella cheese, grated

Toss meat with the next 5 ingredients. Press against sides and bottom of casserole dish or 9-inch pie pan. Spread tomato sauce over meat and sprinkle with remaining ingredients. Bake at 375° for 20 minutes. Do not overbake. Place pan under dish to catch grease drippings. Before serving, drain off some of excess grease. Serves 4.

MRS. GRIMES THOMAS

TAMALE PIE

1 pound ground meat
½ pound bacon
1 large onion, chopped
1 large green pepper, chopped
1 large can tomatoes, drained
1 small can butter beans, drained (or 1 package frozen, cooked)
1 can spaghetti with tomato sauce

Cook bacon, drain off most of grease. Put in onion and pepper and cook until tender. Cook meat in grease until red color is gone. Put in bacon, green pepper, onion, tomatoes, and butter beans. Add spaghetti and salt and pepper to taste. Put in baking dish and bake at 350° for 30 minutes. May be prepared ahead and baked at the last minute. Serves 4 to 6.

MRS. R. E. JONES, JR.

"A'S" BEEF STROGANOFF

2 onions, chopped
⅓ stick butter
1¼ pounds ground meat
2 small cans V-8 juice
Celery salt

1 can sliced mushrooms
1 package thin egg noodles, uncooked
1 carton sour cream
1 cup grated American cheese

Brown onions in butter. Add meat and brown. Add all other ingredients except sour cream. Stir well and simmer for 20 minutes. Add sour cream. Pour in casserole and top with grated cheese. Bake at 350° until cheese is bubbly. Serves 8.

MRS. JOSEPH K. HALL III

HAMBURGER STROGANOFF

1 pound ground beef
3 slices bacon, diced
½ cup chopped onion
¾ teaspoon salt
1 teaspoon paprika

Dash of pepper
1 can mushroom soup
1 can mushrooms (medium)
1 cup sour cream
Hot poppy-seed noodles

In skillet brown beef with bacon. Add onion and cook until tender. Drain off excess fat. Add seasonings to meat mixture. Stir in soup and mushrooms and cook slowly, uncovered, for 20 minutes, stirring frequently. Stir in sour cream and heat through. Do not boil. Serve over hot poppy-seed noodles. Serves 4.

MISS CLAUDIA WATKINS

BEEF 'N' BEAN BAKE

3 slices bacon
1 large onion, sliced
1 pound ground chuck
1 10½-ounce can tomato soup, undiluted
1 1-pound can lima beans, drained

2 tablespoons brown sugar
1½ teaspoons salt
¼ teaspoon pepper
1 tablespoon Worcestershire
Dash of Tabasco

In large skillet sauté bacon until nearly crisp; remove bacon. In bacon fat, sauté onion until golden; add meat and sauté, stirring occasionally, to desired doneness. Remove from heat. Stir in soup, beans, and seasonings. Transfer mixture to 1½-quart casserole. Lay bacon on top. Bake, uncovered, at 325° for 25 minutes. Serves 4.

MRS. THORNWELL G. GUTHERY

BEEF AND RICE DISH

3 tablespoons oil or Crisco
¼ pound mushrooms, chopped
1 pound ground beef
1 or 2 onions, chopped
1 cup rice (uncooked)

2 cans consomme
½ teaspoon Worcestershire
Salt to taste

Sauté onions and mushrooms in oil or Crisco in large iron skillet. When brown, remove from heat and add consomme, uncooked rice, seasonings and uncooked meat. Stir well. Place in covered casserole dish and cook in 300° oven for 1½ hours, or leave in covered skillet and cook on top of the range for 1½ hours, simmering very slowly. Serves 6.

MRS. HUGH M. TILLETT

DIVINE CASSEROLE

1 large package small egg noodles
2 pounds ground beef
2 cans tomato paste
2 teaspoons Worcestershire
Few drops Tabasco
Pinch of oregano
1 carton creamed cottage cheese
1 8-ounce package cream cheese
½ pint sour cream
Salt to taste
2 chopped onions, sauteed in butter
2 sticks butter or margarine

Boil, drain and rinse noodles under hot water. Brown meat well. Add tomato paste, Worcestershire, Tabasco, salt and oregano. Mix cottage cheese, cream cheese (which has been allowed to stand at room temperature until softened), sour cream and onions. Melt butter.

Grease two 2-quart casseroles. Place one-fourth of the noodles in each casserole. Pour a little melted butter over noodles and add half the cheese mixture to each casserole. Add remaining noodles, more butter, and top with meat mixture. Bake in 350° oven for approximately 40 minutes or until bubbly. Freezes well. Serves 8 to 10.

MRS. JAMES CRAIG

EAT MORE

3 pounds lean ground chuck
3 stalks celery (leaves included)
1 large sweet onion, chopped
1 large green pepper, chopped
Garlic salt to taste
1 teaspoon oregano
1 teaspoon basil
1 tablespoon dry mustard
3 tablespoons catsup
2 packages Swiss cheese
1 teaspoon chili powder
1 cap full Liquid Smoke
1 large can tomatoes
2 cartons cottage cheese
2 packages Mozzarella cheese
2 cans mushrooms
Pinch of salt
Parmesan cheese
8-ounce package egg noodles

Brown meat in a large skillet, using a little grease. Stir with a fork to prevent sticking. Add chopped celery and leaves, onion and pepper. Cook until tender. Add tomatoes and cook down until almost dry. Add seasonings. Meanwhile, cook noodles until almost tender.

In three casseroles arrange ingredients in this order: layer of sauce, layer of cottage cheese, sprinkle with Parmesan cheese, layer of noodles, long slices of Mozzarella and Swiss cheeses. End with layer of sauce on top. Sprinkle with Parmesan again. Cook at 350° until bubbly. Casseroles may be frozen. Makes 3 1½-quart casseroles. Serves 12.

MRS. G. B. ADAMS

EGGPLANT PARMESAN

3 medium eggplants
1½ cups flour
3 eggs, beaten
Olive oil
3 packages sliced Mozzarella cheese
Salt and pepper
1½ pounds ground beef
2 cloves garlic
2 cans tomato paste (small)
2 14-ounce cans tomatoes

Peel eggplant and slice about ¼-inch thick. Dip each slice in beaten egg, then flour; salt and pepper well. Brown well on both sides in enough oil to keep from sticking, but don't cook thoroughly. Make a spaghetti-type sauce from the ground beef, garlic, tomatoes and tomato paste, being sure it is not too runny. In a 3-quart casserole, place layers of eggplant, sauce, then cheese until filled. Cook, uncovered, at 325° for about 1 hour—until hot and bubbly. Serves 10.

MRS. JOE LINEBERGER

GROUND BEEF CASSEROLE

1 8-ounce package noodles
2 cans mushroom soup, undiluted
½ pound grated sharp cheese
¾ cup chopped ripe olives
½ cup chopped onion
3 tablespoons chopped parsley
2 pounds ground beef
¼ pound slivered almonds
1 can Chinese noodles

Cook noodles and drain. Brown meat lightly. Add onion, salt and pepper. Drain grease. Add soup to meat mixture and stir until blended. Put in large, greased casserole, adding alternate layers of noodles and ground beef and other ingredients (except for Chinese noodles and almonds, which are added very last). Bake at 350° about 30 minutes. Remove from oven, top with Chinese noodles and almonds. Continue cooking for 15 minutes longer. Serves 6 to 8. Can be prepared ahead.

MRS. JAMES GLENN

TAGLIANI

2 pounds ground beef
1 green pepper, chopped
1 large onion, chopped
½ clove garlic, sliced (optional)
1 small can mushrooms
1 cup sharp cheese, grated
1 8-ounce package egg noodles (¼-inch wide)
2 cans tomato paste
1 qt. 14 oz. can tomato juice
1 #1 can cream style corn (optional)
½ to 1 cup red wine
½ cup Romano cheese, grated
Salt, pepper, Worcestershire to taste

Brown meat, pepper, onion and garlic. Drain off grease. Add mushrooms with liquid, tomato paste and tomato juice and stir well. Add uncooked noodles and cook over low heat, covered, until noodles are tender, about 30 minutes. Mix in corn, sharp cheese and wine. Pour into buttered casserole dish and bake at 325° about 20 minutes, or until lightly browned on top. Top with grated Romano cheese and cook 10 more minutes. Serves 14.

MRS. BRUCE H. RINEHART

TEXAS HASH

1 pound ground beef
3 tablespoons bacon grease
2 large onions, chopped
1 green pepper, chopped
2 cups tomatoes

½ cup uncooked rice
2 teaspoons salt
½ teaspoon black pepper
1 teaspoon chili powder

Cook onions and green pepper slowly in bacon grease until onions turn yellow. Add meat and sauté until it loses red color; add tomatoes, rice, and seasonings. Arrange in large casserole. Cover and cook at 350° about 45 minutes. Remove cover and bake 15 minutes longer. Serves 4.

MRS. JOHN McCANN, JR.

QUICK SAUERBRATEN

2 to 3 pounds beef (ground and shaped like meat loaf)
1 cup sliced carrots
1 teaspoon minced onion
1 teaspoon salt
⅛ teaspoon pepper

2 tablespoons margarine
1 10½-ounce can beef bouillon
¾ cup water
¼ cup lemon juice
8 ginger snaps (crushed)

Brown meat in butter. Add remaining ingredients. Cover and simmer slowly for 2 hours. Just before serving, put in ginger snaps to thicken gravy. Baste frequently. Serves 4 to 6.

MRS. HUGH TILLETT

QUICK SUPPER

1 pound ground beef
½ onion, chopped
½ green pepper, chopped
Salt and pepper to taste

1 14½-ounce can tomatoes
1 can mushroom soup
1 can tomato paste
1 cup instant rice

Brown beef, onion and pepper. Add seasoning. Drain excess fat and add tomatoes, mushroom soup, tomato paste and instant rice. Simmer, uncovered, for 20 to 30 minutes, or until rice is done. Serves 4 to 6.

MRS. THOMAS BARNHARDT, III

PAN FRIED LIVER

1 pound beef liver
¼ cup flour

2 tablespoons fat
Salt and pepper to taste
Bacon, cooked

Have liver sliced thin. Dip liver in flour. Brown in hot fat. Season with salt and pepper. Reduce heat and cook on low heat for 10 to 15 minutes. Serve with crisp bacon strips. Serves 4.

MRS. JOSEPH K. HALL, III

Pork

BAKED STUFFED PORK CHOPS

6 pork chops, cut with deep
  pockets
1 tablespoon margarine
¼ cup hot water
⅔ cup Pepperidge Farm Stuffing
¼ cup onion, choped fine

½ tablespoon sage
Salt and pepper
½ tablespoon Kitchen Bouquet
½ cup crabapple juice
3 tablespoons white corn syrup

Trim excess fat from chops. Melt margarine in hot water; combine with stuffing, onion, and sage; toss to mix. Sprinkle pockets with salt and pepper. Spoon in stuffing. Salt and pepper chops and place in baking dish, being careful that chops do not overlap. Cover and bake at 350° for 30 minutes. Uncover and bake 1 hour more. Baste the last 30 minutes with sauce made from Kitchen Bouquet, crabapple juice and corn syrup. Serves 6.

MRS. CARL HORN, JR.

CHINESE BROILED PORK FILLET

1 pound fresh pork tenderloin
1 tablespoon prepared hot
  mustard
3 tablespoons sherry
2 tablespoons soy sauce

½ clove garlic, crushed
1 teaspoon peanut oil
Salt and pepper to taste
1 cup rice, cooked
1 small can pineapple slices

Cut fillet in half and trim fat. Blend next six ingredients and rub into meat and let stand 2 hours. Cook over charcoal, basting often. Cut in small pieces and serve over rice with broiled pineapple. Serves 4.

MRS. JOSEPH DULANEY

CHINESE RICE CASSEROLE

1 box uncooked wild and white
  rice mixture
1 1-pound can Chinese vegetables,
  drained
1 can mushroom soup

1 can water
6 or 7 pork chops
Soy sauce
Chinese noodles

Mix first four ingredients in a 7 x 11-inch casserole and top with pork chops. Sprinkle with pepper, and bake at 350°, uncovered, for 1 hour and 20 minutes. Serve with soy sauce and heated Chinese noodles. Serves 6-7.

FRANCES WADDILL

EDITH'S GREASELESS PORK CHOPS

8 pork chops, at least ½-inch thick
Salt and pepper
¼ cup strained honey

3 tablespoons sweet basil
¼ cup lemon juice
⅔ cup red wine

Trim fat from chops and place in a single layer in pan or casserole. Salt and pepper one side and add half of the honey and basil. Turn chops over and repeat. Combine lemon juice and red wine. Pour over seasoned chops. Bake, uncovered, at 350° about one hour, turning once for even browning. Serves 4 to 6.

MRS. R. STUART DICKSON, JR.

PORK CHOPS AND SOUR CREAM

4 loin pork chops
1 chicken bouillon cube
½ cup boiling water
3 teaspoons vinegar

1½ to 2 tablespoons sugar
1 cup sour cream
Dried basil
Salt to taste

Brown chops and put in casserole. In a saucepan dissolve bouillon cube in water. When it is dissolved, add vinegar, salt and sugar. Then add sour cream. Sprinkle chops with dried basil and pour sauce over them. Bake in a 350° oven for 30 minutes. Skim off fat from sauce after meat has cooked and thicken with a little flour. Serves 4.

MRS. JAMES R. SHIELDS

PORK CHOPS ST. JOHN

4 lean pork chops
3 tablespoons Madiera wine

⅓ cup sour cream
Salt and pepper to taste

Brown chops over high heat and cook, turning frequently, until tender. Remove from pan, pour off excess fat. Add wine and sour cream to pan, stirring frequently to scrape off brown bits in pan. Return chops to pan, season and simmer 5 to 10 minutes, basting frequently. Serves 4.

MRS. EDWARD J. WANNAMAKER, JR.

POLYNESIAN PORK

1 whole loin of pork (boned and tied securely)
Salt
Pepper
Rosemary

½ cup soy sauce
½ cup catsup
¼ cup honey
2 cloves crushed garlic

Put meat on rack in shallow pan and sprinkle with salt, pepper, and rosemary. Baste frequently with a sauce made from the soy sauce, catsup, honey, and garlic. Transfer pork to heated platter and garnish with preserved kumquats and watercress. Serves 6 to 8.

MRS. THOMAS W. BAKER

SWEET AND SOUR PORK

1 pound pork loin, cubed
1 large can pineapple chunks and syrup
¼ green pepper, diced
½ onion, chopped
½ cup celery, diced
1 tablespoon Worcestershire

3 tablespoons soy sauce
¼ cup vinegar
¼ cup sugar
3 tablespoons cornstarch
1 beef bouillon cube
¾ cup water
Meat tenderizer

Soften bouillon in water. Cut off all fat from pork and cube meat. Sprinkle pork cubes with meat tenderizer. Brown meat well in greased skillet. Drain syrup from pineapple into a small saucepan and set aside. Add onion, celery, and green pepper to meat. Sauté for several minutes. Meanwhile, to syrup add Worcestershire, soy sauce, vinegar, and sugar. Add cornstarch to bouillon cube dissolved in water, then add to other liquids. Heat and stir until thickened. Pour sauce over meat and vegetables, adding pineapple chunks. Stir until well combined. Cover and simmer for 1 hour on low heat. Serve over steamed rice. Serves 4.

MRS. WALTER SCOTT III

CHINESE SPARERIBS

2 pounds fresh pork spareribs
Salt and pepper to taste
½ cup vinegar
1 cup sugar
1 teaspoon cornstarch
¼ cup soy sauce
1 can pineapple chunks, drain and save liquid

1 large onion, sliced
½ bell pepper, chopped
1 garlic clove, crushed
Rice
Chinese noodles

Brown spareribs in heavy skillet. Add salt and pepper. Combine vinegar, sugar, cornstarch, soy sauce, and juice from pineapple into a sauce. Pour mixture into skillet, from which the spareribs have been removed, and simmer for 10 minutes. Add onion, bell pepper, and garlic. Put pork spareribs back into mixture. Cover and allow to simmer 1 hour or more. Add pineapple chunks before serving. Serve with rice and Chinese noodles. Serves 4.

FRANCES WADDILL*

TAHITIAN PORK CHOPS

8 pork chops
¾ cup sherry
¼ cup salad oil
¾ teaspoon ginger, ground

1 tablespoon maple syrup
¼ cup soy sauce
1 clove garlic
¼ teaspoon oregano

Heat oven to 350°. Brown pork chops in a skillet. Place pork chops in a baking dish. Put all other ingredients into blender and mix until smooth. Pour over chops, cover, and bake 1 to 1½ hours or until tender. Turn chops once during baking time to give both sides added browning. Serves 8.

MRS. WILLIAM D. THOMAS

PORK BARBECUE

2 4 to 5 pound pieces of Boston
   Butt (Pork) or Fresh Ham
½ cup barbecue sauce

Hickory smoked salt to taste
Salt, pepper, and red pepper to
taste

Place meat on rack in turkey roaster or heavy covered pan. Use any amount of meat desired. Rub the barbecue sauce in with your hands, completely covering meat. Use more sauce if necessary. Put meat in 250° oven about 11:00 p.m. Remove from oven about 8:00 or 9:00 a.m. When slightly cool, pull off fat from meat. Chop meat in small pieces and place in large bowl. Season heavily with seasonings. (It takes a lot.) Before serving, heat over very low heat. Serve on toasted buns, or by itself with slaw and heated barbecue sauce. If there is any left over, refrigerate or freeze. Serves about 16.   Mrs. Terry Young

HOT BOUCHEES QUICHE LORRAINE

2 pounds plain flour
1 pound butter
Milk
1 pound chopped country or
  baked ham
1 pound swiss cheese, diced very
  small

1 pint half and half
8 whole eggs, beaten
1 teaspoon accent
Salt and pepper to taste
Accent of nutmeg
1 teaspoon Tabasco sauce
(optional)

In advance, work slowly by hand making the butter submerge into the flour. Use enough plain milk to blend for paste. Roll on a big sheet as any dough. Cut into small slices for individual molds (about 6 inch round molds). Bake in mold at 375° for 12 minutes. (This is only half of the required baking time as the dough will continue to bake when filled).

Combine beaten eggs and cream then mix with ham and cheese. Add seasonings. Fill pastry shell with mixture. Bake at 375° for 10 minutes or until top of mixture is golden brown. This should be served immediately. Serves 100. Ideal for Buffet or Cocktail Party.

A must is that baking is done in a bambare, in event of not knowing instructions for the use of a bambare, use a double broiler. This recipe was given to me by Chef Antoine S. C. Micalef, Chef at Quail Hollow Country Club.   Mrs. H. F. Kincey

HAM LOAF

1 pound ham, ground
1 pound pork, ground
1 cup graham cracker crumbs
2 eggs
½ cup milk

1 can tomato soup
¼ cup water
¼ cup vinegar
¼ cup brown sugar
1 teaspoon dry mustard

Combine ham, pork, graham cracker crumbs, eggs and milk and shape into loaf. Make a sauce of the tomato soup, water, vinegar, brown sugar and mustard. Pour over meat loaf in baking dish. Bake in slow oven (300°) for 2½ hours, basting every half hour. Serves 4-6.

Mrs. William Thomas

HAM LOAF WITH SAUCE

2 pounds ground ham
½ pound ground pork
½ pound ground beef
2 eggs

2 cups Post Toasties
1 cup milk
Onion to taste
1 medium green pepper, chopped

Have butcher grind the three meats together. Add beaten eggs, crushed cereal (any similar kind will do), milk (add more if you like it real moist), minced onion and chopped pepper. Mold into shape and bake for 2 hours in 325° oven. Cover with sauce and baste every half-hour. Serves 10-12.

HAM LOAF SAUCE

1½ cups brown sugar
1 tablespoon flour
1 teaspoon ground cloves
½ teaspoon dry mustard
2 tablespoons vinegar

1 tablespoon lemon juice
¼ teaspoon grated lemon rind
1 cup boiling water
½ cup raisins

Cook over low heat until thick. Keep warm (but not over heat) and baste loaf every half-hour.

MRS. TERRY YOUNG

SWISS ALPINE PIE

1 10-inch pastry shell, unbaked
1 package frozen broccoli, cooked
2 cups pre-cooked ham cubes
  (½-inch)
2 cups shredded Swiss cheese

3 tablespoons chopped onion
1½ cups milk, scalded
3 eggs, slightly beaten
⅛ teaspoon salt
⅛ teaspoon pepper

Preheat oven to 450°. Drain and chop broccoli. Layer half of broccoli, ham and cheese in pastry shell. Repeat with second half, sprinkle onion on top. Set aside. Gradually stir milk into eggs, add seasonings. Pour into pastry shell. Bake 10 minutes. Reduce heat to 325° and continue baking for 30 to 35 minutes. Remove from oven, and let stand a few minutes before serving. Serves 4.

MRS. W. V. WILLIAMSON, JR.

SAUSAGE CASSEROLE

1½ pounds lean pork sausage
4 or 5 spring onions (including tender tops)
1 large green pepper
1 medium bunch of celery
  (including tender tops)
2 packages chicken noodle soup

1 cup brown rice (uncooked)
1 can water chestnuts (sliced and drained)
¼ cup slivered almonds
Salt and pepper to taste

Cook 2 packages of soup in 4½ cups of boiling water for 7 minutes. Cook sausage until fat is out. Sauté onions, pepper, celery in 3 tablespoons fat. Add soup, rice and chestnuts. Mix together. Cook, covered, at 350° for 1½ to 2 hours. Remove cover and sprinkle with almonds the last 30 minutes. Serves 6.

MRS. JOHN McCANN

QUICHE LORRAINE

1 9-inch pie crust, unbaked
1 teaspoon butter
3 slices Canadian bacon or ham cut ¼-inch thick and diced
1 medium onion, finely chopped
½ cup Swiss cheese, cut in small pieces

4 eggs, slightly beaten
1 cup milk
1 cup cream
Pinch of grated nutmeg
½ teaspoon salt
¼ teaspoon pepper, freshly ground

Line a 9-inch pie pan with pastry. In a small saucepan heat butter. Add bacon or ham and cook 5 minutes or until golden brown. Remove bacon (or ham) and set aside. Add onions to pan and cook 5 minutes. Cover piecrust with bacon (or ham) and onions and ¼-cup cheese. In mixing bowl, combine remaining cheese, eggs, milk, cream, nutmeg, salt and pepper. Mix well. Pour over bacon mixture. Bake at 450° 15 minutes. Reduce heat to 350° and bake another 15 minutes or until custard is well set. Serve hot. With a green salad this makes a nice luncheon dish. Serves 4-6.

MRS. CARLISLE ADAMS

BAKED PREM

1 can Prem (Spam or similar meat)
⅓ cup brown sugar
½ teaspoon vinegar

1 teaspoon prepared mustard
1 teaspoon water
Whole cloves

Score Prem loaf and dot with cloves. Baste with mixture of sugar, vinegar, mustard, and water. Bake 20 minutes at 375°. Serves 3-4.

MISS CRAIG MASON

Lamb

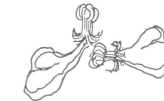

BAR-B-QUED "BUTTERFLY" LAMB

1 leg of lamb, butterfly cut
1 cup dry red wine
½ cup olive oil
2 tablespoons parsley, snipped
2 tablespoons chives, chopped
½ teaspoon Worcestershire
¼ teaspoon pepper
⅛ teaspoon marjoram
⅛ teaspoon rosemary
⅛ teaspoon thyme
2 cloves garlic, crushed
1 teaspoon salt

Combine all ingredients to make marinade. Pour over lamb and marinate overnight in refrigerator. Barbecue on both sides, about 25 minutes per side slowly on an open grill. Baste occasionally. Serves 6-8.

MRS. STEPHEN K. URNER, JR.

LAMB CURRY

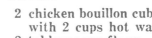

5 tablespoons butter
1 cup sliced onions
2 medium-sized apples, cored, peeled and sliced
2 cups diced cooked lamb
1 teaspoon mild fresh curry
2 chicken bouillon cubes mixed with 2 cups hot water
2 tablespoons flour
1 tablespoon lemon juice
Salt and pepper to taste

Melt 3 tablespoons butter in large frying pan. Add curry. Sauté onions and apples until onions are tender. Remove from pan. Brown lamb in pan. Remove lamb from pan. In same pan, melt 2 tablespoons butter and stir in 2 tablespoons flour. Let this bubble for a minute but do not brown. Add bouillon—must be hot—all at once. Stir until sauce is smooth and thick. Add onions, apples and meat. Stir in lemon juice, and add salt and pepper to taste. Serves 4.

(This can and should be made ahead of time. Reheat when ready to serve, but do not overcook, as apples will become too mushy.)

MRS. BRUCE H. RINEHART

DICED LAMB WITH SAUCE

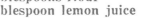

1 pound boned, diced leg of lamb
2 tablespoons butter
1 cup water
1 medium-sized onion, quartered
½ green pepper, coarsely cut
1 stalk celery, coarsely cut
2 slices white bread, torn
1 teaspoon salt
¼ teaspoon pepper
1 tablespoon curry powder

In skillet, melt the butter and add the diced lamb. Sauté over low heat for 20 minutes, stirring occasionally. In a blender, put in remaining ingredients and cover. Blend for 25 seconds at high speed. Pour sauce over lamb, cover, and simmer for 1 hour, stirring occasionally. Serves 4.

MRS. DAVID D. TOWNSEND

LAMB ROAST

7-pound leg of lamb
1 large onion, sliced

Flour
Salt and pepper

Rinse lamb under cold water. On top and undersides, cut slits long and deep enough to insert slices of onion. When onions are in place, salt and pepper lamb generously, then coat it with flour. Place lamb in an open baking pan and fill bottom of pan with at least ½-inch to 1-inch of water. Sprinkle flour into water. Cook, uncovered, on middle rack of 400° oven for one hour. Reduce heat to 350°, cover lightly with foil, and continue cooking for 3 more hours. Add water and flour periodically when you are basting roast, as in this manner the gravy will make itself. Serves 8.

MRS. RODDEY DOWD

LAMB SHANKS

2 or 3 lamb shanks

1 can Campbell's onion soup

Pour soup over lamb. Cover and bake at 325° for 1½ to 2 hours. Uncover and continue baking for half an hour. Serves 4 to 6.

MRS. G. WARING BOYS

Veal

VEAL IN WINE

3 pounds veal, cut in 1½-inch
  cubes
4 onions, whole
2 to 4 ounces pitted green olives
2 to 3 tablespoons olive oil

¾ pound fresh mushrooms
1 cup dry white wine
½ cup water
Salt and pepper

Pour oil in heavy pan and brown veal in it on all sides (holding it down with a wooden spoon). When brown, season with salt and pepper. Add whole peeled onions. Pour wine and water over meat and simmer tightly covered for one hour. After an hour, turn veal; add sliced mushrooms and olives (previously washed to remove salt). If wine has evaporated, add a little water and heat another 10 to 15 minutes, tightly covered. Serves 8-10.

MRS. VANCE KENDRICK, JR.*

VEAL CUTLET NICOISE

1 pound veal cutlet, cut sliver
  thin
½ cup flour
½ teaspoon salt
¼ teaspoon pepper

¼ cup port wine
3 tablespoons olive oil
1 clove garlic, finely chopped
1 4-ounce can sliced mushrooms,
  drained

Combine flour, salt, pepper. Dredge cutlets with flour mixture. Heat oil in large heavy skillet. Add cutlets and garlic. Cook over brisk flame for 10 minutes on each side or until well browned. Remove meat to heated serving dish and keep warm. Add mushrooms to pan and cook 5 minutes. Remove mushrooms to serving dish. Raise heat under frying pan. Add port wine and heat, stirring until brown parts which stick to the bottom of the pan dissolve. Do not allow to boil. Pour over meat. Serve hot. Serves 4.

MRS. ROBERT LYNN

VEAL AND MUSHROOMS

1 pound veal, sliced very thin
Salt, pepper, garlic salt
1 cup sliced mushrooms

½ cup oil
½ cup cooking sherry

Cut veal in small pieces and pound thin. Sprinkle with salt and pepper and a dash of garlic salt. Flour lightly. Cook mushrooms in skillet about 4 or 5 minutes, using ½-cup oil. Take mushrooms out and put meat in. Brown over medium heat. When meat is brown, add mushrooms and sherry. Cook at high heat 2 or 3 minutes. Scrape pan and pour scrapings over meat before serving. Better if you use real cooking sherry. Tasty, but keeps you at the stove until the last minute. Serves 4.

MRS. ELLEN G. GOODE

VEAL STROGANOFF

1½ pounds veal cutlet
⅓ cup flour
1 teaspoon salt
¼ cup butter
1 cup chopped onion

1 6-ounce can sliced mushrooms, undrained
1 can mushroom soup
1 cup sour cream

Cut veal in strips ½-inch thick. Mix flour and salt and dredge meat in mixture. Melt butter in heavy frying pan. Add veal and onion. Brown meat on all sides. Add soup and mushrooms. Stir. Cover and simmer until meat is tender (45 to 60 minutes). Add liquid if too thick. Stir in sour cream. Heat, but do not boil. Serve over rice, noodles, or in patty shells. Serves 6.

MRS. WILLIAM D. THOMAS

VEAL SCALLOPINI FOR FOUR

Veal cutlets—2 pounds
Parmesan cheese
½ cup butter
1 cup B & B Mushrooms, drained
¼ to ½ teaspoon salt

Red pepper
1 can beef consomme
3 tablespoons flour to thicken broth
¼ cup white wine

Have butcher cut thin cutlets off leg and pound them. Cut into small 2 inches long by 1-inch wide pieces, or leave cutlet whole. Dip veal in Parmesan cheese. Fry cutlet in ¼-cup butter. In another pan, put mushrooms and sauté in ¼-cup butter. Add salt and red pepper to taste. Add consomme and thicken with a little flour. Add wine and pour over veal. Serve with white rice. Serves 4.

MRS. HENRY W. MIDDLETON

VEAL SCALLOPINI

1 pound veal cutlet
Flour
½ teaspoon salt
Dash of pepper
¼ cup cooking oil
½ medium onion, sliced thin

1 1-pound can tomatoes, not drained
1 3-ounce can mushrooms
¼ teaspoon garlic salt
¼ teaspoon oregano
4 slices Mozzarella cheese

Cut veal into 4 portions. Combine flour, salt and pepper and lightly coat veal. In skillet, brown slowly in hot oil. Remove meat from pan and cook onions until just tender. Add meat, tomatoes, undrained mushrooms, garlic and oregano. Cover; cook slowly for 20 to 25 minutes, or until veal is tender, stirring occasionally. Just before serving, place slice of cheese on each cutlet and cover until cheese melts. Serves 4.

MRS. ELLEN G. GOODE

VEAL PARMESAN

¼ cup olive oil
½ cup chopped onion
1 pound ground chuck
2 #2½ cans tomatoes, slightly drained
1 teaspoon salt
1 bay leaf
1 6-ounce can tomato paste
2 pounds veal cutlet (very thin)

Seasoned breadcrumbs
Grated Parmesan cheese
3 eggs, well beaten
Salt and pepper
½ cup olive oil
2 packages sliced Mozzarella cheese

SAUCE

Heat in saucepan ¼-cup olive oil. Add and brown lightly ground chuck and onion. Add tomatoes (sieved to discard seeds—optional), 1 teaspoon salt, bay leaf, 6-ounce can tomato paste. Simmer, covered, 2½ to 3 hours or until thickened.

VEAL

Dip veal cutlets into a mixture of seasoned bread crumbs, grated Parmesan cheese, then into eggs, salt and pepper; dip into bread crumbs again. Brown slices on each side in ½-cup olive oil. Alternate in casserole layers of cutlets, sauce, sliced Mozzarella cheese. Top with sauce when ready to serve. Bake at 350° for 20 minutes, or until cheese is melted and brown. Serves 8.

MRS. JOHN G. THOMAS

VEAL PARMIGIANA I

1 cup bread crumbs
¼ cup grated Parmesan cheese
12 thin slices veal
2 eggs, slightly beaten
1 cup finely chopped onion
1 clove garlic, mashed
2 tablespoons olive oil
1 1-pound can tomatoes
2 small cans tomato sauce
1½ teaspoons dried basil

½ teaspoon thyme
½ teaspoon salt
Pepper to taste
½ teaspoon onion salt
2 tablespoons olive oil
2 tablespoons butter
1 8-ounce package Mozzarella cheese
½ cup grated Parmesan cheese

Mix bread crumbs and ¼ cup grated Parmesan. Dip veal slices in egg and coat well with crumb mixture. Let stand. Sauté onion and garlic in 2 tablespoons oil until soft. Add tomatoes, sauce and seasonings. Cover and simmer 15-20 minutes. Preheat oven to 350°. Heat oil and butter until hot and brown a few slices of veal at a time. Arrange veal, sliced Mozzarella, and sauce in shallow long baking dish. Sprinkle with Parmesan. Bake 15 to 20 minutes until bubbly. Makes 6 servings.

MRS. VERNER E. STANLEY, JR.

VEAL PARMIGIANA II

3 tablespoons oil
½ cup chopped onion
1 clove garlic, crushed
2 8-ounce cans tomato sauce
¼ cup water
1 teaspoon oregano
⅛ teaspoon pepper
1 tablespoon chopped parsley
½ cup grated Parmesan cheese
½ cup dry packaged bread
  crumbs

6 slices veal ¼-inch thick
  (about 1 pound)
1 egg, beaten
¼ cup cooking oil
1 8-ounce package Mozzarella
  cheese
2 tablespoons grated Parmesan
  cheese

Heat oil in saucepan. Sauté onion and garlic until brown, stir in tomato sauce, water, oregano, pepper and parsley. Cover and simmer 10 minutes. Combine ½-cup Parmesan cheese and bread crumbs. Dip veal slices in beaten egg, then in the cheese-breadcrumb mixture. Sauté veal in 2 tablespoons oil in skillet until brown, turning only once. Pour half the tomato sauce into shallow dish. Cut Mozzarella cheese into 6 slices and alternate with veal in baking dish. Pour over remaining sauce. Sprinkle with Parmesan cheese. Bake at 350° for 25 minutes. Serves 6.

MRS. RALPH H. ALEXANDER, JR.

CASSEROLE VEAL CHOPS

4 1½" thick Veal Chops
1 stalk celery, minced fine
1 small onion, minced fine
1 small carrot, minced

½ green pepper, minced
Few fresh mushrooms, diced
  (optional)
White wine

Have butcher cut thick chops with a pocket inside, allowing one per person. Sauté in butter the above mixture except wine. Salt and pepper the chops. Fill pockets with mixture. Brown floured chops in hot fat or oleo in heavy frying pan. Place chops in casserole with 1 tablespoon white wine for each chop—about 3 extra tablespoons for casserole. Cover and bake one hour in 350° oven. Chops can be stuffed hours ahead and refrigerated. Serves 4.

MRS. J. R. ADAMS

Poultry

Chicken

LEMON CHICKEN

6 to 8 pieces of frying chicken (breast, legs, thighs)
1 whole lemon
⅓ cup flour
1½ teaspoons salt
½ teaspoon paprika

4 tablespoons salad oil or shortening
2 tablespoons brown sugar
1 lemon, thinly sliced
1 cup chicken broth
2 sprigs fresh mint

Wash chicken and drain on paper towels. Grate the peel from the lemon and set aside; cut lemon in half and squeeze the juice over the pieces of chicken, rubbing each piece with the juice. Shake in a paper bag with the flour, salt and paprika. Brown chicken slowly in the salad oil. Arrange in casserole or baking pan.

Sprinkle grated lemon peel over the chicken, add the brown sugar, and then cover with the thinly sliced lemon. Pour in the broth and place the mint over the top. Cover and bake in a moderately hot oven (375°) until chicken is tender (40 to 45 minutes). Remove mint before serving. Serves 6 to 8 if the chicken pieces are large.

MRS. ERVIN JACKSON, JR.

LEMON BARBECUE CHICKEN

1 chicken cut up, or
6 to 8 chicken breasts
Salt and pepper to taste

6 tablespoons butter or margarine
¾ cup lemon sauce

Salt and pepper chicken. Brown in butter, skin side down. Turn and brown. Pour lemon sauce over chicken. Cover and cook slowly in 325° oven for 50 to 60 minutes. Baste occasionally.

LEMON SAUCE

1 clove garlic
1 teaspoon salt
¼ cup salad oil

½ cup lemon juice
½ teaspoon celery salt
½ teaspoon dried thyme

Mash garlic clove in salt. Add remaining ingredients. If possible, allow sauce to stand overnight. Serves 4-6.

MRS. J. WALTER BARR, JR.

JOHN MARSHALL'S BAR-B-Q SAUCE

6 halves of broiler chicken
Juice of 6 lemons
½ pound butter
2 tablespoons Worcestershire

¾ teaspoon red pepper
Sugar to taste
Dash of Tabasco
Liquid Hickory Smoke (Optional)

Baste chicken with the above sauce after all ingredients are mixed and heated, about every 20 to 30 minutes. Cook, uncovered, at 225° for at least 3 hours. Serves 6.

MRS. DONALD S. McMILLAN

B.B.Q. CHICKEN

1 small chicken or 6 chicken
  breasts
2 tablespoons sugar
1 tablespoon salt

Dash of red pepper
1½ cups water
½ cup vinegar
¾ stick margarine

Place chicken breasts, or chicken that is split up the back, in large roaster or cooking pan. Flour heavily. Place breast or fat side on bottom. Sprinkle with sugar, salt and red pepper. Heat water, vinegar and margarine and pour over chicken. Cover and cook on top of stove slowly for 45 minutes. Remove lid and put in 350° oven for 1 to 1½ hours. Serves 4-6.

MRS. KENNETH R. SMITH, JR.

CHICKEN TERIYAKI

⅔ cup soy sauce
¼ cup white wine
1 clove minced garlic

2 tablespoons sugar
½ tablespoon ginger
1 2½-pound chicken, cut up

Combine first five ingredients. Marinate chicken in this sauce for 1 hour. Bake at 325° for 1 hour, basting several times. Serves 4.

MRS. R. STUART DICKSON, JR.

TURKEY SURPRISE

2 boned turkey breasts
1 8-ounce can jellied cranberry
  sauce
½ cup red wine
2 tablespoons honey

2 tablespoons salad oil
1 tablespoon vinegar
2 teaspoons cornstarch
Salt to taste

Combine sauce ingredients in saucepan, simmer 10 minutes. Place poultry in casserole, pour sauce over. Bake, covered, at 325° for 30 minutes. Any equivalent pieces of left-over turkey can be used. Serves 8-10.

MRS. JOHN A. STEWMAN

SINGAPORE TURKEY BREAST

1 4-to-6-pound turkey breast
1 tablespoon curry powder
1 tablespoon fines herbs, dried
(Spice Island)
1 tablespoon salt substitute
1 teaspoon paprika

1 cup gin
1 cup water
1 onion, sliced
1 carrot, chopped
1 piece celery, chopped
½ an orange, sliced

Wash and dry thawed turkey. Mix curry powder, herbs, salt substitute and paprika. Rub turkey inside and out with this mixture. Place in pan with vegetables and orange. Roast, uncovered, at 350° for 3 hours or until tender. Baste with gin and water. When done, spoon off all fat from juices. Serve sliced thin with the pan juices unthickened. Exotic and low calorie. Serves 6.

MRS. JAMES B. CRAIGHILL

COQ AU VIN

4 slices bacon, diced
2½ to 3 pounds chicken pieces
2 tablespoons butter
Salt and pepper
1 1-lb. jar white onions
1 can mushrooms
½ cup sliced onions

2 garlic cloves, minced
2 tablespoons flour
2 ounces brandy
14 ounces Burgundy
3 sprigs chopped parsley
½ bay leaf
⅛ teaspoon thyme

Brown bacon and set aside. Add chicken pieces and 2 tablespoons butter to fat in skillet and season with salt and pepper. Place chicken in a good-sized casserole after it is browned. Add and brown in skillet: can of onions, can of mushrooms, sliced onions and garlic. Remove to casserole. Add 2 tablespoons flour to skillet. Stir in brandy and Burgundy Pour in casserole. Sprinkle top with chopped parsley, bay leaf and thyme. Add bacon. Cook at 400° for 1½ hours, uncovered. Serves with minced parsley. Serves 4.

MRS. RUFUS SAFFORD

CHICKEN COUNTRY CAPTAIN

16 to 18 chicken breasts,
preferably boned
6 green peppers, chopped
3 large onions, chopped
1 large bunch parsley, chopped
Cooking oil
2 No. 2 cans tomatoes
(approximately 5 cups)
1½ teaspoons mace

3 teaspoons curry powder
¼ teaspoon garlic powder
Salt and pepper
Paprika and flour
1 cup currants
¾ pound blanched almonds
Steamed rice (3 cups raw rice for
12 servings, or 4 cups to have
extra for seconds)

In brown paper bag, shake chicken with salt, pepper, paprika and flour. Fry in hot oil until brown. Put aside. In large frying pan, heat more oil.

Fry slowly the peppers, onions and parsley for approximately 15 minutes. Put this mixture in large casserole or roaster. Add tomatoes, spices and garlic powder. Simmer for 15 minutes. Taste and adjust salt and pepper.

Lay chicken in the sauce. Cover casserole or roaster. Place in 275° oven for 1½ to 2 hours. Stir in currants half-hour before serving. Toast almonds in slow oven. Sprinkle almonds on top of chicken before serving.

Chicken should be served in casserole or deep platter with sauce poured over it. Each guest should serve himself first to rice, then place chicken and sauce on rice; sprinkle almonds on top. Serves 12.

MRS. JOHN J. HANES

CHINESE HOT POT

This is a meal in itself. Everything can be done early. It's fun to use chopsticks and a mongolian cooker (a chafing dish will do). Everything is served raw. Each person picks out a few choice tidbits, drops them into the bubbling broth. In a few minutes fish them out, dip them into the zesty sauces, and eat with rice. At the last you can drop in eggs to be poached, or drink the broth.

Mongolian cooker: Fill chimney with charcoal, add charcoal starter. Pour cold broth into moat of cooker, cover cooker, then light charcoal. When broth is hot, you're ready to cook. Serves about 4.

1 pound clean, raw shrimp	½ head Chinese cabbage, or
2 chicken breasts, skinned, boned, and sliced thin	lettuce heart, cubed
	1 5-ounce can water chestnuts, drained and sliced thin
½ pound beef sirloin, sliced very thin across grain	1½ cups sliced mushrooms
	4 cups small spinach leaves

BROTH:

3 14-ounce cans chicken broth	1 tablespoon Accent
3 chicken bouillon cubes	½ teaspoon ground ginger

SAUCES:

(1) Hot Sauce:	
3 tablespoons catsup	(2) Soy Sauce:
3 tablespoons chili sauce	1 teaspoon lemon juice
1½ tablespoons horseradish	Dash of Tabasco

MRS. FRANK CONNER, JR.

95

CORNISH HENS A LA CISSIE

Cornish Hens
Wesson or olive oil
Seasonings
2 teaspoons Worcestershire

2 tablespoons red wine
(burgundy or claret)
¼ teaspoon thyme
¼ teaspoon poultry seasoning
1 tablespoon chopped parsley

One Cornish hen per person. Have butcher split them down the back—not into two pieces, but so you can open them up. Tear off enough squares of foil to tightly enclose each bird. On each square of foil put 2 tablespoons oil (Wesson or preferably olive), rub the bird around in the oil to cover the meat side well and spread oil over foil. Sprinkle with salt and pepper and paprika. Place hen meat side down. Mix remaining ingredients and put into the cavity.

Wrap foil tightly around bird. Place on cookie sheet in 300° oven for about 45 minutes to an hour. At this point you can vary the time by several hours by turning the oven up or down. The creator of this succulent dish (Cissie) says she has held off as long as three hours. Just before serving, unwrap each package, save juice in a cup. Put birds, meat side up, in broiler and brown. Baste with remaining juice. The rest of juice can be thickened and used as gravy with rice.

MRS. HOWARD YATES DUNAWAY, JR.*

POULET CHASSEUR

6 chicken breasts
1 envelope garlic salad dressing
mix
2 to 4 tablespoons oil
3 tablespoons butter
½ cup sliced spring onions

1 pound sliced fresh mushrooms
1 can whole tomatoes
2 teaspoons dried tarragon
leaves
1¼ cups Sauterne

Sprinkle chicken with half of the salad dressing mix. Brown chicken in oil. Pour off remaining oil and remove chicken from pan. Brown onions and mushrooms in butter over low heat. Add tomatoes, tarragon, remaining salad dressing mix, wine. Blend well. Add chicken, cover, and cook 45 minutes to one hour. Serves 4 to 6.

MRS. THOMAS M. BARNHARDT III*

CHICKEN CHASSEUR

8 to 10 chicken breasts
½ cup flour
6 tablespoons olive oil
6 tablespoons butter
1 medium onion, chopped fine
1 pound mushrooms, thinly sliced
1 cup white wine

1 jigger brandy
1 cup tomato sauce
½ cup canned chicken broth
1 tablespoon Kitchen Bouquet
Juice of 1 lemon
4 tablespoons chopped fresh
parsley

Salt chicken, and dredge in flour; brown in mixture of butter and olive oil. Transfer to casserole and sauté onions until transparent. Add mushrooms to onions, sauté for a few minutes, then add remaining ingredients except parsley. Bring sauce to a quick boil, stirring all the while; pour over chicken. Cover casserole and set aside in a cool place. Before serving, bake, uncovered, in 325° oven for 1½ hours or until tender. Sprinkle with freshly chopped parsley.

With this chicken I serve rice prepared in the following way:

3 cups rice	3 cups canned chicken broth
¼ pound butter	

Wash rice and drain until dry. In a heavy 3-quart pan sauté rice in butter until butter is absorbed. Add chicken broth, stir thoroughly. Cover tightly and bring to a quick boil. Turn heat as low as possible and let rice cook for 30 minutes. Do not remove cover until ready to serve.

This dish may seem complicated to prepare, but is well worth the effort. The chicken can be made the day before, refrigerated and baked just before serving. The rice can be prepared just before your guests arrive. You can keep it warm as long as needed. Serves 8.

A marinated green bean salad is good with this.

MRS. O. HUNTER JONES

CHICKEN IN RED WINE

Chicken, cut into serving pieces	Salt
½ stick butter	Pepper
2 cloves garlic	Accent
1 tablespoon Kitchen Bouquet	Mushrooms (optional)
2 cups dry red wine	

Melt butter in large casserole. Brown chicken pieces on all sides in butter. When brown, add 2 cups dry red wine, garlic cloves, salt, pepper, Accent and Kitchen Bouquet. Simmer over slow fire one hour, or until chicken is cooked. If desired, sauté sliced, fresh mushrooms in butter and add to chicken at serving time. This may be made ahead of time and reheated. Serves 6-8.

MRS. PHILIP G. CONNER

CHICKEN IN WINE

¼ cup butter	¼ teaspoon pepper
4 to 6 chicken breasts, boned	1 chicken bouillon cube
1 medium onion, sliced	1 cup hot water
1 clove garlic, minced (optional)	¼ cup red wine
2 tablespoons flour	Snipped parsley
½ teaspoon salt	

In hot butter in chicken fryer or Dutch oven, sauté chicken until both sides are golden. Add onion and garlic (if desired). Combine flour, salt and pepper. Dissolve bouillon cube in water. Stir in flour. Pour over chicken. Cook over low heat, covered, for 30 minutes or until tender. Stir in wine. Garnish with parsley. Serves 4 to 6.

MRS. WILLIAM W. MARCHANT, JR.

MYSTERY CHICKEN

Breast of 2 roasting chickens,
    halved
1 chicken bouillon cube
1 carrot
1 onion
Celery leaves
Parsley
Salt

Black peppercorn
1¼ tablespoons butter
1 tablespoon flour
¼ cup chopped black walnuts
½ pint sour cream
Paprika
Monosodium glutamate

Put 4 half-breasts of chicken in deep saucepan. Pour over them sufficient cold water to cover—about 3 cups. Add 1 bouillon cube, chopped carrot, 1 quartered onion, celery leaves, sprig of parsley, salt, freshly ground pepper and pinch of monosodium glutamate. Bring to boil, skim, cover, and simmer until chicken is tender. (If you are using second joints, start them a little ahead of the pieces of breast as they take longer.) When chicken is done, remove it from the broth and cool.

Strain the broth. Melt 1 generous tablespoon butter in saucepan and stir in 1 tablespoon flour. When it is smooth, add gradually a cup of the strained broth and cook and stir until thick and smooth. Add a scant ¼-cup powdered black walnuts and ½-pint sour cream. (Put chopped walnuts, found in jars, through food mill or meat grinder.) Skin pieces of chicken and remove the little rib bones from the breasts. Heat the chicken in the sauce. (Since the sour cream has been added to another sauce, it will not separate.) When ready to serve, sprinkle generously with paprika. May be prepared in advance. Serves 4.

MRS. J. PRINCE SEBRELL

SMOTHERED CHICKEN

1 chicken
2 slices bacon

Salt and pepper

Split a well-cleaned bird down the back. Place it in a pan which can be covered. Fill bottom of pan with water up to rack. Salt and pepper bird and lay 2 slices of fat bacon over top of each side. Cover and let steam until well done. When done, add enough butter to make a rich gravy. Place under broiler to brown, basting often to keep bird soft and juicy.

OLD NORTH STATE COOKBOOK

CHICKEN VERMOUTH

1 whole chicken, or 6 breasts
1 can mushroom soup
1 ½-pint half and half cream

1 can drained mushrooms
½ cup dry vermouth
Slivered almonds

Season chicken, put in shallow roasting pan or pyrex dish, pour mixture of other ingredients over chicken and bake in 350° oven, uncovered, for 1 hour. Serves 6.

MRS. FRANCIS M. PINCKNEY, JR.

CHICKEN BREASTS SUPREME

4 chicken breasts, boned and
  halved
8 strips of bacon
2 packages chipped beef (enough
  to cover bottom of baking dish)

½ pint sour cream
1 can mushroom soup
½ can milk

Wrap each half of chicken in a piece of bacon. Place in baking dish lined with 2 layers of chipped beef. Blend sour cream, soup and milk and pour over chicken. *Do not add salt.* Cook, uncovered, for 3 hours in 300° oven. May be cooked ahead and reheated when ready to serve. Serves 8.

MRS. JAMES B. CRAIGHILL

BREAST OF CHICKEN PERIGOURDINE

8 small whole broiler-fryer
  chicken breasts, boned and
  flattened
Salt and pepper to taste
½ teaspoon powdered thyme
¾ cup butter or margarine, divided
½ pound chicken livers, chopped
½ pound mushrooms, chopped

4 shallots (or small spring
  onions) chopped
1 teaspoon salt
1 cup (4 ounces) grated Swiss
  cheese
1 egg, beaten
Fine dry bread crumbs

Sprinkle inside of chicken breasts with salt, pepper and thyme. To prepare stuffing, heat ¼-cup butter in skillet; add chicken livers, mushrooms and shallots; sprinkle with salt. Cook slowly for about 5 minutes, until livers are cooked. Remove from heat and stir in grated cheese. Divide stuffing into 8 portions; place in center of chicken breasts. Fold sides of breasts over stuffing and fasten with skewers or sturdy wooden picks. Roll first in beaten egg, then in bread crumbs. Chill, uncovered, in refrigerator for at least 2 hours, to allow coating to dry.

Heat remaining ½-cup butter in large skillet. Add chicken breasts, a few at a time, and brown on all sides. Remove to shallow pan and bake in 350° oven for about 45 minutes or until tender. Spoon a little cream sauce over chicken breasts and garnish with parsley if desired. Serve remaining sauce in side dish. Serves 8.

CREAM SAUCE

¼ cup butter or margarine or
  drippings from chicken
¼ cup flour

2 cups chicken stock
1 tablespoon lemon juice
½ cup cream

Melt butter in saucepan; blend in flour and gradually stir in chicken stock. Cook, stirring constantly, until mixture thickens and comes to a boil. Cook 3 to 5 minutes longer; add lemon juice. Stir in cream. Heat, but do not allow sauce to boil.

MRS. LAWRENCE REGER

CHICKEN A L'ORANGE

1 fryer chicken
1 clove garlic, minced
Butter, melted

2 oranges, juiced
1 lemon, juiced

Quarter a fryer. Place in 300° oven in covered 9x13-inch casserole with clove of garlic, a bit of melted butter and water. Cook 1 hour. Uncover and continue baking at 300° another hour, basting frequently with juice of 2 oranges and 1 lemon. Serves 3-4.

MRS. HERBERT H. BROWNE, JR.

APRICOT CHICKEN

4 to 6 chicken pieces (boned
breasts for company)
1 package Lipton Onion Soup Mix

1 can peeled apricots
6 tablespoons butter
Rice, cooked

Place chicken on aluminum foil. Sprinkle soup mix on top and add apricots. Spoon about half the apricot syrup over chicken. Dot with butter. Cover tightly with foil and bake at 200° for 3 hours. Serve over rice. Serves 4-6.

MRS. G. WARING BOYS

HAWAIIAN CHICKEN

1 chicken or 12 breasts of
chicken
1 can pineapple chunks, drained
½ cup pineapple juice
1 onion, chopped
¼ cup brown sugar

¼ cup soy sauce
2 tablespoons sliced fresh ginger
(or crystallized ginger)
1 tablespoon fried chicken
drippings

Shake chicken in seasoned flour and brown quickly in skillet. Place in casserole, add remaining ingredients; cover and bake in 350° oven for 30 minutes. If more juice is needed, add water or pineapple juice. Serves 6 to 12, depending on amount of chicken. This may be prepared ahead of time. Liquid from casserole is good served on rice.

MRS. BREVARD S. MYERS*

SOUTH OF THE BORDER CHICKEN

1 can mushroom soup
1 can chicken soup
1 can milk
1 onion, grated
1 pound grated cheese (sharp)

3 or 4 tablespoons hot sauce
12 tortillas or doritas
7 chicken breasts, cooked in
celery, onion, etc. and cubed

Heat milk, soups and salt. When cool, add other ingredients. Save enough cheese for top. Place all in a casserole and let stand overnight. Bake at 350° for about an hour, or until hot. Serves 6.

MRS. JOSEPH DULANEY

CHICKEN KIEV

3 large chicken breasts, split and boned
¼ pound butter, softened
1 clove garlic, mashed
½ teaspoon crumbled rosemary
1 tablespoon minced parsley
1 tablespoon finely cut chives
1 teaspoon Worcestershire
½ teaspoon salt
Dash of pepper
½ cup flour
2 eggs, well beaten
2 cups fine, soft bread crumbs

Flatten the breasts to ¼-inch thickness. Blend the next 7 ingredients well and form into a 6-inch roll and refrigerate in wax paper. Chill until *very* firm. Cut the roll into 6 equal portions and place one on each breast. Tuck ends of breast in and roll tightly, jelly-roll style. Fasten with skewers or string. Dredge in flour, then beaten egg, then crumbs. Repeat egg and crumb coating. Fry the rolls in 2 inches of hot oil for about 12 minutes until golden, turning carefully. Drain on paper towels. Serves 6.

MRS. VERNER E. STANLEY

FRIED CHICKEN I

¾ cup all-purpose flour
1 tablespoon salt
1 tablespoon paprika
¼ teaspoon pepper
1 3-pound ready-to-cook broiler-fryer, cut up

Combine flour and seasonings in paper bag; add pieces of chicken and shake well. Place on rack to let coating dry. Heat fat until it will sizzle a drop of water. (Have fat ¼-inch deep in skillet.) Brown meaty pieces first; then slip others in. Brown one side; turn with tongs. When lightly browned (15 to 20 minutes) reduce heat; cover tightly. Cook until tender (30 to 40 minutes). Uncover for last 10 minutes. Serves 4.

MRS. C. E. WILLIAMS, JR.

OVEN-FRIED CHICKEN PARMESAN

1 broiler-fryer, cut up
1 egg, beaten
2 tablespoons milk
½ cup Kraft Parmesan Cheese
¼ cup flour
2 teaspoons paprika
½ teaspoon salt
½ teaspoon pepper
½ cup margarine, melted

Dip chicken in egg and milk. Dredge in flour mixture and seasonings. Place in shallow baking dish. Pour margarine over chicken. Bake at 350° for 1¼ hours. Serves 4.

MRS. W. KENT COMBS

FRIED CHICKEN II

Chicken, cut up
Self-rising flour
Salt and pepper

Crisco
1 stick of butter

Mix self-rising flour, salt and pepper in a paper bag. Shake chicken pieces in the bag. Drop in large frying pan or hot crisco combined with one stick of butter. Cook fairly fast, covered, for 10 minutes. Turn; cook 5 to 10 minutes more, covered. Drain well on paper towels.

MRS. JOHN L. DABBS III

OVEN-FRIED CHICKEN

Chicken, cut up
Melted butter

Potato chips, crushed

Dry cut-up chicken. Dip in melted butter. Roll in potato chips. Place in foil-lined pan and bake at 350° for 1½ hours.

MRS. BERNARD WRIGHT, JR.

CHARLIE STOWE'S FAVORITE CHICKEN

1 chicken, cut up
1 egg
½ cup milk
1 stick butter

1 cup flour
1 teaspoon baking powder
2 teaspoons salt
4 tablespoons sesame seed

Dip chicken in mixture of egg and milk. Mix all ingredients and roll chicken in this. Place in Dutch oven *uncovered* and add melted butter. Cook half an hour at 375°. Turn and cook another half-hour. Serves 4.

MRS. HARLEY GASTON, JR.

HAM-CHICKEN ROLLS

4 boned chicken breasts
4 slices cooked ham

4 slices Swiss cheese
1 box Chicken Shake 'n Bake

Pound chicken thin. Cover each breast with slice of ham and cheese. Roll breasts and skewer with toothpick. Cover each with Shake'n Bake. Bake, uncovered, for approximately 45 minutes at 350° until brown. Serves 4.

MRS. NOEL LEE DUNN

CHICKEN DELIGHT

⅓ cup melted butter
8 medium-sized chicken thighs

8 slices bacon
Salt and pepper to taste

Salt and pepper chicken lightly. Brush with a little butter. Wrap each in a slice of bacon. Secure with toothpick if necessary. Bake on rack at 375° about 1 or 1½ hours, or until tender. Serves 4.

MRS. GRIMES THOMAS

CHICKEN CROQUETTES

1 cup milk	Salt and pepper
1 tablespoon flour	1 teaspoon chopped parsley
1 tablespoon butter	½ set of brains
Juice of small onion	1 boiled chicken, ground

Parboil brains. Make cream sauce of first 5 ingredients. Add parsley, brains, and chicken. Mix well, shape into croquettes and put into refrigerator until thoroughly cold. Roll in beaten egg and bread crumbs and fry in deep fat.

SAUCE

½ cup chopped celery	3 egg yolks
½ onion, chopped	2 tablespoons flour
Chicken stock	

Cook celery and onion in butter or chicken fat until soft. Sprinkle with flour and add chicken stock. Cool slightly and fold in 3 egg yolks. Pour around croquettes.

OLD NORTH STATE COOKBOOK

CURRIED CHICKEN

4 cups diced cooked chicken	2 teaspoons Worcestershire
2 medium onions, chopped	4 cups chicken stock
1 cup celery, chopped	Salt to taste
¾ to 1 cup tomato juice	1 tablespoon curry powder
1 heaping tablespoon flour	½ cup raisins (optional)
1 stick margarine	

Boil chicken in water, saving 4 cups for stock. Cool and shred in large pieces. Brown onions and celery in margarine. Add flour. Stir in stock slowly until smooth. Add remaining ingredients and simmer for 1 hour. May be made ahead of time and reheated. Serve over rice. Serves 8.

Serve in separate small dishes the following condiments:

Chutney	Cocktail peanuts, chopped fine
Hard boiled eggs, mashed fine	Cooked bacon pieces, crumbled fine
Sweet pickles, cut in strips	

MRS. JOHN L. DABBS III

CHICKEN GUMBO

2 quarts okra, sliced	2 cans tomatoes, mashed fine
2 medium onions, chopped fine	2 small chickens (fryers)
6 large ears of corn (cut off the cob)	1 cup butter
1 pint butterbeans	¾ cup bacon grease

Put butter and grease in deep, large pan. Cut up chicken, season and flour. Put in and fry slowly until brown. Stir in vegetables. Add about 3 quarts of boiling water. Season as you like it and cook, simmering it until it's thick like soup. Before serving, lift bones out of soup. Serves 12.

MRS. H. F. KINCEY

DEEP SOUTH BRUNSWICK STEW

4-pound hen
2 pounds pork (cubed)
2 pounds beef (cubed)
1 large can tomatoes
1 large can corn
1 large can butterbeans
   (or 1 package frozen)
1 large can okra
   (or 1 package frozen)
¼ cup catsup
3 teaspoons Worcestershire

1 to 3 teaspoons Tabasco
3 tablespoons parsley flakes
3 tablespoons celery seed
1 teaspoon chili powder
1 teaspoon mustard seed
1 teaspoon curry powder
1 teaspoon thyme
2 or 3 bay leaves

Cook meats until tender, saving the stock. Shred meat by hand. Mix all vegetables (except butterbeans) with meats and seasonings together in large pot and simmer on top of stove six to eight hours. Add butterbeans the last hour of cooking time. Stir frequently and, if liquid is needed, add some of stock. Serves 10.

MRS. RALPH H. ALEXANDER, JR.

QUICK CREAMED CHICKEN IN PATTY SHELLS

6 frozen patty shells
2 tablespoons butter
2½ cups diced cooked chicken
1 can cream of chicken soup

2 tablespoons sherry
1 3-ounce can sliced or chopped
   mushrooms

Bake patty shells as directed on package. Heat butter in pan. Add chicken, soup, sherry and mushrooms and bring to a boil. Simmer 5 to 10 minutes. Serve in shells. Serves 6.

MRS. EDWIN W. FULLER, JR.

CHICKEN IN SHELLS

3½ pound roasting chicken
1½ teaspoons salt
2 stalks celery
3½ to 4 tablespoons flour
1 lemon

¼ teaspoon paprika
2 hard boiled eggs
Mushrooms
Patty shells

Boil chicken until tender in 1½ quarts salted water with 2 stalks celery. Refrigerate chicken broth until congealed (there should be a little more than 1 pint). Cut up chicken in small pieces. Melt congealed fat in a double boiler. Make sauce by using flour, adding broth. Grate the lemon rind and squeeze in the juice. Add paprika and 2 eggs mashed fine. Stir well. Add chicken and mushrooms. Fill patty shells. (Can be made ahead and frozen.) Serves 8-10.

MRS. MCALISTER CARSON

CHICKEN SUPPER DISH

6 full breasts of chicken, cooked
1 large yellow onion, chopped
1 cup raw rice (white)
1 No. 2½ can solid-packed
tomatoes, not drained

2 cloves garlic
2 small cans mushrooms, drained
½ green pepper, chopped
3 tablespoons oil or butter
salt and pepper to taste

Simmer chicken until tender. Save broth. Remove chicken from bones in large chunks. Fry onion and green pepper in a little oil until glossy. Add raw rice and simmer until golden brown. Add tomatoes, garlic and mushrooms and simmer about 20 minutes. Remove garlic. Place chicken in greased casserole and spread rice mixture over top. Add about 1-inch chicken broth. Bake at 350° for 45 minutes. Add more broth if necessary. Serves 6. (This may be cooked before serving or made ahead.)

MRS. HUGH CAMPBELL

CHICKEN DIVAN

4 pieces of chicken breast,
cooked and cut up
1 package broccoli, cooked until
almost done and drained
1 can mushroom soup

1 tablespoon Worcestershire
2 tablespoons chicken broth
2 tablespoons sherry
¾ cups grated sharp cheese
1 cup Pepperidge Farm stuffing
½ stick butter, melted

Put broccoli in casserole and put chicken on top. Make a sauce, using remaining ingredients. Mix over heat and pour over chicken and broccoli. Before serving, crush 1 cup Pepperidge Farm stuffing and ½-stick melted butter. Mix and spread over casserole. Cook, covered, at 350° for 20 minutes. Uncover and cook 20 minutes more. Serves 6.

MISS CLAUDIA WATKINS

CHICKEN AND SPAGHETTI

6-pound hen
1 8 oz. pkg. thin spaghetti
4 tablespoons flour
1 No. 2 can tomatoes (strained
or blended)
1 large onion

1 bell pepper
2 tablespoons butter
1 can sliced mushrooms
Parmesan cheese
1½ to 2 cups stock
½ jar beef extract (concentrate)

Boil chicken until tender. While it is cooking, brown flour in hot skillet. Remove hen from stock and allow stock to cool so fat will rise to top. Skim off fat and add stock to browned flour slowly, blending until smooth. Then add tomatoes and beef extract. Cut chicken in bite-sized pieces. Chop onion and pepper fine and sauté in butter. Add to sauce.

Cook spaghetti and drain. Grease casserole and layer ingredients in this order: spaghetti, chicken, then mushrooms. Cover with sauce and sprinkle with Parmesan cheese. Continue layering, ending with sauce and cheese. Heat at 425° until brown and bubbling. Serves 8 to 10. Can be frozen.

MRS. C. E. WILLIAMS, JR.

CHICKEN TETRAZZINI

1 5-pound chicken
2 tablespoons butter
2 tablespoons flour
2 teaspoons salt
2 cups milk

1 green onion, chopped
1 small can pimento
1 cup mushrooms
¼ pound grated cheese
½ box spaghetti (approximately 4 oz. to cook)

Boil chicken, then chop when cool. Make a white sauce of butter, flour, salt and milk. Add to the sauce the green pepper, pimento (chopped), chicken, mushrooms and cheese. Meanwhile, cook spaghetti in chicken stock. When tender, add to sauce mixture and place in large casserole. Top with more grated cheese. Bake at 375° until brown (about 25 to 30 minutes). Serves 6 to 8.

MRS. F. A. ADKINS

Game

MRS. STONEWALL JACKSON'S STUFFED PARTRIDGES

Partridges
Bacon, in strips

Salt and pepper
Butter

Select firm, plump birds. Do not split and then draw them down the back, but draw them, stuff them, and bake them in a moderate oven as you would a hen. Lay a strip of bacon across the breast of each. Season with salt, pepper and lumps of butter. Baste frequently. Serve on small triangles of toast which have been buttered on both sides.

OLD NORTH STATE COOKBOOK

HUNTER'S STEW

Doves
2 tablespoons butter
1 large onion
Small slice of ham
2 tablespoons of flour
1 can chicken consomme or
  chicken broth

1 clove garlic
2 bay leaves
¼ teaspoon dried thyme
½ pound (or 1 can) mushrooms
1 lemon
1 cup claret or burgundy
Salt and pepper

Salt and pepper doves; put butter into large skillet and brown doves well. Remove doves from pan. Chop onion fine, add ham that has been cut into cubes, crushed garlic clove, thyme, and bay leaves. Cook together in skillet for a minute or two. Add flour and brown, pour in wine, and simmer 5 to 10 minutes. Add consomme and enough water to make 1 quart of liquid. Add doves; cook gently for one hour Add mushrooms and the grated rind of the lemon. Season to taste; cook half hour longer. This may simmer for a long time if necessary. It is delicious over wild rice, but very good also over brown rice.

MRS. STANLEY W. BLACK, JR.

DOVE

10 to 12 dressed doves
2 tablespoon finely chopped onion
2 large ground bay leaves
½ cup dry white wine (sauterne)

4 or 5 peppercorns, finely crushed
2 tablespoons lemon juice
Flour, salt and pepper

SAUCE:
Franco-American beef gravy
Butter

Sauterne

Place dove on shallow platter; sprinkle with salt, pepper, and pinch of allspice. Mix together next five ingredients and pour over dove. Marinate for at least 2 hours (overnight is better). Drain and roll in flour, salt and pepper. Grease frying pan and sauté doves. Put in casserole (or leave in pan) and bake in 350° oven at least 1 to 1½ hours. Make sauce of Franco-American beef gravy, butter and sauterne to taste; heat and pour over birds (or put in gravy boat and guests may serve themselves). Serve with wine jelly, wild or brown rice. Serves 4 to 6.

MRS. A. L. CHASON, JR.

DOVE OR QUAIL

Birds
Salt, pepper and flour
Corn oil

Water to cover
1 stick margarine
Kitchen Bouquet (optional)

Slightly salt birds, dust with flour, brown in corn oil, turning frequently to brown on all sides. Remove birds from pan. Pour off oil, add enough water to cover birds and 1 stick margarine and heat. Place birds in pan or pyrex dish. Kitchen Bouquet can be added to make gravy brown. Cover and cook slowly in 300° oven until birds are tender. If not covered, baste birds in the gravy.

MRS. JAMES TROTTER

SAUTEED DOVE IN WINE WITH WHITE GRAPES

6 doves (or fill a 10-inch frying pan)
6 tablespoons butter or oil
2 tablespoons chopped onion
1 cup white wine
2 tablespoons chopped parsley (2 teaspoons if dried)
2 tablespoons tarragon (2 teaspoons if dried)
Toast
1 cup white seedless California grapes

Brown doves in butter with onions, salt and pepper. Add ½-cup white wine and simmer, covered, for 15 minutes. (Simmer longer if old doves; test with fork.) Add ½-cup wine, parsley, and tarragon. Simmer, uncovered, for 5 minutes. (Note: ½-cup brandy, blazed, may be substituted for the wine). Before serving, add grapes just long enough to heat but *not* cook. Serve on toast with sauce spooned over it.

MR. O. D. BAXTER, JR.

Meat Temperature Chart

Meat	Oven Temperature	Minutes per Pound	Thermometer Temperature
BEEF			
Roast	300°		
(Add 10 minutes per pound for boned roasts)			
Rare		18	140°
Medium		22	160°
Well Done		30	180°
Rump	300°	25-30	160°
Tenderloin	350°	1 hour	160°
FISH			
Quick-Baked	500°	10	

Meat Temperature Chart

Meat	Oven Temperature	Minutes per Pound	Thermometer Temperature
LAMB			
Leg, Loin	300°	25-30	170-180°
(Add 5 minutes per pound for boned roast)			
Crown	300°	2 hours	
PORK			
Fresh Ham	350°		185°
Under 5 pounds		45	
Over 5 pounds		35	
Cured (Precooked)	350°	30 (including glazing)	
VEAL			
Leg, Loin (Boned)	300°	40	170°
POULTRY AND GAME			
Chicken (Baked)	325°	25	180°
Turkey (Ready to cook, unstuffed weight)	350°		195°
6- 8 pounds		3-4 hours	
8-12 pounds		4-4½ hours	
12-16 pounds		4½-6½ hours	
16-20 pounds		6½-7 hours	
20-24 pounds		7-8½ hours	
(Foil wrapped, unstuffed weight)	450°		190°
8-10 pounds		2¼-2½ hours	
10-12 pounds		2¾-3 hours	
14-16 pounds		3-3¼ hours	
18-20 pounds		3¼-3½ hours	
22-24 pounds		3¼-3¾ hours	

The last 30 minutes turn back foil and brown turkey in 350° oven.
(For stuffed bird: add 30 to 45 minutes to total time)

Seafood

BROILED FLOUNDER

4 pieces of flounder
¼ cup diced celery
3 tablespoons butter
¼ chopped onion

Parsley
Paprika
Lemon slices

Place flounder on greased foil paper, sprinkle with salt and pepper and dot with butter. Cover fish with mixed chopped celery and onion. Sprinkle with parsley and paprika. Squeeze enough lemon juice to moisten fish well. Add about 2 tablespoons of water to pan (not over fish). Cook under broiler and keep basting with juice in the pan for 15-20 minutes. Add more water if juice begins to brown and dry out. Serve with lemon slice and parsley sprigs. Delicious plain, but delectable if served with hollandaise sauce. Serves 4.

MRS. JOE RUSH SHULL, JR.

BAKED FLOUNDER

1 package frozen flounder,
  thawed
1 can frozen shrimp soup, thawed
Lemon juice

Parmesan cheese
Bread crumbs
Butter

Put flounder in greased oblong casserole. Spread soup over fish. Sprinkle lemon juice, cheese, and bread crumbs over all. Dot with butter and bake, uncovered, in 350° oven for 20 to 30 minutes. Serves 4 to 6. (Sometimes I add a small jar of sliced mushrooms, more shrimp soup and sherry.)

MRS. JULIAN W. CLARKSON

BAKED FILLET OF FLOUNDER

1 pound flounder
1 cup water

Salt and pepper

Dip fish in water to which 1 tablespoon salt has been added. Dry and rub with salt and pepper. Bake until tender.

SAUCE

4 tablespoons butter
2 tablespoons flour
1 cup milk
1 egg
½ pound shrimp

½ pound mushrooms
Juice of 1 lemon
Salt, pepper to taste
Dash of paprika

Melt butter, add flour and milk. Cook over low heat until sauce begins to thicken. Remove from heat. Add egg and beat well. Return to heat and cook until thick. Add lemon juice, shrimp, and mushrooms. Place fish on large platter and cover with sauce before serving.

OLD NORTH STATE COOKBOOK

BAKED STUFFED FLOUNDER

6 flounder fillets
Paprika
Lemon juice and butter
1 medium onion, chopped
¾ cup butter
1½ cups cooked shrimp
1½ cups picked-over chunk crab meat

1 well-beaten egg
1 tablespoon water
1 teaspoon parsley
3 tablespoons sherry
Salt and pepper to taste
Bread crumbs

At a seafood market pick out the size pieces of white fillet of flounder that, when folded in half, will be the correct size on a dinner plate. Place a portion of the stuffing on one half of the fillet and fold the other side over. Cover generously with paprika and wrap immediately in waxed paper, tying well at both ends with string. Freeze this a day ahead of time. When ready to bake, remove string and paper. Place on well-buttered baking tray and place in pre-heated oven at 375° for approximately 25 minutes, basting often with lemon juice and butter mixture.

Stuffing: Sauté onion in butter until onion turns transparent. Remove from heat and cool. Add shrimp and crab meat. Stir into this the egg, water, parsley, sherry, salt, pepper, with enough toasted bread crumbs to make dressing consistency. Serves 6.

MRS. A. S. BUMGARDNER, JR.*

SNAPPER NEWBURG

4 tablespoons butter
1 cup cream
3 egg yolks
⅓ teaspoon nutmeg
⅛ teaspoon pepper
¼ teaspoon salt

½ teaspoon Worcestershire
Paprika to taste
¼ cup cooking sherry
4½ pounds boneless red snapper fillets

Melt butter and heat in double boiler. Add cream. Stir in egg yolks and seasonings. Cook slowly until creamy and smooth. Add sherry just before serving.

SNAPPER FILLETS

Place fillets on heavy aluminum foil, shaped to fit each piece of fillet. Turn up edges to hold juice in. Brush with butter. Place in 425° oven and cook until tender and flaky about 10 minutes. Remove from foil with spatula. Serve sauce on fillets. Serves 4.

MR. TERRY YOUNG

FILETS DE POISSON A LA BRETONNE

5 pounds skinless and boneless
flounder fillets, cut into
serving pieces
4 tablespoons finely chopped
green onions

Salt and pepper
3 tablespoons butter
1½ cups dry white wine

Preheat oven to 350°. Poach flounder in white wine, using two 10 or 12-inch baking dishes about 1½-inch deep. Butter the baking dishes; sprinkle half of onions on bottom of baking dish. Salt and pepper fillets and put them in one layer (they may overlap slightly) in dish. Sprinkle remaining onions on fillets and dot with butter. Pour in white wine and enough cold water to barely cover fish. Bring almost to simmer on top of stove. Lay a piece of buttered brown paper or wax paper over the fish. Put dish in bottom third of oven and maintain liquid almost at the simmer for 8 to 10 minutes. The fish is done when a fork will pierce the flesh easily. Drain off the cooking liquid and save in a saucepan. The fish is now poached and ready for the Sauce Bretonne. (Keep fish warm by placing over hot — not simmering — water.)

SAUCE BRETONNE

2 cups of poaching liquid
5 tablespoons flour
6 tablespoons butter

1½ to 2 cups whipping cream
Salt, pepper, lemon juice

Make a paste of flour and butter. Add paste to hot liquid. Add half of cream and bring to boil. Thin the sauce with tablespoons of remaining cream until sauce coats spoon. Season with salt, pepper, and lemon juice.

JULIENNE OF VEGETABLES

½ pound mushrooms
2 carrots

2 yellow onions
2 celery stalks
Salt and Pepper

Cut vegetables into matchstick size and cook slowly for 20 minutes in butter in covered saucepan until tender, but not brown. Add mushrooms and cook 2 minutes. Season with salt and pepper.

½ cup grated Swiss cheese

2 tablespoons butter, cut into
bits

Now place julienne of vegetables over fish. Spoon thickened sauce on top of this. Sprinkle cheese and dot with butter. Place dish 6 inches from broiler for 2 or 3 minutes until sauce is lightly browned. Serve immediately. Serves 12.

MRS. RODDEY DOWD

LOBSTER NEWBURG

1 pound cooked lobster	½ teaspoon salt
½ cup brandy	1 tablespoon Worcestershire
⅛ pound butter	4 egg yolks
2 cups cream	½ teaspoon paprika
4 tablespoons flour	2 dashes Tabasco
1 teaspoon sugar	

Pour brandy over lobster, let stand 15 minutes. Melt butter in skillet, add lobster and brandy, and let simmer 5 minutes. Mix cream and flour to a smooth paste and add to beaten egg yolks; then add sugar, salt, paprika, Worcestershire and Tabasco. Stir well. Pour these ingredients into double boiler, cook until consistency of thin cream sauce. Stir continuously. Add lobster. Cook 2 minutes. Serve.

OLD NORTH STATE COOKBOOK

STUFFED LOBSTER SUPREME

8 frozen Rock Lobster tails	2 cups light cream
1 stick butter	2 tablespoons lemon juice
4 tablespoons flour	¼ cup cracker crumbs
1 teaspoon salt	¼ cup grated Parmesan Cheese
1 teaspoon paprika	1 tablespoon melted butter
Dash of cayenne	(for topping)

Boil lobster according to directions. Cut away meat and dice; save shell. Sauté lobster in butter for 2 to 3 minutes. Remove from heat and blend in flour, salt, paprika, cayenne. Slowly stir in cream. Cook, stirring constantly, until it thickens and boils for 1 minute. Stir in lemon juice. Spoon filling into shells. Sprinkle top lightly with mixture of crumbs, cheese and melted butter. Bake in 450° oven until golden (10 to 12 minutes). (Lobster tails may be cooked and stuffed early and refrigerated. Before heating, top with crumb mixture and bake at 350° for about 40 minutes.) Serves 4.

MRS. RUFUS SAFFORD

BAKED SHRIMP AND LOBSTER EN PERDITA

1 pound shrimp, cooked, shelled	Dash of nutmeg
1 pound lobster, cooked, bite	Dash of paprika
size pieces	1 teaspoon chopped parsley
2 tablespoons flour	Salt and pepper to taste
2 tablespoons butter	1 teaspoon Durkee's mustard
⅔ cup of cream	4 tablespoons Welsh rarebit
⅔ cup white wine (Chablis)	4 thin slices of lemon

Make a cream sauce of butter, flour, cream; then add wine and seasonings. Add Durkee's mustard to taste. Bring almost to boil, then add Welsh rarebit. Cool slightly. Pour over lobster and shrimp. Mix well. Place equal portion of the seafood mixture on 12x12 sheet of aluminum foil. Top with lemon slices. Fold up and seal foil air-tight. Cook in 450° oven 10 to 15 minutes. If frozen, cook 20 to 30 minutes. Serves 4-6.

MRS. JAMES HARRISON WHITNER III

LOBSTER AND SHRIMP

1 pound cooked lobster
1 teaspoon shrimp spice
1 pound medium shrimp,
  cleaned and deveined
8 slices bacon
1/4 cup butter
1/4 cup flour
1 cup light cream
1 1/4 cups milk
3/4 cup dry white wine

2 teaspoons salt
1/4 teaspoon white pepper
1 teaspoon prepared mustard
1 teaspoon Worcestershire
2 tablespoons sherry (optional)
3/4 cup sliced ripe olives
Grated Parmesan cheese
Paprika and parsley
Toast

Cut lobster in bite-size pieces. Tie shrimp spice in a cheesecloth and boil with the shrimp for 5 minutes, until they are pink. Fry bacon, drain and crumble. Melt butter in a large pan; stir in flour; slowly add cream and milk, stirring constantly. Add wine and cook until thick and smooth. Season with salt, pepper, mustard, and Worcestershire. Add bacon and blend, then simmer 20 to 30 minutes. Add sherry if desired. Add lobster, shrimp and olives and cook until very hot. (Sauce part can be made ahead.) Put in ramekins or casserole. Sprinkle with cheese and broil until brown. Dust with paprika. Decorate with parsley. Serve with toast. Makes 8 servings.

MRS. VERNER E. STANLEY, JR.

SHRIMP SCAMPI

2 pounds shrimp, in shells, fresh
  or frozen
2 sticks margarine

2 cloves garlic, minced fine
Salt and pepper to taste

Remove shells from shrimp, except portion which covers tail. Cut down center of back and remove sand vein. Melt butter and add garlic. Simmer 3 minutes. Place shrimp on individual flame-proof platters or large broiling pan. Pour garlic butter over them. Sprinkle with salt and pepper. Place in preheated broiler 3 inches from heat and broil 5 to 7 minutes, or until browned and tender. Makes 4 to 5 servings.

MRS. BONN A. GILBERT, JR.

CHARCOALED SHRIMP KABOBS

1/4 cup onion, chopped fine
1/4 cup celery, chopped fine
1/2 cup melted butter
1/4 cup orange juice
1/4 cup Worcestershire

3 pounds fresh jumbo shrimp, in
  shell with tails on
2 lemons, cut up
2 green peppers

Sauté onion and celery in 1/4 cup butter. Remove from heat. Add remaining butter and orange juice and Worcestershire, mixing thoroughly. Boil shrimp, leaving them in shell and with tails on, with lemons. Cover with sufficient water and cook 7 minutes, or until done. Cool in cold running water and shake dry in colander. Dice green peppers in 1-inch squares. Place about 3 shrimp, then pepper square, then shrimp alternately on skewers until desired number are skewered. Place skewers on charcoal grill 4 to 5 inches above coals. Turn often and baste generously with sauce. Remove from skewers and serve on platter. Serve with cocktail sauce. Serves 6-8.

MR. TERRY YOUNG

BARBECUED SHRIMP

1 pound large raw shrimp in shells
½ cup soy sauce
¼ cup sugar
1 teaspoon grated ginger
1 teaspoon sherry

Remove legs and devein shrimp, leaving tail and shell. Mix marinade and soak shrimp in it for at least 30 minutes. Broil at medium heat until pink (about 5 minutes). They may also be cooked on grill on aluminum foil with holes punched in it so the smoke can come through. These are great for hor d'oeuvres although they are rather messy as they are served in the shell. Serves 3.

MRS. DANIEL T. RUSSLER

ADLAI STEVENSON'S ARTICHOKE AND SHRIMP CASSEROLE

1 #2 can artichoke hearts (or 1 package frozen artichoke hearts, cooked by directions)
¾ pound medium-sized cooked shrimp (if fresh shrimp, use one pound, allowing for shrinkage)
¼ pound fresh or canned mushrooms
2 tablespoons butter
1 tablespoon Worcestershire
¼ cup good dry sherry
Salt and pepper to taste
¼ cup grated Parmesan cheese
Cream sauce (1½ cups)

Drain can of whole artichokes and arrange in buttered baking dish. Spread the cooked shrimp over them. Sauté sliced mushrooms in butter for 6 minutes and add them to baking dish. Add Worcestershire, salt and pepper, and sherry to cream sauce and pour over contents of baking dish. Sprinkle the top with Parmesan cheese and dust with paprika. Bake in 375° oven for 20 minutes. Cover dish with chopped parsley just before serving. Serves 6.

MRS. C. DIXON SPANGLER, JR.

SHRIMP NEWBURG

2 cans frozen shrimp soup
2 garlic cheese rolls
2 cups shrimp
1 can mushrooms, drained
Sherry to taste

Mix all ingredients and heat in double boiler. Serve in patty shells or on toast. Can also be served in chafing dish for cocktail party. Serves 6.

MRS. ROBERT CHERRY

SHRIMP SUPREME

1¾ pounds cooked shrimp
4 tablespoons butter
4 tablespoons flour
1½ cups milk

8 tablespoons tomato catsup
1¼ teaspoons curry powder
4 tablespoons Worcestershire

Blend melted butter and flour in top of double boiler. Slowly stir in milk. Add catsup, curry and Worcestershire. Add shrimp last. Serve over rice. Serves 6.

MRS. J. OVERTON ERWIN

SHRIMP N' EASY

1 pound cleaned cooked shrimp
2 cans Van Camp's Spanish Rice

Slivered, blanched almonds
Buttered bread crumbs

Mix all ingredients together in buttered casserole dish, except a few almonds and the bread crumbs, which should be sprinkled on top. Bake in 350° oven until bubbly. Add more seasoning if desired. Serves 6 to 8.

MRS. JAMES WILCOX, JR.

SHRIMP CREOLE

2 tablespoons margarine, melted
½ cup chopped onions
8 green olives, sliced
½ green pepper, chopped fine
1½ cups tomatoes
1 small can tomato soup

½ teaspoon salt
1 teaspoon sugar
¼ cup chili sauce
Dash of chili powder
2 cups shrimp, cooked
Rice, cooked

Sauté margarine, onions, olives and pepper in large skillet. Add remaining ingredients, except shrimp, and cook together very slowly for 15 to 30 minutes. Add shrimp just before serving. Serve over hot rice. Serves 3 to 4.

MRS. TERRY YOUNG

SHRIMP AND CRAB MEAT A LA RICE

1 pound crab meat
1 pound shrimp, cooked
½ green pepper, chopped fine
½ cup onion, chopped (or 2 tablespoons onion flakes)
½ small can pimento, chopped
1 cup celery, chopped fine

1 4-ounce can mushrooms (or ½ pound fresh mushrooms)
1 cup Kraft mayonnaise
½ teaspoon salt
1 cup half and half cream
1 tablespoon Worcestershire
¾ cup raw rice
Bread crumbs

Cook rice according to directions. Combine first 7 ingredients. Mix mayonnaise, salt, cream, and Worcestershire together. Combine this with meat mixture and cooked rice and place in a 2-quart greased casserole. Sprinkle with bread crumbs. Bake at 375° for 35 minutes. Serves 8.

MRS. EDWIN REESE RENCHER, JR.

SHRIMP CASSEROLE

1 cup onion, chopped
1 cup celery, chopped
1 can tomato soup
1 can mushrooms

1 pound sharp cheese, grated
4 pounds cooked shrimp
1 cup raw rice

Cook rice according to directions. Sauté onions and celery in butter. Add remaining ingredients. Mix well and bake 45 minutes at 350° in individual shells or casserole. Serves 6 to 8.

MRS. THOMAS CUMMINGS

CRAB AND SHRIMP CASSEROLE

2 cups raw rice
1½ pounds crab meat
½ pound small shrimp
½ green pepper, chopped
⅓ cup parsley, chopped
1 can mushrooms

1½ cups Duke's mayonnaise
2 packages frozen peas, thawed
  but not cooked
Salt and pepper, to taste
Spice Island's Fine Herbs, to taste

Cook the rice. Combine all ingredients. Mix lightly. Place in greased casserole. Bake, covered, for 1 hour at 350°. Serves 8.

MRS. G. WARING BOYS

SEAFOOD CASSEROLE

1 6-ounce can crabmeat
1 6-ounce can shrimp
1 medium green pepper, chopped
1 medium onion, chopped
1 cup celery, chopped
½ teaspoon salt

½ teaspoon pepper
1 cup mayonnaise
½ cup crushed cracker crumbs
Worcestershire to taste
Tabasco to taste

Combine all ingredients except crumbs. Add seasoning and mix well. Pour into casserole or individual shells. Spread crumbs on top. Bake at 350° for 25 minutes. Serves 4 to 6.

MRS. THOMAS CUMMINGS

SHRIMP AND CRAB CASSEROLE

1 pound shrimp, boiled and
  cleaned
1 pound crabmeat

1 cup mayonnaise
½ cup Durkee's dressing
Buttered bread crumbs

Mix all ingredients except crumbs. Place in casserole and top with crumbs. Heat in 350° oven about 20 or 25 minutes until bubbly hot. Serves 4 to 6.

MISS CLAUDIA WATKINS

CRAB SPAGHETTI CASSEROLE

½ of 8-ounce package thin
  spaghetti
1 can cream of mushroom soup
3 tablespoons butter
1 cup milk

½ pound grated cheddar cheese
1 pound fresh, flaked crab meat
⅛ teaspoon pepper
¼ cup sherry (or to taste)
Dash of Worcestershire

Cook spaghetti until tender and drain. Heat soup, stir until smooth; add butter, milk and ¾ of grated cheese. Combine this cheese sauce with spaghetti, picked crab meat, pepper and Worcestershire. Place in greased casserole and sprinkle with remaining cheese. Bake at 400° for 30 minutes. Can be made a day ahead. Serves 4.

MRS. DANIEL T. RUSSLER

CRAB MEAT SPAGHETTI

1 8-ounce package spaghetti
½ cup onion, chopped
¼ cup green pepper, chopped
2 tablespoons butter or oil
1 #1 can tomato soup
½ teaspoon salt
Few drops Tabasco

½ teaspoon Worcestershire
⅛ teaspoon paprika
½ pound fresh or canned crab
  meat
½ pound grated cheese
1 can mushrooms, drained

Cook spaghetti in salt water until tender. Drain. Sauté onions in butter. Add soup and seasonings and simmer for 5 minutes. Remove from heat and add crab and mushrooms. Place half of spaghetti in greased baking dish and add layer of crab and part of the cheese. Continue layering until all is used. Bake for 30 minutes in 350° oven. Serves 6 to 8.

MRS. BRUCE H. RINEHART

CRAB CASSEROLE

1½ pounds cooked shrimp
2 lobster tails (or 1 can) cut up
½ pound lump crab meat
  (picked)
1 can frozen shrimp soup
1 can mushroom soup

½ cup toasted almonds
1 cup grated cheese
Worcestershire sauce
Salt and pepper
¼ cup sherry
Bread crumbs

Combine all ingredients, mixing well. Put in casserole, cover with bread crumbs, dot with butter, and bake at 350° for 30 minutes. Serves 8.

MRS. HENRY G. NEWSON

CRAB MEAT CASSEROLE

½ stick butter
1 cup chopped onion
½ cup chopped green pepper
1 cup chopped celery
3 tablespoons flour
2½ cups milk
Salt and pepper to taste

⅓ teaspoon dry mustard
¼ teaspoon red pepper
1 teaspoon Worcestershire
3 well-beaten eggs
2 pounds crab meat
½ cup grated cheese
Cracker crumbs

Melt butter and cook vegetables for 10 minutes at very low heat. Remove vegetables. To the butter left in the pan, add flour and milk to make medium white sauce. Add seasonings, eggs, crab meat, and the vegetables. Put in well-greased casserole. Top with grated cheese and cracker crumbs. Bake at 325° 45 minutes to 1 hour. Serves 10.

MRS. JOHN STEDMAN

CRAB MEAT SYCAMORE

2 pounds white lump crab meat
¾ pound diced Swiss cheese
2 cans artichokes, drained
1½ cups cream sauce
1 tablespoon chopped shallots
1 teaspoon parsley
3 tablespoons butter
2 tablespoons flour
1¼ cups milk
2 tablespoons sherry
Tabasco and Worcestershire to taste
Salt and pepper to taste
½ cup bread crumbs
8 thin slices of lemon
Parsley sprigs

Make sauce by melting butter, adding onions and parsley, blending in flour, and slowly stirring in the milk. Add sherry and other seasonings. Place in large, greased pyrex dish, or individual shells, alternating layers of crab meat, cheese and artichokes. Spoon cream sauce evenly on top. Sprinkle with bread crumbs and bake at 350° for 35 to 40 minutes. Garnish with thin lemon slices and parsley. Serves 6 to 8.

MRS. JOSEPH K. HALL III

CRAB MEAT SOUFFLE

1 cup crab meat
1 minced onion
1 cup thin cream
4 tablespoons cooked rice
¼ cup toasted bread crumbs
2 teaspoons curry powder
8 ounces tomato pulp
4 eggs, separated
Seasonings to taste

Sauté onion slowly, add cream and when hot, stir in rice, bread crumbs, curry powder and seasoning. When thickened, add tomato pulp, flaked crab and beaten yolks. Let cool and add beaten egg whites. Bake in greased dish over hot water in moderate (350°) oven until set—about 30 minutes. Serves 4.

MRS. AMOS BUMGARDNER, JR.

DEVILED CRABS

5 slices bread, toasted until hard (like melba toast)
1 egg, beaten
½ teaspoon Worcestershire sauce
Tabasco sauce (shake)
1 tablespoon prepared mustard
1 clove garlic, chopped fine or pressed
3 tablespoons catsup
1 cup mayonnaise
Juice of 1 lemon
1 teaspoon salt
1 pint crabmeat

Grate bread. Beat egg. Combine all ingredients except half of bread crumbs. Put into shells. Sprinkle remaining crumbs on top. Bake until brown at 325°.

MRS. RUSSELL RANSON

DELUXE DEVILED SEA FOOD

¼ cup minced onion
4 tablespoons butter
4 tablespoons flour
1½ teaspoons dry mustard
2 cups milk
Cayenne pepper
1 teaspoon Tabasco
3 or 4 teaspoons Worcestershire
3 hard boiled eggs, sieved or grated

1½ pounds sea food (shellfish preferred), any combination of shrimp, crab, lobster or oysters, cooked
1 cup very sharp cheddar cheese, grated
1 cup fine buttered crumbs
½ cup pecans, chopped very fine

Grease 2-quart shallow baking dish and rub it with garlic. Cook onion in butter until transparent. Add flour and mustard and cook a minute or two longer. Add milk and seasoning when thickened. Add sieved eggs, sea food and half of cheese. Mix crumbs, rest of cheese and nuts. Put half creamed mixture in dish. Sprinkle half of dry mixture. Repeat. Put melted butter on top. Place in 325° oven for 25 minutes, or until thoroughly heated. Serves 8.   MRS. WALTER B. MAYER

JUMBO IMPERIAL CRAB

1 pound backfin lump crab meat
1½ tablespoons mayonnaise
1½ tablespoons Durkee's Sauce
1 tablespoon Worcestershire

½ cup coarsely rolled cracker crumbs
1 tablespoon paprika
3 tablespoons butter

Combine crab meat, mayonnaise and sauces lightly, and pile into 6 crab shells. Combine cracker crumbs and paprika and sprinkle on top. Pour on melted butter. Place shells in shallow baking pan which contains ¼-inch water. Bake for 15 to 20 minutes, or until browned, in 350° oven. Serves 6.

If you have no crab shells: mix the sauces in a mixing bowl and be generous with the sauces and mayonnaise. (This keeps the mixture from becoming dry.) Add crab meat and mix well. Add cracker crumbs and mix. Add melted butter and blend. Put mixture in an 8-inch pie pan and cover with aluminum foil. Place pan in water, as above, in 350° oven for 20 to 30 minutes.   MRS. BEN TROTTER

CRAB IMPERIAL

2 tablespoons butter
1 cup heavy cream
½ teaspoon salt
½ teaspoon red pepper
½ teaspoon dry mustard

½ teaspoon vinegar
1 tablespoon Worcestershire
1 cup finely minced green pepper
1 cup Pepperidge Farm dressing
1 pound crab meat

Melt butter. Add cream, salt, red pepper, mustard, vinegar and Worcestershire. When heated, add 1 cup green pepper. Cook for 1 minute, then add Pepperidge Farm dressing. Mix well. Remove from heat and add crab meat. Sprinkle top with dressing and bake at 400° for about 15 minutes. Serves 6.   MRS. LYN BOND, JR.

TUNA FLORENTINE

3 packages frozen chopped spinach
2 tablespoons butter
3 tablespoons flour
2 cups milk
¼ cup grated Swiss cheese
⅓ cup grated Parmesan cheese
2 7-ounce cans tuna

Cook spinach according to directions on package. Drain well and keep hot. Melt butter, add flour. Slowly add milk, Swiss cheese, 2 tablespoons Parmesan cheese, and oil from canned tuna. Cook over hot water for 20 minutes. Add flaked tuna. Pour over spinach. Top with rest of Parmesan cheese. Broil until bubbly. Serves 6.

MRS. FRANK H. CONNER, JR.

SCALLOPS BROILED IN GARLIC BUTTER

1 large clove garlic
⅓ cup butter or margarine
2 teaspoons minced chives, scallions or onions
1 tablespoon chopped parsley
¼ teaspoon dried tarragon (if desired)
¼ teaspoon salt
Dash of pepper
1 pound scallops

Split garlic clove and brown in the butter. Remove garlic and add to butter the chives, parsley, tarragon, salt and pepper. Wash and drain scallops. Cut into small pieces. Put in oven-proof shallow pan and pour butter over them. Broil under moderate heat about 5 minutes, until done. Do not overcook. Serve on fresh toast. Serves 4.

MRS. RICHARD K. SIMS

OYSTERS ROCKEFELLER

1 package frozen spinach
12 green onions
4 stalks celery
1 bunch parsley
1 head lettuce
2 sticks butter
1 cup bread crumbs
2 tablespoons Worcestershire
2 teaspoons anchovy paste
3 tablespoons absinthe, if available
½ teaspoon salt
1 clove garlic
Dash of Tabasco
Oysters (number desired)
Parmesan cheese
Rock salt

Defrost spinach and pulverize with onions, celery, parsley and lettuce in blender. Melt butter in large saucepan, add above ingredients and garlic clove, and simmer slowly for half an hour, stirring occasionally. Add bread crumbs. Worcestershire sauce, Tabasco, anchovy and absinthe. Remove from fire. *This part may be frozen.*

Place 8 to 10 oysters in individual baking shells. Put shells on rock salt spread in baking pan. Place under broiler until oysters curl. Pour off excess liquor. Top generously with sauce and sprinkle with Parmesan cheese. Return to broiler until sauce is bubbly. Serves 6-8.

Alternate for hors d'oeuvres: Chop 3 dozen oysters fine and broil in butter on top of stove. Add 1 cup of sauce. Place on toast rounds and sprinkle with Parmesan. Place under broiler.

MRS. MIKE BACCICH

SCALLOPED OYSTERS I

1 pint oysters
6 tablespoons evaporated milk
2 cups crushed saltines

½ cup melted butter
⅔ cup grated American cheese
Salt and pepper

Drain oysters, saving ½-cup liquor. Grease casserole. Add a layer of crumbs, then oysters. Make 3 layers of crumbs, 2 of oysters. Salt, pepper, and pour butter on each layer of oysters. Pour cream and oyster liquor on top layer of crumbs. Dot with butter and sprinkle with cheese. Bake 20 minutes in 400° oven. Serves 4.

MRS. FRANK CONNER, JR.

SCALLOPED OYSTERS II

1 quart oysters
Salt and pepper

Thick white sauce
1 cup toasted bread crumbs

Put oysters into the saucepan with salt and pepper to taste. Cook until edges curl (about 5 minutes). Fold in the sauce. Add most of the bread crumbs, reserving a little to sprinkle on top. Bake in moderate oven about 15 minutes.

SAUCE
3 tablespoons flour
6 tablespoons butter
1 cup milk
2 egg yolks

2 teaspoons lemon juice
2 teaspoons Worcestershire
1 teaspoon celery salt
Salt and pepper

Combine flour, butter, and milk over medium heat. Add egg yolks and beat until smooth. Add lemon juice, Worcestershire, celery salt, salt and pepper. Sauce should be quite thick.

OLD NORTH STATE COOKBOOK

SCALLOPED OYSTERS III

1 pint oysters
1 tablespoon oyster liquid
2 tablespoons milk or cream
½ cup stale bread crumbs

1 cup cracker crumbs
½ cup melted butter
Salt and pepper

Mix bread and cracker crumbs and stir in butter. Spread a thin layer of crumbs in bottom of buttered shallow baking dish. Cover crumbs with a layer of oysters. Sprinkle with salt and pepper. Add half of each: oysters, liquid and cream. Repeat and cover with remaining crumbs. Bake 30 minutes at 400°. Do not use more than two layers of oysters, as middle one will be undercooked. Serves 4.

MRS. RICHARD K. SIMS

CHAFING DISH OYSTERS

1 pint oysters
1 tablespoon butter
2 tablespoons Worcestershire

4 tablespoons tomato catsup
Salt and red pepper to taste
¼ cup celery (optional)

Put butter, oysters, celery, salt and pepper in chafing dish and cook until oysters curl. Add Worcestershire and catsup; let simmer about 3 minutes. Serves 3.

MRS. R. E. JONES, JR.

WILD RICE AND OYSTERS

1 cup raw wild or brown rice
¼ cup butter
1 8-ounce can sliced mushrooms

¼ cup chopped green pepper
1 cup sauterne
2 cups oysters

Cook rice in boiling water until tender; drain. Melt butter and add sliced mushrooms, green pepper, salt and pepper to taste. Add sauterne and simmer mixture for 15 minutes. Mix with rice. Spread half of this mixture in a 2-quart casserole. Dip oysters in melted butter and arrange 1 cup of them over rice in casserole. Spread remainder of rice, then another layer of oysters. Bake at 350° for 30 minutes. Serves 6.

MRS. HENRY G. NEWSON

SALMON PUFFS

½ pound canned salmon
   (hunk will do)
½ cup fresh bread crumbs
2 tablespoons grated onion
1 tablespoon lemon juice

1 tablespoon melted butter
½ teaspoon salt
¼ teaspoon pepper
1 egg, beaten
½ cup milk

Remove skin and bones from fish. Blend in next 6 ingredients. Beat egg with milk and combine it with all other ingredients. Place in two ramekins or a small baking dish. Bake in 350° oven for 40 minutes in pan of hot water. Serves 2.

MRS. WALTER B. MAYER

CLAM FRITTERS

1 cup flour
½ teaspoon salt
½ cup milk
1 teaspoon baking powder

1 tablespoon melted shortening
2 eggs, beaten
1 cup (approximately) clams, chopped

Sift dry ingredients. Add eggs, melted shortening and milk and mix well. Add clams. Drop by small spoonfuls into hot fat. Brown on both sides. Serve hot. (Substitute for clams: Corn). Serves 4 to 6.

MRS. LYN BOND, JR.

Eggs

ALIBI EGGS

2 tablespoons butter or oleo
½ teaspoon Worcestershire sauce
½ teaspoon dry mustard or 1
    tablespoon prepared mustard
4 tablespoons catsup

4 tablespoons water
4 eggs
2 pieces toast
Parmesan cheese to taste

Melt butter in skillet. Stir in Worcestershire, mustard, catsup and water. Carefully break in the eggs. Cook slowly, spooning sauce over eggs until they are set. Serve on buttered toast, sprinkling with cheese. Good for brunch or quick lunch. Serves 2.

MRS. WALTER BREM MAYER

BAKED EGGS

1 cup canned tomatoes
½ onion, chopped
3 whole cloves
1 bay leaf
Salt and pepper to taste

1½ tablespoons butter
1 tablespoon flour
4 hard-cooked eggs, sliced
¼ cup buttered bread crumbs

Cook tomatoes ten minutes with chopped onion, cloves and bay leaf. Add salt and pepper to taste. Strain. Melt butter and stir in flour. Add tomato liquid, stirring until thickened. Slice eggs into baking dish. Pour tomato sauce over eggs. Sprinkle with buttered bread crumbs. Bake at 400° for 15 minutes. Good luncheon dish. Serves 2.

MRS. J. OVERTON ERWIN

CREAMED EGGS

3 tablespoons butter
3 tablespoons flour
1½ cups whole milk
1 small onion
5 cloves

5 hard-cooked eggs, diced
3 large slices of Swiss cheese
3 pieces of toast, buttered
Salt and pepper to taste

Make cream sauce with 3 tablespoons butter, 3 tablespoons flour and one and one-half cups whole hot milk. After sauce becomes thick and smooth, add onion which has been studded with cloves. Add diced eggs and heat thoroughly. Butter toast and place a piece of Swiss cheese to fully cover toast. Add eggs, pour sauce over mixture. Sprinkle paprika on top and add a sprig of parsley to make it look pretty. Good Sunday evening supper. Serves 3.

MRS. BRUCE H. RINEHART

DEVILED EGGS

6 hard cooked eggs
¼ cup mayonnaise or salad dressing
1 teaspoon vinegar

1 teaspoon prepared mustard
½ teaspoon salt
Dash of pepper

Halve eggs lengthwise; remove yolks, and mash; mix with mayonnaise, vinegar, mustard, salt and pepper. Refill egg whites. (Pastry tube is good to do this, if available.) Chill, and trim with pimento strips or sliced olives and sprinkle with paprika.

MRS. C. E. WILLIAMS, JR.

EGGS HUSSARD FOR TWO

2 rounds Holland Rusk or toasted English muffins
Grilled ham

2 large slices ripe tomato
2 poached eggs

On each Holland Rusk or muffin, place slice of ham, tomato, poached egg and sauce in that order.

MARCHAUD DE VIN SAUCE

2 tablespoons butter
2 small finely chopped shallots
¼ pound mushrooms, chopped
½ cup cooked ham, finely chopped
⅛ teaspoon garlic, minced

2 tablespoons flour
1 cup hot beef stock
¼ cup red wine
2 teaspoons parsley, finely chopped

Melt butter and sauté shallots, mushrooms, ham and garlic until shallots are tender. Stir in flour and blend well. Stir in gradually hot beef stock, stirring constantly until slightly thickened. Stir in wine and parsley. Add more blended flour if desire it thicker. Bring to a boil again. Pour sauce over above recipe. Serves 2.

MRS. GEORGE IVEY, JR.

EGGS MORNAY

8 eggs
½ cup green peas
¼ teaspoon curry powder
¼ teaspoon salt
¼ teaspoon red pepper
¼ teaspoon celery salt
¼ cup parsley, chopped
¼ cup onion, chopped

2 tablespoons half and half cream
1½ cups milk
1½ tablespoons butter
1½ tablespoons flour
Sharp cheese, grated
Ground cooked ham

Hard boil eggs. Remove yolks, mash and blend in green peas, curry powder, salt, red pepper and celery salt. Add parsley, onion, and cream. Refill egg whites and place in casserole. Make a cream sauce of milk, butter and flour. Cover eggs and sprinkle the top with cheese and ham. Heat about ten minutes in 450° oven. Serves 8.

MRS. ROBERT P. WILSON

EGG-MUSHROOM CASSEROLE

2 tablespoons butter
1 large onion, chopped
2 cans sliced B&B mushrooms
18 hard boiled eggs, coarsely
chopped
2 cans cream of mushroom soup,
undiluted

Sherry, to taste
Salt and pepper to taste
Worcestershire sauce
Tabasco sauce
Buttered bread crumbs

Melt butter in saucepan. Add onions and mushrooms; sauté until onions are transparent. Combine this with eggs, soup and sherry. Season with salt and pepper, Worcestershire and Tabasco. Pour mixture into individual ramekins and top with buttered bread crumbs. Bake at 350° until thoroughly heated and bubbly. May be prepared the previous day. This is a good brunch dish, served with buttered toast triangles. Serves 10.

MRS. J. FRANK TIMBERLAKE

BRUNCH CASSEROLE FOR EIGHT

16 soft scrambled eggs
2 cans mushroom soup
¾ cup milk
1 tablespoon minced chives

1 jar Vera-Sharp Cheese
1 can sliced B&B mushrooms
½ can water chestnuts
2 tablespoons Parmesan cheese

Place scrambled eggs in buttered shallow baking dish. Add milk gradually to mushroom soup and heat. Add Vera-Sharp cheese and stir until melted. Pour over eggs. Top with mushrooms, water chestnuts, and Parmesan cheese. Place in 350° oven for 5 minutes, or until thoroughly heated. Serve with crisply fried chicken livers and bacon curls. Serves 8.

MRS. E. J. WANNAMAKER

OVEN OMELET

6 eggs, separated
6 tablespoons milk

¾ teaspoon salt
1½ tablespoons butter

Beat egg yolks; add heated milk and salt. Fold in stiffly beaten egg whites Heat butter in 10-inch pan on surface burner. Brown slightly. Pour mixture into dish and bake in 325° oven for 20 minutes. Serves 4 to 6. (This can be made with 4 eggs for 2 servings. Grated cheese or small can of mushrooms can be added for Sunday night supper.)

MRS. JOHN C. MARKEY

Cheese

CHEESE SOUFFLE I

½ cup grated sharp cheese
¼ cup flour
3 eggs, separated
Paprika

¼ cup butter
1 cup milk
Few drops onion juice (optional)

Prepare a white sauce with butter, flour and milk. Add cheese and cook until thick, stirring constantly. Add well beaten yolks and let cool. Beat egg whites until stiff and fold in gently. Turn into greased baking dish and place in pan of boiling water and bake 45 minutes at 375° until golden brown. Serve at once. Serves 4.

MRS. WILLIAM S. PIERCE

CHEESE SOUFFLE II

8 slices buttered bread, cut in
  fourths
2½ cups milk
4 eggs

1 teaspoon dry mustard
1 teaspoon salt
½ pound American cheese,
  grated

Remove crusts from bread and cut in fourths. Place half the bread in greased 2-quart casserole and cover with half the cheese. Alternate with remaining bread topped with cheese. Beat remaining ingredients together and pour over bread mixture. Let set in refrigerator, covered, 12 to 24 hours. Bake in pan containing small amount of water at 350° for one hour. Tastes like a cheese soufflé, yet can be made a day ahead. Serves 8.

MRS. DENNIS MYERS

CHEESE SOUFFLE III

1 cup soft bread crumbs
½ cup milk
⅔ cups grated mild or medium
  sharp cheese (according to
  taste)

4 tablespoons butter
1 teaspoon salt
2 eggs, separated

Heat first five ingredients in double boiler until cheese is melted. Remove from fire and cool slightly. Add beaten egg yolks. Fold in beaten whites. Pour into buttered baking dish. Bake at 350° about 30 minutes or until firm. Serves 4-5.

MRS. STUART W. ELLIOTT*

BLENDER CHEESE SOUFFLE

8 ounces sharp cheddar cheese
10 slices buttered bread
4 eggs
2 cups milk

1 teaspoon salt
½ teaspoon dry mustard
Dash of Worcestershire sauce

Put half of cheese (which has been cubed), bread, eggs and milk into blender. Turn on high speed until thoroughly mixed. Pour into large mixing bowl. Stir in remaining ingredients. Pour into greased 2-quart casserole dish. Bake uncovered for 1 hour at 350°. Serves 4.

MRS. JOSEPH D. DULANEY

CHEESE AND ONION PIE

3 eggs
½ cup milk
½ cup light cream
¾ teaspoon salt
½ teaspoon Tabasco
⅛ teaspoon nutmeg

¼ pound Swiss cheese, grated
¼ pound Gruyere cheese, grated
1 tablespoon flour
1 9-inch unbaked pastry shell
1 large onion, thinly sliced and
    cut in quarters

Beat together eggs, milk, cream, salt, Tabasco and nutmeg. Combine grated cheeses and flour. Sprinkle evenly in pastry shell. Pour in cream mixture. Top with onion slices. Bake at 400° for 15 minutes, then reduce heat to 325° and bake 30 minutes longer, or until point of knife inserted in center comes out clean. Serves 6. This is an interesting change from pizza.

MRS. AMOS BUMGARDNER, JR.

Vegetables and Fruits

Vegetables

ASPARAGUS CASSEROLE

3 tablespoons butter
4 tablespoons flour
2 cups milk
⅔ cup sharp cheese, grated
½ teaspoon salt

¼ teaspoon paprika
2 hard boiled eggs, sliced
2 cans green asparagus, drained
Buttered bread crumbs

Melt butter in a saucepan. Stir in flour until smooth. Pour in milk gradually. Stir over medium heat until thickened. Blend in cheese, stirring until melted. Season with salt and paprika. In 2-quart baking dish layer sauce, asparagus and sliced eggs, ending with sauce. Top with buttered bread crumbs. Cover with foil and bake at 350° for one hour. Serves 6.

MRS. WALTER SCOTT III

ASPARAGUS-PETIT POIS CASSEROLE

1 #300 can all green asparagus
1 #300 can tiny green peas
½ cup juice from peas
½ cup juice from asparagus
2 tablespoons butter
2 tablespoons flour

½ cup slivered toasted almonds
¼ cup cracker crumbs
¾ cup grated cheese
2 eggs, separated
Salt and red pepper to taste

Drain vegetables and measure liquid. Make a cream sauce of butter, flour and juice in top of a double boiler. Add ½ cup cheese and well beaten egg yolks, and stir until the cheese is melted. Beat the egg whites until stiff and add to the sauce. In the casserole, alternate layers of the asparagus, peas, almonds and sauce. Sprinkle the cracker crumbs and rest of the cheese on top. Bake in a hot oven (425°) for 15 to 20 minutes or until firm. Serves 6.

MRS. GARLAND B. GARRETTE*

GREEN BEAN CASSEROLE

2 cans French style green beans, drained
1 tablespoon sugar
1 onion, chopped

Salt and pepper to taste
1 small can mushrooms, drained
1 can mushroom soup, undiluted
2 slices crisp bacon, crumbled

Place all ingredients except bacon in 1½-quart greased casserole and mix well. Top with bacon crumbs (add more if desired). Bake at 350° for 30 minutes. Serves 6-8.

MRS. JOHN R. CAMPBELL

GREEN BEANS, FRENCH STYLE

2 to 3 pounds green beans, fresh or canned
1 small can water chestnuts, drained
½ 4-ounce can mushrooms, drained
6 slices bacon

If fresh beans are used, cook them your favorite way. Put water chestnuts and mushrooms through a food chopper or blender. Partially cook bacon. Add chopped chestnuts and mushrooms and sauté with the bacon. Add cooked beans and season to taste. Serves 8 to 10.

MRS. JOHN M. ARCHER

GREEN BEANS VINAGRETTE

1½ pounds green beans
Water enough to cook beans
1 teaspoon salt
⅛ teaspoon pepper
1 teaspoon paprika
1½ teaspoons dry mustard
¼ cup vinegar
¼ cup bacon drippings or salad oil
1 tablespoon chopped green olives

Remove ends from beans. Slice lengthwise, then cut in desired bean size. Place beans in saucepan with water. Combine dry ingredients. Stir in vinegar. Add remaining ingredients and pour over beans. Cook, covered, until beans are tender. Serves 6.

MRS. WILLIAM A. WHITE, JR.

ORIENTAL BEAN CASSEROLE

2 pounds string beans
1 can water chestnuts, drained
1 can bean sprouts, drained
1 can mushrooms, drained
1 can mushroom soup
Grated onion
Parmesan cheese
1 can French fried onion rings

Cook and drain beans. Combine in large casserole beans, water chestnuts, bean sprouts, mushrooms, and soup which has been moistened slightly with milk. Put grated onion and Parmesan cheese on top. Bake at 350° until bubbly. Add onion rings to the top a few minutes before removing from oven. Serves 8.

MRS. ROBERT LYNN

STRING BEAN AND TOMATO BAKE

2 tablespoons bacon drippings
¼ cup chopped onion
1¼ teaspoons salt
2 cups canned tomatoes (#303) can
½ teaspoon paprika
¼ teaspoon curry powder
2 tablespoons brown sugar
2 tablespoons green pepper, finely chopped
Garlic salt to taste
1 pound cooked string beans, drained

Heat bacon drippings. Sauté the onion in drippings until brown. Add tomatoes, seasonings, brown sugar and green pepper. Simmer this sauce a half-hour. Pour sauce over green beans in a 2-quart casserole and bake at 325° for one hour. Serves 6.

MRS. WALTER BREM MAYER

PATIO BEANS

4 slices bacon
1 medium onion, chopped
1 1-pound can baked beans in
tomato sauce
1 1-pound can kidney beans,
drained
1 1-pound can lima beans,
drained
¼ pound sharp cheese, cubed
½ cup brown sugar
⅓ cup catsup
2 teaspoons Worcestershire

Fry bacon until crisp. Sauté onion in bacon drippings. Combine in large casserole the beans, cheese, brown sugar and seasonings. Stir in the onion and bacon which has been crumbled. Sprinkle with Parmesan cheese. Bake at 350° until heated thoroughly and bubbly. Serves 6.

MRS. ROBERT LYNN

HARVARD BEETS

3 cups canned or freshly cooked
beets, sliced or diced
½ cup sugar
1 tablespoon cornstarch
½ teaspoon salt
2 whole cloves
¼ cup mild cider vinegar
2 tablespoons butter

Prepare beets and set aside. In top of double boiler, stir until smooth sugar, cornstarch, salt, cloves and vinegar. Stirring constantly, cook these ingredients over boiling water until smooth and clear. Add the beets and continue cooking over hot water for 30 minutes. Then stir in the butter. Serves 6.

MRS. GEORGE IVEY, JR.

BROCCOLI CASSEROLE I

2 eggs, well beaten
1 stick butter
1 cup mayonnaise
1 can mushroom soup
1 cup sharp cheese
2 tablespoons chopped onion
2 packages frozen chopped
broccoli
Ritz crackers

Cook and drain broccoli. Mix everything together in greased dish, top with crumbled Ritz crackers and bake in 350° oven for 1 hour. Serves 8.

MRS. FRANCIS M. PINCKNEY, JR.

BROCCOLI CASSEROLE II

3 packages frozen broccoli
florets
1 can cream of mushroom soup
1 stick butter
¼ cup almonds
1 roll Cheddar cheese
Bread crumbs

Cook broccoli according to directions on the package. Drain. Melt butter in skillet over low flame. Add mushroom soup, almonds, and cheese (cut up into small pieces). Stir until smooth. Put the broccoli into a buttered baking dish, cover with the sauce, and top with the bread crumbs. Bake at 350° for 30 minutes or until brown. Serves 6 to 8.

MRS. JULIAN J. CLARK, JR.*

BROCCOLI GARNI

2 packages frozen broccoli
¼ cup lemon juice
¼ cup salad oil
¼ teaspoon paprika
1 teaspoon sugar

½ teaspoon salt
½ teaspoon garlic salt
2 tablespoons onion, chopped **fine**
2 hard boiled eggs, chopped **fine**

Cook and drain the broccoli. Omitting eggs, place the remaining ingredients in a jar and shake well, or mix in blender. Pour dressing over broccoli and sprinkle with finely chopped eggs. Sprinkle with paprika. Serves 6.

MRS. BEN C. ASHCRAFT

BROCCOLI AND ONION CASSEROLE

2 packages frozen broccoli
½ regular can whole onions, drained
1 can celery soup

1 cup cheese, grated
Salt to taste
Paprika

Cook broccoli according to directions, but do not overcook. Drain broccoli and put in buttered casserole with onions. Pour undiluted soup over vegetables and top with cheese and paprika. Bake at 350° for 20-30 minutes, until soup bubbles and cheese is melted. Serves 6 to 8.

MRS. ELLEN G. GOODE

BROCCOLI SOUFFLE

4 packages frozen broccoli
1 cup mayonnaise
1 can cream of mushroom soup
6 eggs

4 tablespoons grated sharp cheese
Salt and pepper to taste
Onion juice, if desired

Cook broccoli, let cool and mash into small pieces. Add soup, then mayonnaise. Break one egg at a time, beating (I use mix-master) after each egg. Add cheese, salt and pepper to taste (also a little onion juice if desired). Pour into buttered casserole (2-quart round). Bake in oven at 300° for 45 minutes. Serves 10 or 12.

MRS. R. E. JONES, JR.

SHRIMP SAUCE FOR BROCCOLI

1 can frozen shrimp soup
½ cup milk
3-ounce package cream cheese

1 tablespoon chives
Juice of ½ lemon
Slivered toasted almonds

Dissolve soup in ¼-cup milk in top of double boiler. Soften cheese with rest of milk. Add cheese to soup. Stir in lemon juice and chives. Heat thoroughly. (May thin sauce with extra milk if necessary.) Pour over cooked broccoli spears. Top with almonds.

MRS. WALTER SCOTT III

CABBAGE SURPRISE

1 head cabbage, quartered   6-8 slices bacon

Cook cut cabbage in salted water (about 1 cup) for 5 minutes. Fry bacon, saving the drippings. Drain cabbage and stir in the bacon drippings just before serving. Crumble bacon on top of cabbage. Serves 6.

MRS. R. E. MASON

CARROT BALLS

2 cups cooked carrots, sieved
1½ cups fresh, fine bread crumbs
1 cup sharp cheddar cheese, grated

1 egg white
Salt and pepper to taste
Dash of Tabasco
Corn flake crumbs

Combine carrots, bread crumbs, and cheese. Fold in stiffly beaten egg white and seasonings to taste. Form into 12 balls, roll in finely crushed corn flake crumbs. Place on greased baking sheet. Bake at 375° for 30 minutes or until brown. Serves 4 to 6.

MRS. WALTER SUMMERVILLE, JR.

CARROT CASSEROLE

3 cups canned sliced carrots
4 slices bacon, crumbled
1 tablespoon minced onion
½ teaspoon salt

¼ teaspoon pepper
3 tablespoons brown sugar
3 tablespoons melted butter

Drain carrots. Combine all ingredients except sugar and butter. Grease casserole. Sprinkle sugar and butter on top and cover to cook. Bake in 375° oven for 25 minutes. Serves 6.

MRS. JOHN PURDIE

CARROT SOUFFLE

1½ cups soft bread crumbs
1 cup milk
3 egg yolks
2 cups raw grated carrots
½ cup celery, chopped fine
1 tablespoon grated onion
3 tablespoons parsley

1 teaspoon monosodium glutamate
½ teaspoon white pepper
1 teaspoon salt
⅛ teaspoon paprika
3 egg whites
¼ teaspoon cream of tartar

Soak bread crumbs in milk until thoroughly moistened. Add slightly beaten egg yolks. To mixture, add remaining ingredients except egg whites and tartar. Beat egg whites with cream of tartar until stiff. Fold into mixture. Pour into a greased baking dish. Bake at 325° for 45 to 50 minutes. Serves 4.

MRS. BRUCE RINEHART

135

GLAZED CARROTS

1½ cups water, boiling
1 teaspoon salt
1 pound carrots, cut in 2-inch sticks

5 tablespoons white sugar
5 tablespoons brown sugar
5 tablespoons butter

To boiling salted water, add the carrots. Cover and cook 10 to 15 minutes. Drain off liquid. Add sugars and butter. Reduce heat and cook 20 to 30 minutes, stirring occasionally. Serves 6.

MRS. FRANCIS M. PINCKNEY, JR.

CARROTS AND ORANGE SECTIONS

6 medium carrots, sliced
¼ cup sugar
2 tablespoons butter

3 large oranges, sections and juice
Salt to taste

Cut sections from 3 oranges and squeeze membranes for juice. Cook carrots until tender. Bring to a boil the sugar, butter, and orange juice. At serving time, add carrots (drained) and orange sections to boiled sugar mixture and season with salt. Heat just long enough to warm through. Serves 4 to 5.

MRS. JOHN A. STEWMAN III

CAULIFLOWER WITH SHRIMP SAUCE

1 medium (or 2 packages frozen) cauliflower broken into florettes
1 can frozen condensed shrimp soup

½ cup sour cream
¼ cup toasted almonds
Salt and pepper to taste

Cook cauliflower and drain. Heat soup and cream over low heat and stir constantly. Do not boil. Season and add almonds. Pour sauce over cauliflower. Garnish with parsley or chopped chives. Serves 6 to 8.

MRS. A. S. BUMGARDNER, JR.*

COMPANY CAULIFLOWER

2 packages frozen cauliflower
2 eggs, separated
2 tablespoons cream
½ teaspoon salt
½ teaspoon sugar

½ teaspoon Accent
Paprika
2½ tablespoons lemon juice
¼ cup butter

Cook cauliflower according to directions on package. Meanwhile, separate eggs, putting yolks in top of double boiler and whites in bowl of electric mixer. In top of double boiler, beat yolks and cream until thickened. Add salt, sugar, Accent and paprika. Place over hot water. With a wire whisk, gradually beat in lemon juice. Cook, beating constantly, until thick. Remove double boiler from heat, leaving over hot water. Add butter, one half at a time, beating until each addition is melted. Remove from hot water. Beat egg whites until soft peaks form. Fold in lemon-egg yolk mixture. Pour sauce over cooked and drained cauliflower. Serves 6.

MRS. HENRY W. RIGBY

CORN PUDDING I

6 ears of fresh corn, or 4 cups frozen uncooked corn
½ cup butter
¼ cup sugar
1 tablespoon flour
½ cup cream or evaporated milk
2 eggs, well beaten
1½ teaspoons baking powder
Salt to taste
Dash of cinnamon

Scrape uncooked corn from the cob. Heat butter until melted. Stir in sugar, flour and remove from the heat. Gradually stir in cream. Add well-beaten eggs and baking powder and salt. Mix well. Fold in corn, stir until well mixed. Grease a 2-quart casserole. Pour in corn mixture. Bake 45 minutes at 350°. Sprinkle with cinnamon. Serves 6.

MRS. MARK P. JOHNSON

CORN PUDDING II

6 eggs, well beaten
1 cup milk
1 stick butter
Salt and pepper
2 packages frozen cream style corn
1 package frozen cut corn

Three or four hours ahead, take corn out to thaw. Beat eggs, add milk, melted butter, salt and pepper and then the corn. Mix well and put in long pyrex casserole. Cook at 325° 1 hour or more. Serves 8-10.

MRS. PERRIN Q. HENDERSON

FRESH CORN PUDDING

6 eggs
1 cup sugar
2 cups milk
1 teaspoon vanilla
Nutmeg
Salt
2 sticks butter
12 ears of corn

Beat eggs. Add sugar and milk, stirring well. Season with vanilla, nutmeg, and salt. Melt butter and stir into egg mixture. Cut corn (uncooked) from cob, scraping the ears. Fold corn into egg mixture. Bake in 1 large or 2 medium casseroles in a slow (300°) oven for 45 minutes. The secret is in the slow cooking. Serves 12.

MRS. PHILIP SMALL

CORA'S SOUTHERN SKILLET CORN

8 ears corn
1-1½ cups water
2 tablespoons flour
1 tablespoon butter
1 teaspoon salt
1 teaspoon sugar
½ teaspoon pepper
1 tablespoon bacon grease

Shuck and wash corn ears. Scrape corn ears into a large bowl. Rescrape each ear to release corn "milk". Add water, flour, butter, salt, sugar and pepper. Heat bacon grease in a large skillet. Pour in corn, stirring until well mixed and corn begins to boil. Turn down heat to simmer and cook, covered, until corn is tender—30 to 45 minutes. Should be stirred occasionally. Serves 4.

MRS. WALTER SCOTT III

CORN SOUFFLE

2 tablespoons butter or margarine
2 tablespoons flour
1 cup milk
1 #303 can (2 cups) whole kernel
   corn

1 teaspoon salt
¼ teaspoon pepper
2 slices pimiento
2 eggs
½ cup grated cheese

Melt the butter or margarine in a saucepan and smooth in the flour. Pour in milk gradually and cook over a low heat, stirring constantly, until sauce thickens and bubbles. Add grated cheese and mix well with sauce. Remove from heat, add drained corn, salt, pepper and finely chopped pimiento. Separate eggs, beat yolks slightly and stir into the corn mixture. Beat egg whites until stiff and fold into souffle. Spoon or pour into a greased 1½ quart casserole dish, or 6-custard cups. Place dish in small amount of hot water. Bake at 325°. Bake casserole 45 minutes. Bake custard cups 25-30 minutes. Serves 6.

MRS. TERRY YOUNG

CREOLE CORN CASSEROLE

3 tablespoons bacon drippings
⅓ cup flour
1 package frozen white corn,
   thawed
1 1-pound can tomatoes, drained

1 rib of celery, finely chopped
1 large onion, finely chopped
¼ pound cheese, grated
Salt and pepper

Heat bacon drippings. Add flour and stir until flour is browned. Add corn, tomatoes, celery and onion. Mix well and remove from heat. Make layers in a 2-quart casserole dish, alternating vegetables and grated cheese. Bake one-half hour (or until thoroughly heated) in a 350° oven. This can be prepared ahead of time. Serves 8.

MRS. JOHN HILLHOUSE

GREEN CORN CAKES

1 cup grated corn (4 ears)
1 tablespoon flour
1 tablespoon milk
2 tablespoons melted butter

½ teaspoon salt
Pepper
2 eggs, beaten separately

Grate corn off cob and scrape ears. Mix corn, flour, milk, butter, salt and pepper and egg yolks. Fold in egg whites just before cooking. Fry on a greased griddle, dropping by tablespoonsful. Makes about 15 cakes.

MRS. WALTER SCOTT, JR.

GASTON'S GUMBO

12 ears corn
2 pounds okra
3 large and 1 regular cans
   tomatoes

¼ cup bacon grease or butter
Salt and pepper to taste

Cut corn off the cob. Cut okra in wheels. Melt grease in large pot. Pour in tomatoes, corn and okra. Slowly cook over low heat until done, stirring often as it sticks easily. This freezes well. Makes 8 pint size containers. One pint serves four people.

MRS. WALTER SCOTT III

NOTRE DAME SUCCOTASH

2 tablespoons butter
2 tablespoons flour
1½ cups milk
1 teaspoon salt
1 cup grated cheddar cheese
1 package Fordhook Lima beans (frozen)

1 package cut corn (frozen)
½ cup sliced green onion tops
¼ cup chopped pimento
Buttered bread crumbs

Make a cream sauce by melting butter in a saucepan, adding flour and mixing well. Slowly stir in milk. Cook over medium heat, stirring constantly, until thickened. Add cheese and salt, stir until cheese is melted. Cook the frozen vegetables until tender. Drain off the liquid. Add onions and pimento to cheese sauce. Pour sauce over succotash in a greased casserole. Top with buttered bread crumbs. Bake at 350° for 30 to 40 minutes. Serves 6-8.

MRS. JOHN R. CAMPBELL

CUCUMBERS AND SOUR CREAM

3 or 4 medium cucumbers
1 cup of celery, cut up
1½ cups water
1 teaspoon salt

Taste of dill seed
2 tablespoons vinegar
1 pint sour cream

Score with fork and slice cucumbers. Simmer together with all ingredients except sour cream for about 5 minutes. Drain and mix with sour cream. Serve hot or cold. Serves 6.

MRS. R. E. MASON

EGGPLANT CASSEROLE

1 large eggplant (peeled, cooked, drained and seasoned)
½ can mushroom soup
½ cup mayonnaise
1 egg, beaten

1 onion, chopped fine
¾ cup cracker crumbs
⅓ stick butter
½ cup grated cheese

Cook and mash eggplant. Mix with soup (undiluted), beaten egg, onion, salt and mayonnaise. Pour in buttered casserole, cover with crumbs, dot with butter and cheese. Bake at 350° 15-20 minutes. Serves 4.

MRS. JOHN A. BRABSON

EGGPLANT SOUFFLE

1 large eggplant
½ stick butter
Salt and pepper to taste
2 eggs, beaten

¾ cup milk
8-10 saltines, crumbled
¼ cup onion, chopped
1 cup grated cheese

Peel and boil eggplant until done. Mash with potato masher. Stir in butter while hot. Season with salt and pepper. Stir in eggs, milk, saltines and onion. Put into casserole and top with cheese. Bake at 350° for 40 minutes. Serves 6-8.

MRS. RALPH H. ALEXANDER, JR.

EGGPLANT PROVENCALE

2 eggplants
Ice water
¼ cup olive oil
6 ripe tomatoes, peeled, seeded
and chopped
1 teaspoon salt
1 teaspoon freshly ground
pepper

Oregano
3 cloves garlic, chopped
Buttered crumbs
Chopped parsley (or use dried if
fresh is unavailable.)

Cut the eggplants into 1-inch slices. Soak for a few minutes in ice water. Drain dry and brown quickly in the olive oil. Transfer the slices to a baking dish. Add more butter or oil to the pan and cook the chopped tomatoes. Season with salt and pepper and oregano. Add it to the baking dish with the chopped garlic. Top with buttered crumbs and chopped parsley. Bake at 350° for 35-40 minutes. Can be prepared in advance. Serves 6.

MRS. R. STUART DICKSON, JR.

FRIED EGGPLANT

1 small eggplant
⅓ cup flour
1 egg, beaten

⅓ cup milk
Salt and pepper
⅓ cup breadcrumbs

Peel, slice and soak eggplant in a large bowl of salt water for 3 or 4 hours. Drain on paper towels. Dip each piece in flour, then in the egg and ⅓ cup milk, which has been thoroughly beaten together. Dip into breadcrumbs. Fry in hot oil. Drain. Serve hot. Serves 2.

MRS. HENRY W. RIGBY

SCALLOPED EGGPLANT

1 medium eggplant
1 small onion, chopped
1 tablespoon butter
½ cup bread crumbs

3 tablespoons melted butter
½ cup milk
Grated cheese

Peel, dice eggplant. Cook in boiling, salted water until tender. Drain. Beat with fork until mashed and fluffy. Sauté onion in 1 tablespoon butter. Stir breadcrumbs into 3 tablespoons melted butter. Put layer of eggplant mixed with onion in baking dish, then layer of buttered crumbs. Pour ½-cup milk over this. Sprinkle with grated cheese. Bake at 375° for one-half hour. Serves 4.

MRS. ROBERT P. BAYNARD

LIMA BEANS WITH SOUR CREAM

1 pound dried baby limas
1 onion, chopped
½ cup butter, melted
2 teaspoons dry mustard

1½ teaspoons salt
1 tablespoon molasses
2 cups sour cream

Soak limas overnight. Boil with chopped onion in water until tender (for one hour). Drain well. Add butter, mustard, salt, molasses and sour cream to beans, stirring until well mixed. Rub casserole well with garlic. Bake at 350° for 1½ hours. Serves 3 or 4.

MRS. G. RANDOLPH BABCOCK

MUSHROOM SOUFFLE

½ pound canned mushrooms,
  drained
5 tablespoons butter
Shallots, minced (optional)
1 teaspoon salt

Dash of cayenne
2 tablespoons flour
1 cup milk
4 egg yolks
5 egg whites

Chop mushrooms fine. Sauté mushrooms in butter. If desired, add small amount of shallots. Do not overcook. Season with salt and cayenne. Sprinkle flour over mushrooms and stir. Slowly add milk and simmer until thick. Separate eggs, lightly beating yolks. Beat egg whites until stiff. After cooling mushrooms, stir in egg yolks and egg whites. Grease a 1-quart souffle dish. Pour in mushroom-egg mixture. Bake at 375° for 30 minutes. Serve with Hollandaise Sauce. Serves 4-6.

MRS. RUFUS SAFFORD

GLAZED ONIONS

1 small jar currant jelly
1 teaspoon vinegar or lemon
  juice
2 tablespoons chicken fat or 2
  chicken bouillon cubes

1 cup water
2 jars small onions, drained
Red food coloring (optional)

Heat together the jelly, vinegar, chicken fat and water. Add onions and baste until well glazed. Good as a garnish for beef or chicken or to serve as a vegetable. Serves 4 to 6.

MRS. JOHN A. BRABSON

HONEYED ONIONS

8 medium size onions
3 tablespoons butter, melted
4 tablespoons tomato juice

3 tablespoons strained honey
1 teaspoon salt
¼ teaspoon paprika

Pare onions and cut in half. Place onions in buttered casserole. Mix remaining ingredients and pour over the onions. Bake 1 hour and 15 minutes in 350° oven. Serves 4.

MRS. WM. D. THOMAS

ONIONS SUPREME

4 cups onions, sliced
½ cup butter
1 can undiluted onion soup
½ cup mushrooms, sliced

⅓ cup blanched almonds
1 cup bread crumbs
Melted butter

Sauté onions in ½-cup butter. Combine onions, soup, mushrooms and almonds in 1½-quart oblong dish and lightly mix. Top with crumbs and dribble melted butter around. Bake at 350° for 30 minutes. Serves 6.

MRS. JOHN R. CAMPBELL

YUMMY BAKED ONIONS

4 large onions
½ teaspoon butter per onion slice
½ teaspoon brown sugar per onion slice

½ teaspoon chicken stock base per onion slice
¼ teaspoon hickory smoked salt per onion slice

Peel onions and slice one-half inch thick, placing slices in large shallow pan. Dot each slice with butter. Sprinkle each with brown sugar, chicken stock base, and hickory-smoked salt. Bake uncovered in 350° oven until tender (approximately one hour). (This may also be done on a grill by leaving onions whole and wrapping each in foil.) Serves 2 to 3.

MRS. NOEL LEE DUNN

CREAMED PEA CASSEROLE

1 stick butter
1 medium onion, chopped fine
1 can cream of chicken soup
1 cup or more sharp cheese, grated
4 hard cooked eggs, finely chopped

⅓ cup chopped almonds
1 4-ounce can sliced mushrooms, drained
2 cups green peas, drained
Potato chips

Melt butter in skillet; add onion and sauté. Stir in soup, cheese, eggs, almonds and mushrooms, mixing well. Add peas and pour into a well-buttered 2 quart casserole. Bake at 300° for 20-30 minutes. Cover with crushed potato chips the last 5 minutes. Serves 8-10.

MRS. JOHN L. McCANN, JR.

GREEN PEA CASSEROLE

1 package frozen peas
1 stick butter
2 medium onions, chopped
1 stalk celery, chopped
1 can water chestnuts, sliced
1 4-ounce can mushrooms

½ tablespoon flour
Salt and pepper and Accent
Pepperidge Farm Stuffing or Bread crumbs
1 teaspoon soy sauce

Cook peas and drain. Sauté onions and celery in ¾ stick butter until soft. Add mushroom juice thickened with flour, peas, mushrooms, water chestnuts and seasoning. Put in baking dish, cover with stuffing, dot with butter. Bake at 350° until thoroughly heated. Serves 4 to 5.

MRS. ROBERT CHERRY

PETIT POIS

1 1-pound 1-ounce can Le Sueur
   Peas
1 leaf of lettuce
¼ teaspoon salt

¼ teaspoon sugar
1 tablespoon butter
Dash of pepper

Drain liquid from peas into a saucepan. Add remaining ingredients and simmer for ten minutes. Then add the peas and continue cooking until thoroughly heated. This takes the canned taste from the peas. It is the French way to fix peas. Lettuce may or may not be removed, according to one's preference. Serves 4.

MRS. WALTER SCOTT III

SPINACH AU GRATIN

2 packages frozen chopped
   spinach
½ stick butter or margarine
2 tablespoons flour
1 cup of milk or cream
Salt

Pepper
Accent
Cayenne pepper
1 cup sharp cheese, grated
2 hard-boiled eggs
3 slices bacon, fried

Cook the spinach and drain well. Melt butter, blend in flour and add milk until smooth. Add the seasonings and stir well. Mix this with spinach. Then stir in the grated cheese. Finely chop hard-boiled egg, crumble the bacon, and mix the two well. Grease a 2-quart casserole. Pour in spinach and top with bacon-egg mix. Bake at 350° for 25-30 minutes. Serves 6. (May be prepared and frozen.)

MRS. JAMES CRAIG

SPINACH CASSEROLE

1 package frozen chopped spinach
1 egg
1 cup grated sharp cheese
1 can cream of chicken soup

3 tablespoons melted butter
Dash of garlic salt
Dash of red pepper
2 slices bread, cubed

Cook spinach, using ½-cup water and 1 teaspoon sugar. Drain thoroughly, mashing out all liquid. Combine spinach, soup, egg, and cheese. Pour into greased 1½-quart casserole. Toss the bread cubes in the butter, to which the garlic and red pepper have been added. Place on top of the spinach and bake 1 hour at 350°. Serves 4.

MRS. MOFFATT G. SHERARD

CLEO'S SPINACH CASSEROLE

1 package chopped spinach
2 tablespoons grated onion
2 tablespoons butter
½ teaspoon salt

2 tablespoons flour
1 cup milk
½ cup cheddar cheese, grated
2 eggs, separated

Cook spinach until tender. Drain. Mash it in mixing bowl or blender after spinach is cool and onion has been added. Make cheese cream sauce. When cool, beat in egg yolk. Add cream sauce to spinach. Whip egg whites. Fold spinach and sauce into egg whites. Blend by hand, folding in. Add pinch of pepper. Cook in greased casserole dish at 325° for 30-40 minutes. Serves 4.

MRS. HENRY W. RIGBY

SPINACH RING

2 packages frozen chopped
  spinach
2 eggs, separated
1 can mushroom soup
½-¾ cup homemade breadcrumbs
Salt and pepper to taste

1 cup sharp cheese, grated
Juice of 1 large onion
Worcestershire sauce
Juice of 1½ lemons
1 scant teaspoon baking powder

Cook spinach, according to directions; drain well. Separate eggs. Beat yolks and add mushroom soup, bread crumbs, salt and pepper, mixing well. Grate the onion, then press it into a strainer, collecting the juice. Stir into the soup mixture the onion juice, cheese, Worcestershire sauce and lemon juice. Then fold spinach into this mixture. Beat egg whites, adding baking powder. Fold them into spinach. Pour into a buttered ring mold. Place mold in pan to which it is added water. Bake in 350° oven for 45 minutes. Check water to be sure there is always some in the pan. Serve with small whole beets or finely chopped hard-boiled egg in center of ring. Serves 8.

MRS. JOHN A. BRABSON

SPINACH SOUFFLE

3 tablespoons butter
3 tablespoons flour
1 cup milk
½ teaspoon salt
4 egg yolks

5 egg whites
1½ cups spinach, cooked and well
  drained
Sauteed mushrooms

Grease and lightly flour a 2-quart casserole. Make a cream sauce of butter, flour, and milk. Add salt. Cool for half a minute, then stir in well-beaten egg yolks. Add the cooked, drained spinach. Fold in egg whites that have been beaten until stiff but not dry. (Add immediately after beating.) Put in casserole and bake at 375° for 35 to 50 minutes, or until top is lightly browned. Watch closely after 35 minutes. Serve with sautéed mushrooms. Serves 6.

MR. O. D. BAXTER, JR.

SPINACH SOUFFLE MADELEINE

2 packages frozen chopped
  spinach
4 tablespoons butter
2 tablespoons flour
2 tablespoons chopped onion
½ cup evaporated milk
½ cup vegetable liquid
½ teaspoon black pepper
¾ teaspoon celery salt
¾ teaspoon garlic salt
½ teaspoon salt
6-ounce roll of Jalapenos cheese
1 teaspoon Worcestershire
Red pepper to taste

Cook spinach according to directions on package. Drain and reserve liquid. Melt butter in saucepan over low heat. Add flour, stirring until blended and smooth, but not brown. Add onion and cook until soft, but not brown. Add liquid slowly, stirring constantly to avoid lumps. Cook until smooth and thick, continue stirring. Add seasonings and cheese which has been cut into small pieces. Stir until melted. Combine with cooked spinach. This may be served immediately or put into a casserole and topped with buttered bread crumbs. The flavor is improved if the latter is done and kept in the firgerator overnight. This may also be frozen. Serves 6.

MRS. WILLIAM A. NICHOLS*

SPINACH AND SOUR CREAM CASSEROLE

3 packages frozen chopped
  spinach, cooked and drained
½ package dry onion soup mix
1 pint sour cream
⅓ cup buttered bread crumbs

Combine the spinach and onion soup mix and let stand for 2-3 hours. Add the sour cream and buttered bread crumbs. Pour into casserole and bake for 30 minutes at 350°. Serves 6-8.

MRS. THORNWELL G. GUTHERY

CLEO'S SQUASH CASSEROLE

6 squash, diced
1 large onion
1 teaspoon pepper
2 teaspoons salt
3 cups water
3 tablespoons butter
2 tablespoons flour
1¼ cups milk
½ teaspoon salt
⅓ cup grated sharp cheddar
  cheese
2 eggs
12 Ritz crackers, crumbled

Wash and cut squash. Put in saucepan. Peel and chop onion; add to squash along with pepper, salt and water. Cook until done. Make a cream sauce of butter, flour, milk and salt. Add cheese, stirring until melted. Butter a 2-quart casserole. Drain squash in colander, then mash squash through colander into a bowl placed under colander. Mix cream sauce with squash. Break eggs over squash and mix well into squash. Pour into casserole. Top with cracker crumbs. Bake at 350° for 30 minutes. Serves 6 to 8.

MRS. BONN A. GILBERT

AUNT FANNY'S BAKED SQUASH

2 pounds yellow squash
2 cups chopped onion
Butter
½ cup milk

Salt and pepper
¼ cup butter
2 large eggs
½ cup bread crumbs

Wash and cut squash. Cook with onion in butter until tender. Season with salt and pepper. Stir in milk, measured butter, eggs and bread-crumbs. Pour into a buttered casserole and bake at 350° until brown (30 minutes or longer). Serves 5 to 6.

MRS. STEPHEN K. URNER, JR.

BATTLETOWN INN YELLOW SQUASH

7 small yellow squash
1 small diced onion
½ cup cream

¼ cup saltine cracker crumbs
2 tablespoons butter

Boil squash in salt water until tender. Drain and mash. Sauté onion in butter. Add cream and cracker crumbs. Mix with squash. Pour into 1½-quart buttered casserole dish. Top with additional crumbs and dot with butter. Bake at 350° for 30 minutes. Serves 4.

MRS. JOHN R. CAMPBELL

BAKED STUFFED SQUASH I

6 medium (yellow) squash
2 medium onions
4 tablespoons butter

1 cup bread crumbs
½ teaspoon salt
Dash of pepper

Boil squash and onions (whole) in salted water until tender. Scoop out middle of each squash. Mash up with chopped onions, add butter, salt and pepper, and part of bread crumbs (save some for topping). Stuff squash shells. Put remaining bread crumbs on top. Bake until brown. Serves 6.

MRS. WALTER SCOTT, JR.

BAKED STUFFED SQUASH II

6 small yellow crookneck squash
4 tablespoons butter
½ cup fine breadcrumbs
2 tablespoons minced onion
  (dehydrated, in jar)
½ teaspoon salt
1 tablespoon minced parsley
  (fresh is best)

⅛ teaspoon black pepper
Generous pinch sage
Dash of thyme
1 bouillon cube
1 cup boiling water

Drop whole squash in boiling salted water for 10 minutes, or until tender but not soft. Remove from heat. Cool and drain. Slice a portion from top and scoop out pulp. Melt butter, and add remaining ingredients (except bouillon cube and water) to butter. Mix with mashed squash.

Pack mixture into squash. Dissolve bouillon cube in 1 cup boiling water. Place squash in baking dish and pour bouillon around them. Bake at 350° for 20-25 minutes. Serves 6.

MRS. JOHN L. DABBS, III

SQUASH CASSEROLE AU GRATIN

2½ pounds yellow squash
2 pounds zucchini, peeled
1 large onion, finely chopped
2 tablespoons sugar
1 teaspoon salt
2 cups water
1 cup American cheese, grated
1 cup Cheddar cheese, grated
2 tablespoons margarine
Salt to taste
¼ cup cream

Cube yellow squash and peeled zucchini. Put in large saucepan. Add onion, sugar, salt and water. Simmer until squash is tender (about 12 minutes). Drain and mash. (Can be mashed in blender.) In buttered 2-quart casserole alternate layers of squash, cheese and extra salt. Top with butter. Pour cream over casserole. Bake at 325° for 20 minutes until bubbly hot. Serves about 10.

MRS. WM. D. THOMAS

SQUASH SOUFFLE

8 small squash, cut up
1 medium size onion, cut up
2 eggs, separated
1 can mushroom soup

Cook squash and onion together in boiling salted water until done. Drain well and season. Beat egg yolks and egg whites separately. Combine squash, yolks and mushroom soup. Fold in egg whites. Grease a 1¾-quart casserole and pour in squash. Place casserole in pan of water in 350° oven and cook 1 hour or until done in center. Serves 6.

MRS. R. E. MASON

TOMATOES PROVENCALE

4 to 5 tomatoes, halved
2 slices white bread, crumbled
½ teaspoon onion salt
½ teaspoon garlic salt
½ teaspoon seasoned salt
½ stick butter, melted

Arrange tomato halves in shallow baking dish. Mix bread crumbs with seasoning, then stir in melted butter. Mound crumbs on top of tomatoes. Add a little water to bottom of pan. Bake at 350° for 30 minutes until well browned. Serves about 8.

MRS. WALTER SCOTT, III

SAUTEED COCKTAIL TOMATOES

15 cocktail tomatoes
2 tablespoons butter, melted
2 teaspoons sweet basil
2 teaspoons chopped parsley
Salt to taste
Cracked pepper to taste

Place tomatoes in frying pan with melted butter. Sauté over low heat until tender (about 4 minutes). Add seasonings and sauté 4 minutes longer. Serves 3 to 4.

MRS. NOEL LEE DUNN

SQUASH AND TOMATO CASSEROLE

8 to 10 squash (small to medium)
2 eggs, beaten
1 medium onion, chopped fine
½ stick butter, melted

Fresh tomatoes, sliced thin
Sharp cheese, grated
Paprika

Slice squash and cook in salted water until tender. Drain in colander. Beat eggs together with finely chopped onion; add squash and butter. Cover bottom of casserole with squash mixture. Slice fresh tomatoes thinly on top of squash; sprinkle with grated sharp cheese. Repeat layers, ending with cheese on top. Sprinkle with paprika and bake for 20 to 30 minutes at 350°. Serves 8.

MRS. JOHN DABBS, III

SCALLOPED TOMATOES

1 cup celery
½ cup minced onion
2 tablespoons butter
1 tablespoon flour
1 #2½ can tomatoes (3½ cups)

2 cups ½-inch toast cubes
1 tablespoon sugar
1 teaspoon salt
Dash of pepper
2 teaspoons prepared mustard

Cook celery and onion in butter until tender but not brown. Push onion and celery to one side and blend in flour. In 1½-quart casserole, combine onion-celery mixture with tomatoes, half the toast cubes, sugar and seasonings. Bake in moderate oven (350°) for about 30 minutes. Top with remaining cubes and bake 10 more minutes. Serves 6.

MRS. VERNER STANLEY

TOMATOES WITH ANCHOVIES

8 medium-size tomatoes
Salt
1 teaspoon sugar
4 tablespoons butter
1¼ cups cooked rice
1 2-ounce can anchovy fillets,
    finely chopped, or 6
    teaspoons anchovy paste

2 cloves, garlic, finely minced
2 tablespoons chopped basil
4 tablespoons chopped parsley
Freshly ground black pepper
¼ cup olive oil
2 tablespoons grated Parmesan
    cheese

Preheat oven to 350°. Cut tops off the tomatoes and scoop out centers, leaving a reasonably thick shell. Chop the scooped-out pulp. Sprinkle the inside of each tomato with salt and a little sugar. Add half a tablespoon of butter to each tomato. Mix the rice with approximately half of the chopped tomato, then blend in the anchovies, garlic, basil, parsley, pepper and oil. Stuff tomatoes with mixture. Sprinkle the stuffed tomatoes with cheese and bake in a greased dish about 15 minutes. Serves 8.

MRS. ALEX McMILLAN, III

ZUCCHINI CASSEROLE

2 pounds zucchini
1 onion, sliced
1 medium green pepper, chopped

1 clove garlic
1 can Spanish style tomato sauce
½ cup grated cheddar cheese

Sauté onion, green pepper and garlic in olive oil until tender. Cook zucchini until tender and mash. Add cheese, onion, pepper, garlic, and tomato sauce. Bake in 400° oven until hot—add more grated cheese on top and let it brown. Serves 4.

MRS. DESMOND SAVER

BAKED VEGETABLES

4 medium potatoes
5 large carrots
1 large onion

⅓ cup oleomargarine
Salt and pepper to taste

Peel and slice thin potatoes, carrots and onions. Use any proportions of vegetables and seasonings you desire. Generously butter 1½-quart casserole or 8-inch square pan. Place layers of uncooked vegetables alternately, buttering and seasoning liberally after each layer. Repeat this process until dish is full. This tends to shrink, so piling them in a deeper dish is best. Cover tightly and seal with aluminum foil. This is the secret. Bake at 350° for 2 hours. Uncover only when ready to serve with steak, chicken or roast. Serves 6-7.

MRS. JAMES J. ELLIOTT

SPECIAL TIPS

Add honey (instead of sugar) and sweet basil leaves to stewed tomatoes. Add a touch of marjoram when cooking carrots.

MRS. JOHN STEWMAN III

Starchy Vegetables

MACARONI AND CHEESE DELUXE

1 7-ounce package elbow
  macaroni
2 cups small-curd cream-style
  cottage cheese
1 cup dairy sour cream
1 egg, slightly beaten

¾ teaspoon salt
Dash of pepper
2 cups sharp American cheese,
  shredded
Paprika

Cook and drain macaroni. Combine macaroni, cottage cheese, sour cream, egg, seasonings, and American cheese. Turn into a greased 9x9x2 baking dish. Sprinkle with paprika. Bake at 350° for 45 minutes. Serves 8.

MRS. JOHN C. MARKEY

CRISPY MACARONI AND CHEESE

1 can cream of celery soup
½ cup milk
½ teaspoon prepared mustard
  generous dash pepper

3 cups cooked macaroni
2 cups shredded cheddar cheese
1 cup French fried onions

In 1½ quart casserole, blend soup, milk, mustard, pepper until smooth. Stir in macaroni, 1½ cups cheese. Bake at 350° for 20 minutes. Top with French fried onions and remaining cheese. Bake ten minutes more. Serves 4. Excellent substitute for rice or potatoes.

MRS. JAMES H. GLENN, JR.

COUNTRY NOODLES

½ pound sliced bacon
1 package (1-pound) vermicelli
  noodles (fine)
3 cups cottage cheese
3 cups sour cream
2 cloves garlic, crushed
2 onions, minced
2 tablespoons Worcestershire
  sauce

Dash of Tabasco
4 teaspoons salt
3 tablespoons prepared
  horseradish
1 cup grated Parmesan cheese
Extra sour cream, if desired

Fry bacon until crisp, drain on paper towels, and crumble. Cook noodles "al dente". Drain well. Mix all ingredients except Parmesan cheese in a large bowl. Add noodles and bacon and toss with two forks until well mixed. Turn into deep 3½-quart buttered casserole, cover, and bake at 350° for 30-40 minutes, or until heated through. Remove cover, sprinkle with half the Parmesan cheese, broil until golden. Serve with extra cheese and sour cream. Serves 12. Delicious with steak or roast.

MRS. VERNER STANLEY

BAKED POTATO MOLD WITH GREEN PEAS AND ONIONS

1 potato for each serving
Hot milk
Butter

Salt and pepper
Green peas
Very small onions

Boil potatoes until tender. Rice the potatoes, then mash until creamy with hot milk, butter, salt and pepper. Do not add too much milk as it will make the potatoes soupy. Butter the bottom and sides of a round casserole. Mold the potatoes around the inside of the dish, packing with your hands and hollowing out the center. Spread butter on top and bake in a 400° oven until golden brown. Fill center with hot buttered peas and onions. Potato mold may be prepared ahead of time.

MRS. AMOS BUMGARDNER, JR.

ROQUEFORT BAKED POTATOES

6 baking potatoes
½ cup Roquefort cheese, crumbled

1 cup sour cream
1 tablespoon chopped parsley

Select uniform sized potatoes. Scrub well and rub with shortening before baking. Bake at 400° 1 hour or until tender. Combine remaining ingredients and blend until smooth. Remove potatoes from oven and cut lengthwise and crosswise slits in top of each potato. Press potato to spread opening. Fill with dressing. Place under broiler until dressing melts and potatoes are hot. Be sure to watch it carefully. Serves 6.

MRS. WILLIAM A. WHITE, JR.

TASTY STUFFED POTATOES

6 baking potatoes
4 strips of bacon
5 tablespoons bacon drippings
2 tablespoons salad oil
4 tablespoons vinegar
1½ teaspoons salt

Pepper to taste
1 teaspoon sugar
2 tablespoons grated onion
3 tablespoons minced green pepper
3 tablespoons pimento, chopped fine

Bake potatoes. Fry bacon. Cut thin slice from top of baked potato while potato is still warm. Scoop out inside. Combine all ingredients, except bacon, mixing well. Blend potatoes well with this mixture. Stuff back into potato shells. Just before serving heat in broiler for 6-8 minutes or until heated through and slightly browned. Top with crumbled bacon. Serves 6.

MRS. TERRY YOUNG

PARTY POTATOES

8-10 medium size potatoes
1 8-ounce package Philadelphia
   cream cheese
1 carton sour cream

4 tablespoons butter
1/3 cup chopped chives
Paprika, salt, and pepper to taste

Boil peeled potatoes until tender. Beat sour cream and cheese together, add hot potatoes and beat until smooth. Add butter, chives and salt and pepper to taste. Pour into a well-greased 2-quart casserole, dot with butter and sprinkle paprika on top. Bake at 350° for 25 minutes. Serves 8-10. Wonderful do-ahead dish for company. Men love it.

MRS. BEN ASHCRAFT

AU GRATIN POTATOES

6 large Idaho potatoes
1 stick of butter
3 tablespoons flour
1 teaspoon salt
1/4 teaspoon black pepper

Dash of paprika
Dash of nutmeg
2 cups milk
Sharp cheese, grated

Peel and dice raw potatoes and cook in boiling, salted water about 15 minutes. When crispy and tender, drain in colander. Blend butter and flour over low heat until bubbly. Add seasonings. Add 2 cups of milk, 1/3-cup at a time, stirring constantly. It will be a thin sauce. Add cheese. Place potatoes in shallow, oblong casserole dish. Pour sauce over potatoes (should be runny). Top with a lot of grated cheddar cheese. Bake about 30 minutes at 350° until cheese is bubbly and mixture hot. Delicious with steak, roast beef and fried chicken. Serves 8.

MRS. J. R. ADAMS

CANDIED SWEET POTATOES

4 large or 5 small sweet potatoes
1 cup white sugar
1/2 stick butter

1/2 cup water
Cinnamon

Peel, slice and layer raw potatoes in 1¾ or 2-quart casserole. Sprinkle sugar over top, dot with butter, and sprinkle with cinnamon. Add water around edges of casserole so as not to wash off sugar. Cook, uncovered, at 400° for about an hour. (Can be cooked day before and marshmallows added when heated.) Pile potatoes in, because they really shrink, or else cut down on sugar and water. Serves 6.

MRS. W. WELLS VAN PELT

CANDIED SWEET POTATOES AND APPLES

4 medium sweet potatoes
3 apples
1/2 cup butter
1/2 cup sugar

1/2 cup brown sugar
1/4 cup water
1/2 teaspoon salt

Boil potatoes until slightly tender, but not well done. Peel and slice apples. Arrange layers of potatoes and apples in well-greased 2-quart casserole. Melt butter, add sugar, water and salt. Pour over potatoes and apples. Cover and bake for 1 hour in 350° oven. Serves 6.

MRS. WILLIAM A. WHITE, JR.

FRIED SWEET POTATOES

Peel raw, sweet potatoes and cut in slices. Place them in hot fat and, when slightly brown, turn. Keep skillet covered, as the steam cooks the potato slices tender. When lightly brown and apparently tender, sprinkle with sugar and add about 2 tablespoons of hot water. Put on lid and allow to cook about 2 minutes longer.

OLD NORTH STATE

ORANGE SWEET POTATOES

6 medium sized sweet potatoes
1 cup orange juice
2 teaspoons grated orange rind
1 tablespoon cornstarch

3 tablespoons melted butter
⅓ cup brown sugar (firmly packed)
⅓ cup granulated sugar

Cook potatoes in jackets. Peel and cut in half. Meanwhile, combine remaining ingredients in a saucepan and cook. Stir until thickened. Arrange potatoes in baking dish, pour sauce over them. Cover and bake in moderate oven (350°) for 20 minutes. Uncover and bake 15 minutes longer. Can be prepared ahead. Serves 6.

MRS. WALLACE B. BRADFORD

SPICY SWEET POTATOES

½ stick butter
5 to 6 good size sweet potatoes, cooked
½ cup orange juice
1½ teaspoons orange flavoring

⅓ cup firmly packed brown sugar
1 teaspoon nutmeg
3 teaspoons cinnamon

Mix cooked potatoes with electric mixer until smooth and all lumps gone. Add remaining ingredients after you have mixed for about 5 minutes. Heat in 350° oven until hot, about 20 minutes. Serves 6 to 8.

MRS. CAMERON FAISON

BAKED RICE

1 cup rice
2 tablespoons butter
2 cups hot water
1 teaspoon salt

1 package Old Fashion French Dressing Mix
2 3-ounce cans sliced mushrooms with liquid
Tomato wedges

Lightly brown rice in butter. Add the water, salt, dressing mix and mushrooms. Remove from heat and pour into 1½-quart casserole. Cover tightly and bake at 350° for 30 minutes. Cover with tomato wedges (leave skin on), recover casserole and bake 10 minutes longer. Serves 6-8.

MRS. JULIAN W. CLARKSON

BAKED STEAMED RICE

1 stick margarine
1 medium onion, chopped
2 cans beef consomme, undiluted
1 cup uncooked rice
1 can chopped mushrooms

Sauté chopped onion in margarine until tender. Combine other ingredients and pour into casserole. Cover and bake at 350° for 1 hour (in 1½-quart dish). Serves 5-6.

MRS. I. NATHANIEL HOWARD

DIVINE RICE

1 medium onion, sliced thin
½ cup almonds
½ cup raisins
1 teaspoon salt
1 cup long-grain rice
½ stick butter or margarine

Sauté onions and almonds in butter, add raisins and salt. Cook rice and have it steaming hot. Mix with onions, mixture just before serving. This really is divine, especially with Cornish hen or broiled chicken. Serves 4.

MRS. JULIAN W. CLARKSON

EMERALD RICE

4 cups cooked rice
4 eggs, separated
1 cup minced raw spinach
   (fresh)
½ cup minced green pepper
¼ cup minced onion
1 cup heavy cream, whipped
½ cup grated Parmesan cheese
1 teaspoon paprika
1 teaspoon salt
1 cup sour cream
3 tablespoons minced chives

Beat egg yolks. Add the rice, spinach, pepper, onion, whipped cream, cheese, paprika and salt. Stir. Fold in the stiffly beaten egg whites. Pour into a greased ring mold, set in a pan of water, and bake at 350° for about 45 minutes (until knife inserted comes out clean). Serve with sour cream and chives. Serves 6.

MRS. VERNER STANLEY

GREEN RICE CASSEROLE

1 cup uncooked rice
2 well-beaten eggs
¾ cup milk
¼ cup shortening
¼ cup grated sharp cheese
1 small onion
1 cup finely chopped parsley
1 teaspoon Worcestershire
1½ teaspoons salt

Cook rice. Stir in the remaining ingredients. Pour in greased casserole. Bake 45 minutes at 350°. This dish can be made in advance, and is also an excellent accompaniment for seafood. Serves 5-6.

MRS. HUGH M. TILLETT*

QUICK RICE CASSEROLE

1 to 1⅓ cups Minute Rice, uncooked
1 10-ounce can beef consomme
⅓ stick butter
1 teaspoon onion salt
1 teaspoon garlic salt

Grease well a 1-quart casserole. Pour in rice; sprinkle with seasoned salts. Dot with butter. Pour consomme over this. Cover tightly with foil and bake at 350° to 375° (depending on what else may be in oven) for 30 minutes, until rice has absorbed all liquid. Remove foil and fluff with fork. Serves 4.

MRS. WALTER SCOTT, III

RED RICE

1 small onion, chopped
Bacon grease or oil
1 #303 (medium) can tomatoes
1¼ cups rice
1 teaspoon salt
Dash of pepper
1 teaspoon or more of sugar

Sauté onion in about 1 tablespoon grease, in top of double boiler. When yellow, add tomatoes, salt, pepper, and sugar (taste). Bring to boil, add rice and cover. Lower heat and allow to boil over direct heat about 10 minutes. Start water boiling in bottom of double boiler and put pan in it. Keep top on pan and cook for one hour. If rice is not done, add a teaspoon of water.

Can be varied by adding mushrooms, ripe olives, or sliced stuffed olives, parsley or anchovies. Add these after liquid is absorbed, and add anchovies *just* before serving.

MRS. W. WELLS VAN PELT

SPANISH RICE PRONTO

¼ cup fat
1 medium onion, sliced thin
½ medium green pepper, diced
2 cups Minute Rice
1¾ cups hot water
2 8-oz. cans Hunt's Tomato Sauce
1 teaspoon prepared mustard
1 teaspoon salt
Dash of pepper

Melt fat in skillet. Add onion, green pepper, and rice. Stir over high heat until lightly browned. Add water, tomato sauce and seasonings. Mix well. Bring quickly to boil. Cover tightly and simmer about 10 minutes. Serves 8.

MRS. WM. D. THOMAS

WILD RICE IN ORANGE SHELLS

3 cups cooked wild rice (wild rice and white rice combination can be used)
6 large oranges
½ cup pecans, chopped

Prepare 3 cups of wild rice, cooked. Slice top off oranges and remove insides. (Use this for ambrosia.) Fill oranges with hot rice. Sprinkle pecans on top. Great with wild fowl or duck, especially if it has an orange sauce. Serves 6.

MRS. BRUCE RINEHART

HAWAIIAN FRIED RICE

1 cup rice, uncooked
2 tablespoons vegetable oil
1 large onion, chopped fine
1 teaspoon dried marjoram
1 teaspoon dried rosemary

½ teaspoon dried summer savory
Diced chicken (optional)
2 cups chicken broth
2 ounces soy sauce

Fry raw rice in oil with onion until chalk white, not brown. Stir in herbs (and chicken). Cover with liquid. Bring to a boil and cover. Reduce heat, simmering for 20 minutes. Caution: Do not remove lid while rice is simmering. Serves 5-6.

MRS. JOHN A. STEWMAN

WILD RICE CASSEROLE

1 cup uncooked wild rice or
"Chilton House" wild rice
blend (8 oz.)
1 teaspoon salt
3 cups boiling water
2 tablespoons butter
4 tablespoons minced onion
2 tablespoons green pepper,
chopped
1 4-ounce can sliced mushrooms,
drained

1 10-ounce can cream of
mushroom soup, undiluted
¾ cup half and half cream
¼ teaspoon dried marjoram
⅛ teaspoon dried basil
⅛ teaspoon dried tarragon
½ teaspoon curry powder
½ teaspoon salt
¼ teaspoon pepper

Garnish: 6 or 8 whole, medium size, fresh mushrooms that have been greased with butter make a lovely garnish. Place these on the casserole the last 8 minutes of cooking time. *Not before.*

Wash the rice in three or four changes of cold water. Then, to the boiling water in a saucepan, add 1 teaspoon salt and stir in rice. Cook covered at a simmering stage about 30 minutes, or until all water is absorbed.

While rice is cooking, prepare the following: In another saucepan melt 2 tablespoons butter and sauté the onion, green pepper, and drained canned mushrooms for about 5 minutes. Then stir in the cream of mushroom, cream, marjoram, basil, tarragon, curry, salt and pepper. Heat the combined mixture *slowly* for about 10 minutes. When wild rice is ready, rinse it in a colander and then add the rice to the cream sauce mixture. Pour into a greased 2 qt. casserole, add the fresh mushrooms for garnish, and heat 8-10 minutes in pre-heated 350° oven. (Better made the day before so herbs can blend better.) Serves 8. When adding meat to casserole, allow 1 cup meat for each cup of cooked rice. This will increase the number of people that may be served.

MRS. AMOS BUMGARDNER, JR.

CHEESE GRITS

4 cups boiling water
1 teaspoon salt
1 cup quick-cooking grits
1 stick butter or margarine

1 roll garlic cheese
2 eggs, lightly beaten
Milk

Bring water and salt to boil, slowly stir in grits. Cook for 3 minutes, stirring constantly. Remove from heat. Stir in margarine and garlic cheese. Place eggs in a measuring cup and fill with milk to make one cup. Add to grits mixture. Pour into greased casserole dish. Bake at 300° for one hour. Serves 6.

MRS. BONN A. GILBERT

SPOON BREAD

1 cup corn meal
1 pint milk
1 teaspoon sugar

½ teaspoon salt
4 eggs, separated
½ stick butter

Mix meal, milk, sugar, salt in top of double boiler. Cook until thick. Melt butter in 2 qt. baking dish. Pour excess in thickened mixture. Add unbeaten egg yolks. Fold stiffly beaten whites into above and cook slowly for one hour in 300° oven. Serve immediately. Serves 6.

MRS. JAMES CARSON

BETH'S SPOON BREAD

1 cup corn meal
2 cups salted (½ teaspoon) boiling water

2 tablespoons butter
4 beaten eggs
1 cup milk

Stir corn meal into boiling water for 1 minute. Remove from heat, add butter. and beat well. Add beaten eggs; beat well. Beat in milk. Mix well and pour into hot buttered baking dish. Bake in uncovered 3-quart Pyrex dish in preheated 400° oven for 40 minutes. Serves 6.

MRS. ERVIN JACKSON, JR.

GRANNY SHEPHERD'S SPOON BREAD

1 cup sifted cornmeal
3 cups sweet milk
3 eggs, beaten separately
1½ teaspoons salt (or more to taste)

2 tablespoons butter
1 teaspoon baking powder
1 teaspoon sugar

Scald milk, add meal, cook until "mush" thickens. (This batter should not be thick, add more milk to thin if necessary.) Remove from heat. Add salt, baking powder, butter and blend. Add sugar, egg yolks, and blend. Fold in egg whites. Bake in greased 2-quart casserole (heavy) in 350° oven for 45-60 minutes, until nicely browned. Serve with butter. Serves 8.

MRS. DONALD MCMILLAN

Fruit

HOT APPLE SAUCE

1 medium can apple sauce
2 tablespoons lemon juice
½ cup brown sugar

Lemon slices, sliced very thin
Cinnamon

Grease baking dish with butter. Mix brown sugar, lemon juice and apple sauce to taste. Place in baking dish, cover top with lemon slices, and sprinkle generously with cinnamon. Bake in a slow 275° oven for 1½ hours (or as long as possible). Serve with the meal or as a dessert. Serves 4.

RED CINNAMON APPLES

1 cup water
1 cup sugar
⅓ cup red heart cinnamon
candies

6 apples, peeled and cored
Dash of salt

Cook water, sugar and cinnamon candies about 10 minutes. Peel and core apples and slice in medium sized pieces. Place in syrup, add a dash of salt, and simmer very slowly for about 15 minutes, or until apples are tender. Cool apples in syrup. When partially cool, put apples in dish and cook syrup down, pouring glaze over apples several times. (If glaze is already thick enough, it isn't necessary to recook it.) Serve warm or cold. Serves 4 to 6.

MRS. BRUCE H. RINEHART

SOUTHERN FRIED APPLES

⅓ cup sugar
1 teaspoon ground nutmeg
½ teaspoon ground cinnamon

⅛ teaspoon salt
4 large cooking apples
5 tablespoons butter

Mix together sugar, spices and salt. Wash, core and slice apples in half-inch thick rings. Heat butter in a heavy skillet. Add apple rings and half of sugar mixture. Cook for about 3 minutes. Turn over, sprinkle with rest of sugar and continue cooking until apples are almost transparent. Serve hot. Serves 4-6.

SWEET COOKED APPLES

8 medium apples
½ cup red currant jelly
¼ cup water

1 tablespoon lemon juice
⅛ teaspoon nutmeg
Drop of red food coloring

Peel, core, and slice apples in eighths. Place in 8-inch or 9-inch baking dish. Heat jelly and water slowly until jelly is partially melted. Remove from heat. Add lemon juice and nutmeg and red coloring. Pour over apples, completely covering apples with liquid. Cover with foil and bake at 350° for 45 minutes or until tender. Baste liquid over apples once or twice while cooking. Serves 6.

MRS. CHARLES WARNER

CURRIED FRUIT

1 #2 can pineapple slices
1 #303 can peach halves
1 #303 can pear halves
1 #303 can apricot halves
Small bottle maraschino cherries

⅓ cup butter
¾ cup light brown sugar, firmly packed
3 teaspoons curry powder

Drain fruit and dry on paper towels. Melt butter, add sugar and curry. Arrange fruit attractively in large shallow pyrex dish. Pour curry mixture over it and bake uncovered at 325° (or less) for 1 to 1½ hours. Serves 8-10.

MRS. THOMAS W. DAVIS

HOT FRUIT DISH

1 1-pound can sliced or chunk pineapple, drained
1 1-pound can pears, drained
1 1-pound can peaches, drained
1 1-pound can apricots, drained
1 1-pound jar spiced apple rings, drained

1 can seedless grapes, drained
1 stick margarine
½ cup sugar
2 tablespoons flour
1 cup sherry

Melt margarine in saucepan. Add sugar, flour and sherry. Stir constantly over very low heat until thick (about 5 minutes). Arrange drained fruit in a 2-quart casserole. Pour sauce over fruit. Heat in 350° oven for 30 minutes. Serve at once. This can be fixed the day before serving and be refrigerated, then reheated just before serving. Serves 10-12. Good with ham or chicken.

MRS. EDWIN R. RENCHER, JR.
MRS. ALSTON RAMSAY

GRAPEFRUIT SUPREME

3 large grapefruits
1 pint strawberries

¼ cup orange juice
½ cup sugar

Cut grapefruit in halves; section them and remove seeds. Set aside. Mix washed, capped strawberries with sugar and orange juice. Heat for a few minutes, stirring constantly. Chill in the refrigerator and serve cold over grapefruit. Serves 6.

MRS. ERWIN JONES

MINTED CANTALOUPE BALLS

½ cup mint jelly
⅔ cup water

⅓ cup sugar
Cantaloupe balls

Melt jelly over low heat. Beat until smooth. Combine water and sugar and boil about 5 minutes. Add to jelly. Chill. Scoop out cantaloupe with melon ball cutter. Arrange 5 to 6 balls in cocktail glass. Pour chilled syrup over fruit.

MRS. TERRY YOUNG

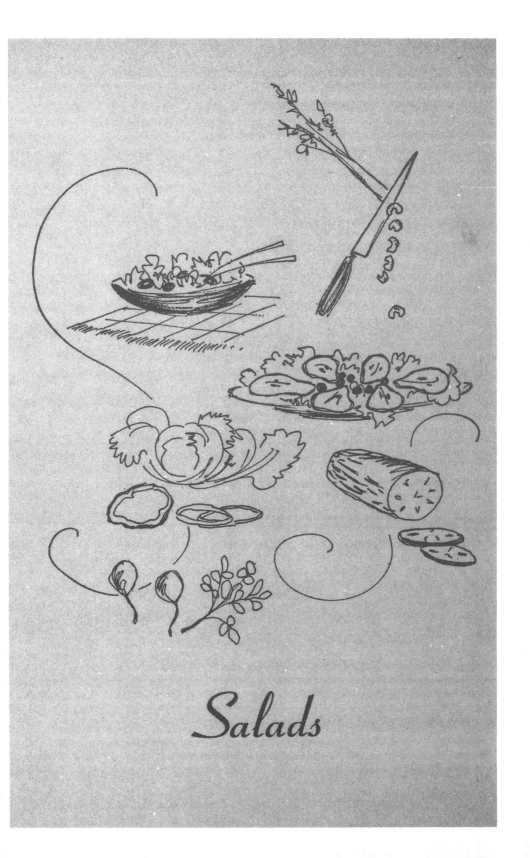

Salads

Fruit Salads

APRICOT SALAD

1 small package lemon or apricot Jello
1½ cups mashed cooked apricots, or 1 large can peeled apricots, drained
2 tablespoons lemon juice
⅓ cup orange juice
1 cup sliced blanched almonds (optional)
1 3-ounce package cream cheese
½ cup Ginger Ale

Cook package of apricots according to directions on package, drain and puree, or puree canned apricots. Dissolve Jello in hot puree. Add juices and nuts. Put small ball of cream cheese in center of molds. Pour in Jello mixture. Refrigerate. Serve with mayonnaise. Serves 6 to 8.

AVOCADO RING

1 small package lemon gelatin
1 cup boiling water
1 cup mayonnaise
3 tablespoons lemon juice
1 teaspoon salt
1 cup mashed avocado
1 cup whipped cream

Dissolve Jello in boiling water and chill until partially set. Add lemon juice and salt to mayonnaise and whip gelatin mixture. Fold in avocado and whipped cream. Put in mold. Serves 6-8. OLD NORTH STATE

BANANA-STRAWBERRY SALAD

6-ounce package strawberry Jello
Liquid from fruit combined with enough water to make 2 cups liquid
2 10-ounce packages frozen strawberries
1 12-ounce can crushed pineapple
2 large ripe bananas, chopped
1 cup sour cream

Mix Jello with 2 cups boiling liquid. Add strawberries, stir until strawberries are thawed. Add pineapple and bananas. Pour half into large pyrex dish. Chill until firm. Spread sour cream over this and add remainder of Jello mixture. Chill again. Serves 10-12.

MRS. ROBERT FREEMAN

COLA SALAD

1½ cups cola
1 small package lemon Jello
1 cup chopped nuts
1 small can crushed pineapple

Heat ¾ cup of cola. Pour lemon Jello in it and heat until dissolved. Do not boil. Cool. Add remaining cola, drained crushed pineapple, and nuts. Chill until firm. Serve on lettuce. Serves 6.

MRS. WILLIAM A. WHITE, JR.

BING CHERRY SALAD

1 tablespoon gelatin
½ cup cold water
1 cup hot cherry juice (or juice and water combined)
⅓ cup sugar
½ teaspoon salt

¼ cup lemon juice
1 medium can Bing cherries
1 small can crushed pineapple
2 small packages cream cheese
½ cup crushed pecans

Soak gelatin in cold water, dissolve in hot juice. Add sugar, salt, and lemon juice. Stir. Add cherries, pineapple. Make cream cheese balls by softening cream cheese with small amount of milk. Add nuts. Put cheese balls in center of mold. Pour gelatin mixture around carefully. Refrigerate. Serves 6 to 8.

OLD NORTH STATE

CONFETTI CHEESE SALAD MOLD

1 3-ounce package lemon Jello
1 cup hot water
½ teaspoon salt
1 5-ounce jar pimento cheese spread
½ cup mayonnaise
¾ cup cold water

1 tablespoon vinegar
Dash of Tabasco
½ cup celery, chopped fine
2 tablespoons chopped green pepper
¼ cup pecans, chopped

Dissolve Jello in hot water. Add salt, pimento cheese, mayonnaise, water, vinegar and Tabasco to Jello and beat until smooth. Chill until partially set. Fold in remaining ingredients, stirring in well, and pour in 1 or 1½-quart mold. Serves 6-8.

MRS. ROBERT FREEMAN

CONGEALED CRANBERRY SALAD

1 pint cranberries, ground
1 cup hot water
1 cup sugar
1 cup nuts, chopped

Juice of 2 oranges
Grated rind of 1 orange
2 packages cherry gelatin
1 diced apple

Mix all ingredients except gelatin and apple. Bring to a boil. Add gelatin and stir until dissolved. Add apple. Pour into mold and refrigerate. Serves 10.

CRANBERRY SALAD RING

1 envelope gelatin
¼ cup cold water
1 can whole cranberry sauce

2 tablespoons lemon juice
¼ cup chopped nuts
8 marshmallows

Place gelatin in cold water and dissolve. Let stand 2 minutes. Place cup in pan of boiling water until gelatin dissolves. Stir into cranberry sauce. Add lemon juice and nuts. Chill until mixture begins to jell. Fold in marshmallows cut in small pieces. Put in ring mold or individual molds. Makes 4 molds.

MRS. WILLIAM D. THOMAS

CRANBERRY-MARMALADE SALAD

1 can whole cranberry sauce
½ cup water
¼ cup orange marmalade
1 teaspoon grated lemon rind
1 tablespoon gelatin

2 tablespoons cold water
1 cup seedless grapes
½ cup diced celery
½ cup chopped nuts

Heat cranberry sauce and water to boiling. Add marmalade and lemon rind. Soften gelatin in cold water and dissolve in hot cranberry mixture. Chill until slightly thickened. Pour a thin layer of gelatin mixture in bottom of ring mold and arrange grapes in circle to form topping. Chill. Fold celery and nuts into remaining mixture and add to ring mold. Chill until firm. Unmold and fill center with lettuce or small dish of mayonnaise. Surround ring with cream cheese balls rolled in chopped parsley or nuts. Especially good for the Christmas season. Serves 6.

MRS. TERRY YOUNG

QUICK MOLDED CRANBERRY SALAD

1 can (9-ounce) crushed pineapple
Water
1 envelope unflavored gelatin

1 can (1 pound) whole cranberry sauce
1 tablespoon lemon juice

Drain pineapple and add enough water to liquid to make one cup. Sprinkle gelatin on liquid in saucepan to soften. Place over slow heat, stirring constantly until gelatin dissolves. Break up whole cranberry sauce. Stir in pineapple and lemon juice. Stir in gelatin mixture. Turn into molds and chill. Unmold on salad greens and serve with dressing. Fills 6 to 8 molds, depending on size.

MRS. R. E. JONES, JR.

FLORIDA GARDEN SALAD

1 cup hot tea
1 package orange Jello, dissolved in hot tea
1 cup crushed, drained pineapple
1 can mandarin oranges, drained

1 cup drained juices added to tea and Jello
1 cup water chestnuts, ground or chopped

Add pineapple and oranges and chestnuts to tea-Jello mixture. Pour in mold and refrigerate until firm. Top with whipped dressing. Serves 6.

WHIPPED CREAM DRESSING

¼ cup cream, whipped
½ cup mayonnaise

Dash of mace
Grated rind of 2 oranges

Fold mayonnaise into whipped cream. Mix in seasoning.

MRS. THOMAS CUMMINGS

FROSTED FRUIT SALAD

1 package lemon Jello	Juice of 1 lemon (or
1 package orange Jello	2 tablespoons)
2 cups hot water	2 bananas, diced
1½ cups cold water	2 cups bite size marshmallows
	1 #2 can crushed pineapple, drained

Dissolve orange and lemon jello in 2 cups hot water. Add 1½ cups cold water and lemon juice. Chill. When partially thickened, add remaining ingredients. Congeal in 9 by 13-inch pan. When ready to serve, top with the following:

TOPPING

2 tablespoons flour	1 egg, slightly beaten
½ cup sugar	2 tablespoons butter
Juice from crushed, drained	1 cup cream, whipped
pineapple	½ cup grated sharp cheese

In heavy pan, mix flour and sugar. Add pineapple juice and egg. Cook until thick and add butter. Cool and fold in whipped cream (may use Dream Whip). Spread on salad and sprinkle with cheese. Serves 10-12.

MRS. GEORGE CROUCH, JR.

FULTON SALAD

3 egg yolks, well beaten	1 small can crushed pineapple
2 tablespoons sugar	1 cup chopped pecans
3 tablespoons vinegar	1 cup small marshmallows
½ cup cold water	1 cup cream, whipped
1 tablespoon gelatin, dissolved in ½-cup cold water	

Mix first four ingredients and cook in double boiler until thickened. Add gelatin and beat until cool. Add remainder of ingredients and pour into mold. Serves 6.

MRS. JOHN L. HILLHOUSE, JR.

GINGERALE SALAD

1 package orange Jello	1 can white Royal cherries, seeded
1 package lemon Jello	
Grated rind and juice from one	½ cup chopped pecans
orange and one lemon	2 cups chilled gingerale
1 small can crushed pineapple	

Dissolve gelatin in juices from orange and lemon and from the canned fruit, which have been heated to boiling. Add grated rinds. Add chilled gingerale. Place in refrigerator until it begins to thicken. Add cherries, crushed pineapple and nuts. Pour into mold or individual molds. Serves 8 to 12. Makes 12 individual molds or 1 large ring mold.

DRESSING
Mix sour cream and mayonnaise. Add a little grated orange rind.

MRS. ARTHUR CULBERTSON*

LIME AND LEMON JELLO SALAD

2 packages lime Jello
2 packages lemon Jello
1 large can crushed pineapple,
  not drained

½ pint whipping cream
1 package cream cheese
5 cups water

Dissolve lime Jello in 2½ cups hot water. When cool, pour in crushed pineapple and juice. Congeal. Dissolve lemon Jello in 2½ cups hot water. Let get real cold. Whip cream and mix with softened cream cheese. Add to lemon Jello, and pour on top of lime Jello which has already congealed firmly. Serves 20.

MRS. WALLACE B. BRADFORD

HEAVENLY ORANGE FLUFF

2 small packages orange Jello
2 cups hot water
1 6-ounce can frozen orange juice,
  undiluted

2 cans mandarin oranges, drained
1 medium can crushed pineapple,
  not drained

Dissolve Jello in boiling water. Add orange juice, stirring until melted. Cool. Add oranges and pineapple. Congeal in 13 by 9-inch pan or molds. Before serving, mix topping and add on top of Jello.

TOPPING
1 package instant lemon pudding
1 cup milk

½ pint whipping cream or
  Smooth Whip
6 maraschino cherries

Beat pudding and milk until slightly firm, about 4 minutes. Whip cream. Fold into pudding mixture. Spread on Jello. Top with maraschino cherries cut in half and drained well. Serves 12.

MRS. TERRY YOUNG

MOLDED FRUIT SALAD

1 large grapefruit, cut in sections
  or 1 can grapefruit and orange
  sections mixed
1 small can crushed pineapple

1 small package lemon Jello
1 small package orange Jello
⅓ cup lemon juice
⅓ cup orange juice

Use all juice from drained fruit, lemon and orange juice. Add enough water to make 3 cups liquid. Dissolve Jello in a portion of the hot liquid. Add fruit to all the liquid and pour into molds. Congeal. Serve with Sweet Salad Dressing. Serves 12.

SWEET SALAD DRESSING
½ cup Hellman's mayonnaise
2 tablespoons cream
2 teaspoons lemon juice

¼ teaspoon poppy seeds
½ teaspoon sugar
Few grains salt

Mix all together. Keeps well in refrigerator. Stir before serving.

MRS. MCALISTER CARSON

ORANGE, PINEAPPLE AND CARROT SALAD

1 package orange gelatin
1½ cups boiling water
1 cup finely grated raw carrots
(can be grated in blender)

1 small can crushed pineapple,
not drained
1 tablespoon vinegar

Dissolve gelatin in boiling water. Add remaining ingredients. Chill. Serves 4 to 6. "Little people seem to like it."

MRS. LEE A. FOLGER III

ORANGE SHERBET SALAD

2 small or 1 large package orange Jello
1 cup boiling water
1 pint orange sherbet
1 large can (2½ cups) crushed pineapple, drained

2 small cans (11 ounces) mandarin orange sections, drained
1 cup sour cream
1 cup miniature marshmallows

Dissolve gelatin in boiling water. Add orange sherbet. Stir until mixed and partially set. Add sour cream and other ingredients. Pour in 12 lightly oiled molds and refrigerate. Serves 12.

MRS. BEN TROTTER, JR.

PEACH AND GINGER SALAD

1 1-pound can cling peach slices
1 3-ounce package cream cheese
1 3-ounce package peach-flavored gelatin

1 cup hot water
1½ tablespoons lemon juice
3 tablespoons chopped crystallized ginger

Drain peaches, reserving syrup. Allow cream cheese to stand at room temperature until soft. Dissolve gelatin in hot water, add cream cheese in chunks. Beat with rotary beater until smooth. Combine peach syrup and lemon juice and add water to make 1 cup. Stir into gelatin mixture. Chill in refrigerator until partially set. Fold in peaches and ginger. May be put into 4-cup mold or individual molds. Chill until firm. Unmold and serve on lettuce. Top with mayonnaise. Serves 8.

MRS. JAMES CRAIG

SPICED PEACH JELLO

2 large jars spiced peaches
1 cup pineapple chunks, no juice or 1 cup white grapes in season
½ to 1 cup pecans, chopped

2 cups peach juice
2 packages lemon Jello
1 cup orange juice
1 cup water or ginger ale

Drain peaches, saving 2 cups juice. Cut pineapple chunks in half pieces. Heat juice and dissolve Jello. Add orange juice and water and cool. Add fruit and nuts. Congeal in 12 molds or 12 by 7-inch pan. Serves 12.

MRS. TERRY YOUNG

RED RASPBERRY RING

1 10-ounce package frozen
   raspberries, thawed
2 3-ounce packages raspberry
   gelatin
2 cups boiling water

1 pint vanilla ice cream
16-ounce can frozen lemonade
   concentrate, thawed
¼ cup chopped pecans

Drain raspberries, reserving syrup. Dissolve gelatin in boiling water. Add ice cream by spoonfuls, stirring until melted. Stir in lemonade and reserved syrup. Chill until partially set. Add raspberries and pecans. Turn into a 6-cup ring mold and chill until firm. Serves 10.

MRS. SAMUEL R. SLOAN

RASPBERRY AND CHERRY JELLO SALAD

1 10-ounce package frozen
   raspberries, thawed
½ cup currant jelly
2 cups water
2 3-ounce packages red raspberry
   gelatin

½ cup sherry
¼ cup lemon juice
1 1-pound can pitted dark sweet
   cherries, drained

Drain raspberries, reserving the syrup. Combine jelly and ½-cup water. Heat and stir until jelly melts. Add remaining 1½ cups water and gelatin. Heat and stir until gelatin dissolves. Remove from heat, add sherry, lemon juice, and the reserved raspberry syrup. Chill until partially set. If desired, reserve a few raspberries for garnishing mayonnaise. Add cherries and raspberries, pour in a 6-cup mold, chill until firm (6 hours). Serve with mayonnaise or salad dressing. Serves 10.

MRS. LOUIS ROSE*

STRAWBERRY NUT SALAD

2 3-ounce packages strawberry
   Jello
1 cup boiling water
2 10-ounce packages frozen sliced
   strawberries, thawed

1 1-pound 4-ounce can crushed
   pineapple, drained
1 cup pecans, chopped
1 pint sour cream
Lettuce

In large bowl combine Jello, boiling water, and stir until dissolved. Fold in strawberries and their juice, drained pineapple, and nuts. Turn half of strawberry mixture into 12x8x2 pyrex dish and refrigerate until firm. Spread top with sour cream. Gently spread on remainder of strawberry mixture. Refrigerate again. When firm, cut in squares and serve on lettuce. Serves 10-12.

MRS. NATHANIEL HOWARD

WINE SALAD

2 3-ounce packages raspberry
  Jello
2 cups boiling water
1 cup port wine

1 #2 can crushed pineapple
  (do not drain)
1 can cranberry sauce
½ cup nuts, chopped

Dissolve Jello in boiling water. Cool slightly. Add remaining ingredients and mix thoroughly or put in blender to dissolve cranberry sauce. Place in 12 slightly oiled molds and chill until firm. Serves 12. Excellent with turkey or chicken.

MRS. BRUCE H. RINEHART

YUM YUM SALAD

2 cups crushed pineapple and
  juice
2 tablespoons gelatin
½ cup cold water
Juice of 1 lemon

1 cup sugar
1 cup water
1 cup grated sharp cheese
1 cup whipped cream

Soften gelatin in ½-cup water. Bring to a boil lemon juice, sugar and 1 cup water. Pour in gelatin and let dissolve. When cool and beginning to thicken, add pineapple, cheese and whipped cream. Pour in large mold or 8 small ones.

DRESSING

Combine:

¼ cup celery, chopped fine
1 tablespoon chopped parsley
¼ cup green pepper, chopped fine

4 to 6 drops onion juice
1 cup mayonnaise

Make 24 hours ahead and store in refrigerator.

MRS. WILLIAM S. PIERCE

AVOCADO WITH HOT SAUCE

Half an avocado
2 tablespoons confectioners'
  sugar
2 tablespoons vinegar
2 tablespoons catsup
2 tablespoons Worcestershire
  sauce

2 tablespoons butter
Salt and pepper to taste
Dash of paprika
Lettuce leaf

Peel half an avocado and place on lettuce leaf. Chill until serving time. Fill the cavity with the hot sauce which has been mixed together and heated. Serves 1.

MRS. CARLISLE ADAMS

AVOCADO SURPRISE SALAD

2 avocados
½ package cottage cheese
1 3-ounce package cream cheese
1 teaspoon onion, grated

1 teaspoon lemon juice
½ teaspoon salt
½ teaspoon celery salt
½ teaspoon Worcestershire

Peel avocados, halve lengthwise, and hollow out the stem ends slightly. Sprinkle inside and out with lemon juice and salt. Combine remaining ingredients and blend thoroughly. Fill halves with cheese mixture and press halves together. Wrap and chill in the refrigerator. Cut into thick crosswise slices and lay on lettuce-garnished salad plate. Allow 1 oval to each serving. Top with mayonnaise and the following dressing. Any left-over filling makes a good dip. Serves 8.

MAYONNAISE DRESSING

1 cup sour cream
½ tablespoon onion
Dash of cayenne pepper

1 tablespoon Worcestershire
1 tablespoon lemon juice
Salt to taste

Blend, and serve as topping on avocado salad. Dressing good on other salads, too.

MRS. HUGH TILLETT

CAVIAR-AVOCADO SALAD

2 avocados
2 3-ounce packages cream
   cheese
Cream to soften cream cheese

½ cup mayonnaise (or more)
Lemon juice to taste
Salt and white pepper to taste
1 small jar caviar

Soften cream cheese and mash with small amount of cream and seasonings. Add mayonnaise and lemon juice until mixture is consistency of heavy mayonnaise. Add caviar and mix well. Fill cavities of peeled avocado halves with mixture. Serve, very cold, on lettuce. Serves 4.

COCONUT FRUIT BOWL

1 #2 can chunk pineapple, drained
1 11-ounce can mandarin oranges, drained
1 cup white seedless grapes (canned or fresh)

1 cup small marshmallows
½ can (3½-ounce size) Angel Flake Coconut
1 carton sour cream

Mix all together and chill overnight. Do not serve on lettuce. Serves 8.

MRS. BREVARD S. MYERS

QUICK AND DELICIOUS FRUIT SALAD

1 cup drained crushed pineapple
1 cup orange sections, drained
(canned or fresh)

1 cup miniature marshmallows
1 cup sour cream
½ cup coconut

Stir these ingredients together and serve on lettuce leaves. It is better to mix them together shortly before serving, but it can be done ahead of time. Serves 6 to 8.

MRS. HENRY WELFARE

GRAPEFRUIT SALAD AND DRESSING

4 or 5 sections of fresh grapefruit
per person (approximately
4 grapefruit)
1 cup small pickled onions

1 cup diced celery
1 cup olive oil
1 cup chili sauce or catsup
1 cup broken pecans

Cut all white membrance from grapefruit sections. Arrange sections on lettuce. Combine dressing ingredients, mixing well, and before serving place on grapefruit. Serves 8.

MRS. GEORGE CROUCH, JR.

GRAPEFRUIT AND AVOCADO SALAD WITH CELERY SEED DRESSING

Arrange grapefruit sections and slices of avocado alternately on crisp lettuce or watercress. Serve with Celery Seed Dressing.

CELERY SEED DRESSING
½ cup sugar
1 teaspoon mustard
1 teaspoon salt
½ tablespoon onion juice

⅓ cup vinegar
1 cup salad oil
1 tablespoon celery seed

Combine sugar, mustard, salt, onion juice and half of the vinegar. Beat well. Gradually add the oil alternately with the remaining vinegar and beat until a stable emulsion has been formed. Add the celery seed.

MRS. DENNIS MYERS

WALDORF SALAD

2 large red apples
½ cup diced celery
1 small can pineapple, drained
½ cup walnuts or pecans, chopped
½ cup seedless grapes (optional)

1 banana (optional)
¼-½ cup mayonnaise
½ cup raisins
½ cup miniature marshmallows
Dash of salt

Wash and peel and core apples, cutting into medium sized pieces. (Leave peel on if desired for color.) Cut pineapple into small pieces and cut grapes in half. Slice banana into small pieces. Add all ingredients together, using amount of mayonnaise desired. Serve on crisp lettuce. Serves 6.

MRS. CHARLES WARNER

FROZEN BANANA SALAD

1 tablespoon lemon juice
1 teaspoon salt
4 tablespoons mayonnaise
2 small packages Philadelphia
  Cream Cheese
1 large can crushed pineapple,
  drained

½ cup maraschino cherries,
  drained
½ cup nuts (pecans or English
  walnuts
1 cup whipping cream
3 bananas

Add lemon juice and salt to mayonnaise. Mix well with cream cheese. Add broken nut meats, quartered cherries, and pineapple. Stir well to blend. Add well-beaten whipped cream (fold in). Add bananas, cut in small chunks. Put in freezer tray and freeze. Serves 6 to 8.

MRS. W. KENT COMBS

FROZEN FRUIT SALAD

1 3-ounce package cream cheese
1 tablespoon cream
⅓ cup mayonnaise
1 tablespoon lemon juice
Dash of salt
1 cup canned pineapple, drained
1 cup orange sections, drained

1 cup Royal Ann cherries,
  drained or green seedless
  grapes
½ cup maraschino cherries,
  drained
1 cup whipped cream
3 tablespoons sugar
1 cup miniature marshmallows

Blend softened cream cheese, cream and mayonnaise. Add lemon juice and salt. Add fruit, which has been cut in small pieces. (Any fruit may be substituted.) Whip cream, folding in sugar. Fold whipped cream, marshmallows, and fruit mixture together. Pour into refrigerator trays or square pan and freeze until firm. Serves 8.

MRS. CHARLES WARNER

CRANBERRY SALAD

2 3-ounce packages cream cheese
2 tablespoons mayonnaise
2 tablespoons sugar
1 can whole cranberry sauce

1 9-ounce can drained crushed
  pineapple
½ cup chopped pecans
1 package Dream Whip (2 cups)

Soften cheese, add mayonnaise and sugar. Add fruit and nuts, mixing all well. Fold this into whipped cream. Freeze in 12 to 14 molds. (Very lightly oil molds so they will come out easily by going around each with a knife.) Do not thaw before serving.

MRS. J. WILLIAM LINDSAY, JR.

FROZEN CRANBERRY SALAD

1 can cranberry sauce (jellied)
3 tablespoons lemon juice
1 cup heavy cream (whipped)
1 3-ounce package cream cheese

¼ cup mayonnaise
¼ cup confectioners' sugar
1 cup chopped pecans
8 paper cups

Mix cranberry sauce and lemon juice. Fill cups nearly half full (or pour in a dish approximately 8 inches square). Mix softened cream cheese and mayonnaise with confectioners' sugar and nuts. Fold in whipped cream. Spread mixture on top of cranberry sauce. Freeze until firm. Peel cups away from salad and serve on lettuce. Let stand a few minutes before serving. Good with food and especially pretty during the Christmas season. Serves 8.

MRS. J. FRANK TIMBERLAKE, JR.

FROZEN BLUEBERRY SALAD

12 ounces cream cheese
1½ cups mayonnaise
2 teaspoons grated lemon rind
¼ cup confectioners' sugar
1 cup fruit cocktail or any fruit, drained

1 cup banana (or other canned fruit, drained)
2 cups fresh blueberries
1 pint heavy cream, whipped

Blend softened cream cheese with mayonnaise. Beat in lemon rind and sugar. Whip cream and fold into drained fruits and cream cheese mixture. Pour in refrigerator trays or square pan and freeze until firm.

MRS. BRUCE H. RINEHART

Meat Salads

CHICKEN AND PECAN SALAD

3 cups cubed chicken or turkey
1 cup diced celery
¼ cup broken pecans
½ cup mayonnaise

2 tablespoons salad oil
1 tablespoon vinegar
1 teaspoon salt

Combine first 3 ingredients. Make dressing out of remaining ingredients. Pour over chicken mixture and toss lightly. Place on lettuce leaf. Garnish with fresh peaches. Serves 4.

MRS. TORRENCE HEMBY, JR.

HAWAIIAN CHICKEN SALAD

2 quarts coarsely cut, cooked
chicken breast
2 cups celery, sliced
1 5-ounce can water chestnuts,
sliced
1 pound seedless grapes
2-3 cups toasted, slivered almonds

3 cups mayonnaise
1 tablespoon curry powder
1 tablespoon soy sauce
1 teaspoon lemon juice (optional)
pineapple chunks
paprika

Combine cubed chicken, celery, water chestnuts, grapes and most of the almonds. (Reserve a few of the almonds for later garnishing.) Mix mayonnaise with curry and soy sauce and a little lemon juice, if desired. Mix mayonnaise mixture with chicken-fruit mixture, and chill several hours or overnight. When ready to serve, garnish with paprika, reserved almonds, and drained pineapple chunks. Serves 18.

MISS FRANCES WADDILL

HOT CHICKEN SALAD

2 cups chopped cooked chicken
or turkey
2 hard boiled eggs, chopped or
sliced
1 cup chopped celery
½ cup mayonnaise

1 tablespoon lemon juice
1 can cream of mushroom soup
½ cup sliced water chestnuts
Salt and pepper to taste
Crushed potato chips

Mix all ingredients except potato chips. Put in greased 1½-quart casserole and top with potato chips. Bake at 375° for 30 minutes or until it bubbles. Serves 6.

MRS. KENT WALKER

JELLIED MAYONNAISED CHICKEN

1 hen (4 pounds) cooked and diced
1 #2 can green peas
2 cups celery, chopped fine
4 hard boiled eggs, chopped
4 tablespoons chow chow
1 cup blanched almonds, cut in
small pieces

4 tablespoons plain gelatin
dissolved in ½-cup cold water
1 cup hot chicken broth
1 pint mayonnaise

Add dissolved gelatin to hot broth. Cool, add mayonnaise. Stir in other ingredients. Mold in large flat pan. When ready to serve, cut in squares and place small piece of parsley on each square. Mayonnaise may be served with it, if desired. This will make 16 generous or 24 small servings.

OLD NORTH STATE

CORNED BEEF AND POTATO SALAD

2 teaspoons celery seed
2 teaspoons mustard seed
1 tablespoon vinegar
1 can corn beef
¼ cup dill pickles (finely
chopped)

2 cups green cabbage, shredded
¼ cup green onions, diced
3 cups diced warm potatoes
1 teaspoon sugar
½ teaspoon salt

Soak the celery seed and mustard seed in vinegar, then drizzle over potatoes. Sprinkle sugar and salt over potatoes and chill. (This part can be done the day before.) Combine the corn beef, pickles, cabbage, and onion; add to the potatoes. Last, blend this mixture with the dressing below.

DRESSING

¾ cup salad oil
3 tablespoons milk

1 tablespoon vinegar
½ teaspoon salt

MRS. C. E. WILLIAMS, JR.

ROAST BEEF OR HAM SALAD

2 cups cooked roast beef
(or ham) cubed
½ cup celery, chopped
¼ cup onion, chopped fine
½ to 1 cup Kosher dill pickles,
chopped and drained

½ cup mayonnaise
1 teaspoon prepared mustard
1 teaspoon Worcestershire
1 teaspoon salt

Mix together beef (or ham), celery, onion and pickles. Combine remaining ingredients together and mix wth beef mixture. Serve on lettuce leaf. (Tomatoes can be stuffed with this mixture.) Serves 6.

MRS. CHARLES WARNER

CRAB AND TOMATOES DELUXE

6 large tomatoes
½ cup mayonnaise
⅛ cup finely chopped shallots
or scallions
1 tablespoon chopped chives
1 teaspoon tarragon
½ tablespoon chopped parsley

1 tablespoon basil
½ tablespoon finely minced garlic
1 hard-cooked egg, finely sieved
½ pound lump crab meat
Salt and freshly ground black
pepper

Pare away core of tomatoes and scoop out pulp. Salt the inside of the tomatoes and turn them upside down to drain. Combine remaining ingredients and use to fill centers of tomatoes. Garnish with parsley sprigs. Serve cold. Serves 6.

MRS. ERWIN JONES

CRAB MEAT SALAD

1 10-ounce can tomato soup
2 tablespoons (2 envelopes)
unsweetened gelatin
1 cup (8-ounce jar) mayonnaise
3 3-ounce packages cream cheese
½ cup cold water
1 teaspoon grated onion

Worcestershire sauce to taste
(about a teaspoon)
Dash of Tabasco, if desired
1 cup chopped celery
1 small bottle stuffed olives,
sliced
1 can crab meat

Let soup come to a boil, add cheese and blend. Stir well until all cheese is melted and blended. Add to this the gelatin which has been soaked in the ½-cup of cold water for about five minutes. Stir and set aside to cool a little; then add all other ingredients and pour in mold. Serves 10 to 12.

MRS. DOUGLAS BOOTH

SALMON MOUSSE

2 envelopes gelatin
½ cup cold water
1 cup boiling water
1 tablespoon vinegar
3 tablespoons lemon juice
1 1-pound can salmon

1 cup mayonnaise
1 cup cream, whipped
½ teaspoon salt
1 tablespoon Worcestershire
1 medium onion, grated
2 cups diced celery or cucumber

Soak gelatin in cold water, then dissolve in hot water. Add vinegar and lemon juice and place in refrigerator to thicken. Whip cream. Flake salmon and combine with mayonnaise and cream. Add all ingredients. Pour into a 2 quart oiled mold. I use 5½ cup fish mold plus 4 individual molds. Chill until firm. When serving, turn out on chilled platter. Place olive slice for eye, if fish mold is used. It is best if prepared a day ahead. This is delicious served as an hors d'oeuvre with crackers. Serves 8-10.

MRS. JOHN SCOTT CRAMER

SHRIMP CHILI MOLD

1 envelope unflavored gelatin
1½ tablespoons sugar
½ teaspoon salt
Dash of pepper
1¼ cups water, divided,
   or ½ cup water and ¾ cup
   tomato juice

¼ cup lemon juice
¼ cup chili sauce
1 cup cooked or canned shrimp
2 tablespoons pickle relish

Mix gelatin, sugar, salt and pepper thoroughly in small saucepan. Add ½-cup water. Place over low heat, stirring constantly, until gelatin is dissolved. Remove from heat and stir in remaining ¾-cup water (or tomato juice), lemon juice and chili sauce. Chill to consistency of unbeaten egg white. Fold in shrimp and pickle relish. Turn into 3-cup mold and chill until firm. Unmold on serving platter and garnish with salad greens. Serves 6.

MRS. BEN TROTTER, JR.

SHRIMP SALAD

4 cups cooked shrimp
2 teaspoons lemon juice
3 cups celery, chopped fine
2 to 3 cups dill or sweet pickles,
   chopped and drained well
1 cup olives, chopped and
   drained well

6 hard boiled eggs, chopped
½ teaspoon celery salt
Salt and pepper to taste
Mayonnaise

Moisten shrimp with lemon juice. Add together all ingredients and mix well. Add enough mayonnaise for personal preference. Chill. Serves 10.

MR. TERRY YOUNG

NEW ORLEANS SHRIMP SALAD

2½ pounds clean, cooked shrimp
⅓ cup oil
3 tablespoons vinegar
1 tablespoon paprika
½ teaspoon white pepper

2 tablespoons mustard
½ cup finely chopped celery
2 tablespoons finely chopped
   onion
1 teaspoon parsley

Combine all ingredients except shrimp, mixing well. Add shrimp, blending thoroughly. Marinate all day. Serve on lettuce, or as hors d'oeuvre with toothpicks.

MRS. NORMAN S. RICHARDS

CURRIED SHRIMP AND MUSHROOM SALAD

1 6-ounce can sliced mushrooms (drained)
¾ pound cooked shrimp
¼ cup well-seasoned French dressing

1 cup toasted sliced almonds
1 cup diced celery (optional)
½ teaspoon salt
¼ teaspoon curry powder
¼ cup mayonnaise

Mix mushrooms and shrimp with French dressing. Cover and let stand in refrigerator at least two hours. Drain off excess dressing. Add almonds and celery. Blend together mayonnaise, salt and curry powder. Pour over salad and toss lightly. Serve on salad greens.

MRS. J. FRANK TIMBERLAKE, JR.

Vegetable Salads

ASPARAGUS SALAD

3 tablespoons butter
2 tablespoons flour
4 eggs
½ teaspoon salt
1 tablespoon gelatin, dissolved in ½-cup water

Juice of 1 lemon
½ pint heavy cream
1 large can asparagus
Paprika

Melt butter. Add flour and stir until smooth. Slowly add asparagus juice, lemon juice and seasoning. Cook until thick, stirring constantly. Remove from fire; add well-beaten eggs. Place in double boiler and stir until eggs are done (thick and creamy). Add dissolved gelatin. When cool, add the cream, whipped. Arrange alternate layers of asparagus and sauce in flat dish or individual molds. Chill. Serve on lettuce and top with mayonnaise. Serves 8.

MRS. MOFFATT SHERARD

179

ASPARAGUS SALAD MOLD

1 package cream cheese
1 package lemon Jello
½ pint boiling water
⅓ pint mayonnaise

1 17-ounce can green asparagus
¼ cup almonds
1 tablespoon almond extract

Drain asparagus, saving juice. Whip juice and cream cheese together. Add well-mashed asparagus and mayonnaise. In separate pan, dissolve Jello in boiling water. When cool, add to cheese mixture. Add almonds and almond extract and place in mold. Makes 1 medium-sized ring mold or 8 individual molds. Serves 8.

MRS. J. OVERTON ERWIN

CONGEALED BEET SALAD

1 cup boiling water
1 package lemon Jello
¾ cup beet juice
3 tablespoons vinegar
½ teaspoon salt

½ teaspoon grated onion
1 to 2 teaspoons horseradish
¾ cup diced celery
1 cup chopped cooked beets

Dissolve Jello in boiling water. Add beet juice, vinegar, salt, onion and horseradish. Chill until mixture thickens slightly. Fold in celery and beets and pour in 6 lightly oiled molds or a 1½-quart mold. Serves 6.

MRS. WILLIAM A. WHITE, JR.

BROCCOLI MOLD

1 envelope gelatin
¼ cup cold water
1 cup hot consomme
¼ teaspoon salt
¾ cup of mayonnaise

Juice of ½ lemon
⅛ teaspoon pepper
2 hard-cooked eggs, mashed
1 package frozen broccoli

Soak gelatin in cold water. Dissolve in hot consomme. Cook broccoli until very tender. Drain well and mash. Combine with other ingredients and pour into 1-quart mold. Refrigerate until serving time. Nice for a luncheon.

MRS. GEORGE IVEY, JR.

MOLDED CUCUMBER SALAD

2 cups boiling water
1 6-ounce package lemon or
  lime Jello
⅓ cup white wine vinegar
¼ teaspoon salt
2 medium cucumbers

½ cup celery, chopped fine
  (optional)
1 tablespoon horseradish
  (optional)
1 tablespoon grated onion

Dissolve Jello in boiling water. Stir in vinegar and salt. Chill slightly. Peel 1 cucumber and grate it fine. Do not peel other cucumber, and grate it. Drain well. Mix cucumbers with remaining ingredients. (Can beat all in blender.) Combine all with Jello mixture. Slightly oil 8 molds and fill with mixture. Chill until set. Serve with mayonnaise or green goddess dressing. Serves 8.

MRS. CHARLES WARNER

WHIPPED CUCUMBER SALAD

1 3-ounce package lime Jello
1 cup boiling water
1 cucumber
1 small onion
1 cup cottage cheese
½ cup mayonnaise
½ cup pecans, chopped (optional)
Dash of salt

Dissolve Jello in boiling water. Peel ¾ of cucumber. Add all ingredients, including cucumber, together in blender or electric mixer and beat until pulp. Add to Jello mixture and congeal. Serves 6-8.

MRS. CHARLES WARNER

QUICK TOMATO ASPIC

1 small package lemon Jello
1¾ cups V-8 juice
½ cup olives, chopped
⅓ cup celery, chopped fine
¼ cup onion, minced fine
Drop of Worcestershire
Salt to taste

Bring 1 cup V-8 juice to boil. Dissolve Jello in it. Remove from heat and add remaining ingredients. If you prefer a plain aspic, add only remaining V-8 juice, salt and Worcestershire. Place in molds. When serving, top with drop of mayonnaise.

TOMATO ASPIC

2 packages gelatin
½ cup cold water
2 cups (#2 can) tomato juice
2 tablespoons minced onion
  or 2 teaspoons dried minced
  onion
Juice of 2 lemons (5 tablespoons
  lemon juice)
2 tablespoons vinegar
1 teaspoon salt
2 tablespoons sugar
Dash of red pepper and allspice
  for taste

While gelatin is soaking in cold water, heat rest of ingredients with tomato juice. Simmer 5 minutes. Add gelatin to juice mixture and dissolve thoroughly. Pour into mold and chill. (Sliced stuffed olives or small shrimp are a nice addition.)

MRS. LEE FOLGER III

TOMATO ASPIC MOLDS

½ large can (23-ounces) tomato
  juice
1½ tablespoons Worcestershire
Dash of Tabasco
1 small onion, grated
Salt to taste
8 artichoke hearts (canned)
1½ packages gelatin
  (1½ tablespoons)
Lemon juice to taste
8 molds

Soak gelatin in ½-cup cold tomato juice. Heat remaining tomato juice to boiling. Remove from heat, add gelatin, Worcestershire, Tabasco, salt and lemon juice. Cool. Rinse molds with cold water. Put ¼-teaspoon grated onion in each and 1 artichoke heart. Pour cool aspic on top and place in refrigerator. Top with mayonnaise. Can be prepared a day ahead. Serves 8.

MRS. AMOS BUMGARDNER, JR.

ASPIC-ASPARAGUS MOLD WITH ROQUEFORT DRESSING

4 to 6 cups tomato aspic salad
3 cans asparagus, drained
¼ pint whipping cream
1 3-ounce package cream cheese

¾ cup roquefort cheese, crumbled
¼ teaspoon lemon juice
Salt to taste

Prepare favorite tomato aspic recipe yielding about 4 to 6 cups. Partially jell. Lightly oil a large ring mold or bundt pan. Line sides with cold cooked asparagus. (Use only 2 cans if you don't want asparagus almost touching.) Leave stem end on top. Pour tomato aspic carefully in mold and refrigerate until serving time.

Make dressing by combining softened cream cheese and roquefort cheese, lemon juice, salt, mixing thoroughly. Whip cream and mix all together. Unmold salad and place dressing in center. Serves about 14.

MRS. EDWARD J. WANNAMAKER

CONGEALED VEGETABLE SALAD

¼ cup water
2 envelopes plain gelatin
2 tablespoons sugar
2½ tablespoons vinegar
2 teaspoons salt
¼ teaspoon black pepper

1 cup grated cabbage
1 bunch carrots
½ cup green pepper
1 cup celery
1 small onion
¾ cup mayonnaise

Combine first six ingredients in small sauce pan. Cook the ingredients in saucepan over medium heat until gelatin dissolves and all ingredients are blended. Then fill blender half full of water. Add singly, remaining ingredients blending for 3 seconds, and drain the vegetables. Add gelatin mixture to vegetables, then add ¾-cup mayonnaise and chill until firm. Makes 8 to 10 servings.

MRS. WALTER RAY CUNNINGHAM*

PARTY VEGETABLE MOLD

2 cups English peas (save liquid)
1 cup cooked chopped carrots
1 cup chopped celery
1 teaspoon chopped green pepper
¼ cup pea liquid
4 teaspoons vinegar
1 teaspoon sugar

1 teaspoon salt
1 teaspoon mustard
1 tablespoon chopped onion
1 cup mayonnaise
1 package lemon Jello
1½ cups boiling water

Dissolve Jello in 1½ cups boiling water and cool. Add other ingredients and refrigerate. Serves 6-8.

MRS. ROBERT FREEMAN

ARAB SALAD

½ cup olive oil or salad oil
1 cup chopped onion
2 pounds fresh, or 2 packages frozen, green beans

1 cup canned tomatoes
1½ teaspoons salt
½ teaspoon pepper
½ teaspoon oregano

Heat olive oil in sauce pan. Add onions, sauté 10 minutes, but do not allow to brown. Add beans. Cover and cook over low heat for 10 minutes, stirring occasionally. Add tomatoes, salt, pepper, oregano. Cook for 20 minutes. Chill and serve with lemon wedges. Serves 6.

MRS. WALTER SUMMERVILLE, JR.

CALICO BEAN SALAD

1 1-pound can (2 cups) cut green beans, drained
1 1-pound can (2 cups) cut wax beans, drained
1 1-pound can (2 cups) kidney beans, drained
½ cup chopped green pepper
¾ cup sugar

⅔ cup vinegar
⅓ cup salad oil
1 teaspoon salt
1 teaspoon pepper
3 or 4 sliced spring onions
1 small can of sugar peas (1 cup), drained, optional

Combine all ingredients. Toss lightly. Refrigerate overnight. Drain before serving. Makes 6 to 8 servings. Good for picnics or buffets — a marvelous hot-weather dish.

MRS. SHADE I. WOOTEN
MRS. HUNDLEY R. GOVER*

MARINATED STRING BEAN SALAD

2 packages frozen French style string beans
½ cup French dressing (see recipe below)
½ to ¾ cup chopped Spanish onion

6 slices cooked bacon
4 to 6 hard cooked eggs
2 teaspoons fresh parsley, chopped
⅓ cup mayonnaise
Salt to taste

Cook and drain beans. Prepare French dressing as listed below. Mix drained beans, French dressing, and onion together and let stand 24 hours. Before serving, drain bean mixture and add the remaining ingredients. Serves 6.

FRENCH DRESSING

1 cup olive oil or salad oil
¼ cup cider vinegar
¼ cup lemon juice

1 teaspoon salt
½ teaspoon paprika
½ teaspoon dry mustard

Put all ingredients into jar with tight top. Shake very thoroughly or mix in blender.

To make a good Roquefort Dressing, put a package of roquefort cheese into blender or mixer, add just enough of this French dressing to cover and blend until smooth.

MRS. J. OVERTON ERWIN

GOURMET'S CAESAR'S SALAD

2 cups French bread croutons
or Kellogg Croutettes
Olive oil
Split clove of garlic
2 heads romaine lettuce
¼ teaspoon dry mustard
¼ teaspoon black pepper

½ teaspoon salt
½ cup Parmesan cheese
6 tablespoons olive oil
Juice of 2 lemons
4 or 5 anchovy fillets
1 egg

Brown lightly croutons in olive oil flavored with a split clove of garlic. Rub salad bowl with garlic. Tear 2 heads of romaine lettuce into medium-size pieces and put in bowl. Add dry mustard, black pepper, salt and cheese. Sprinkle with olive oil, lemon juice and anchovy fillets cut into small pieces. Break one egg in and toss lightly until all trace of egg is gone. Add croutons last, toss briefly, and serve.

MR. ROBERT FRANCIS

CABBAGE SLAW

1 large head cabbage, shredded
1 large minced onion
½ cup vinegar
1 cup Wesson Oil

1 tablespoon mustard
2 tablespoons sugar
1 teaspoon celery seed
½ teaspoon dry mustard

Mix and bring to a boil all ingredients except cabbage and onion. Pour boiling mixture over cabbage and onion. Stir well and store in air-tight container in refrigerator for 24 hours. Stays fresh for several days.

MRS. ROBERT FREEMAN

COLE SLAW I

1 large head white cabbage
1 large onion
1 large green pepper
1 cup sugar
¾ cup salad oil

1 cup vinegar
1 teaspoon dry mustard
1 teaspoon celery seed
1 tablespoon salt

Shred cabbage in large bowl. Shred (or thin slice) onion and pepper on top of cabbage. Sprinkle sugar to cover entire top. Do not stir! Bring to a boil — salad oil, vinegar and dry seasonings. Pour over other ingredients while hot. Do not stir. Refrigerate at least 4 hours. Overnight is better. Keeps for days. Delicious. Serves 6-8.

MRS. W. W. VAN PELT

COLE SLAW II

1 medium cabbage
2 tablespoons sugar
1 teaspoon salt
½ teaspoon celery seed

2 tablespoons tarragon vinegar
1 teaspoon prepared mustard
½ cup mayonnaise

Grate cabbage, doing half head at a time. Combine the rest of ingredients to make dressing and pour over cabbage. Stir until well mixed. Refrigerate before serving. Serves 6-8.

MRS. WALTER SCOTT III

GERMAN CUCUMBER SALAD

4 cucumbers
1 tablespoon salt
1 cup sour cream
Juice of ½ lemon
Grated rind of one lemon
2 tablespoons caviar

1 tablespoon horseradish
1 tablespoon minced onion
Salt and pepper to taste
2 tablespoons parsley
1 hard cooked egg

Sprinkle cucumbers, peeled and thinly sliced, with salt. Let stand for 3 hours. Drain. Add other ingredients except parsley and egg. To serve, sprinkle the salad with 2 tablespoons finely chopped parsley and the riced yolk of 1 hard-cooked egg. Serve very cold.

EAST INDIAN SALAD

1½ cups brown or wild rice
2 tablespoons chopped onion
2 6½ oz. cans solid white tuna fish
1 bottle Kraft Sweet & Sour Dressing
¼ cup blond raisins

½ cup chutney
¾ cup chopped celery
¼ cup chopped green pepper
½ cup pineapple tidbits
½ cup chopped cashew nuts
1 small jar chopped pimento
1 tablespoon minced parsley

Cook rice and marinate in above bottled dressing several hours. Drain off dressing. Add other ingredients, except cashews, and chill. Add nuts at last minute. Serve on salad greens. (This can be one dish main course, accompanied by toasted rolls and followed with a light dessert.)

MRS. E. J. WANNAMAKER

WILTED LETTUCE

3 or 4 pieces bacon
¼ cup vinegar, diluted slightly
2 teaspoons sugar
½ teaspoon salt

½ teaspoon mustard
1 raw egg
1 head lettuce

Fry bacon and drain. While bacon grease is cooling, mix together other ingredients. Stir this mixture into slightly cooled bacon grease and pour this dressing over shredded lettuce. Crumble bacon over the top. Serves 4-6.

OLD NORTH STATE

IDA'S PERFECTION SALAD

1 cup shredded cabbage
2 cups celery, diced fine
1 4-ounce can pimentos (less if desired), drained
2 envelopes plain gelatin, soaked in ½ cup cold water

2 cups boiling water
½ cup vinegar
½ cup sugar
Juice of 1 lemon
1 teaspoon salt

Mix boiling water, vinegar, sugar, lemon juice, salt, with the dissolved gelatin. Cool mixture, then pour over celery, cabbage, and pimento mixture. Put in individual salad molds. Makes about 10 servings.

MRS. SAM H. MCDONALD

LINDA'S POTATO SALAD

3 or 4 large new potatoes, cooked
   until firm but not mushy
½ onion, chopped fine or grated
½ teaspoon celery seed
1 teaspoon salt

2 teaspoons sugar
¼ teaspoon pepper
2 chopped hard cooked eggs
2 stalks celery, chopped

Combine above ingredients and seasonings. Add dressing made with:

½ cup mayonnaise
½ cup thousand island dressing

1 tablespoon vinegar

A nice variation of normal potato salad.

MRS. MARK P. JOHNSON, JR.

POTATO SALAD

4 baking-sized potatoes or
   equivalent (approximately
   2 pounds)
½ cup French dressing (recipe
   below)
1 cup chopped celery

3 hard cooked eggs
2 tablespoons sweet pickle relish
Grated onion to taste
2 tablespoons mayonnaise
Salt and pepper

Boil potatoes in skins until tender. Let cool, then peel and slice. Marinate potatoes for several hours in French dressing, stirring once or twice. After marinating, pour off excess dressing, add celery and two of the eggs. Reserve third egg for garnish. Add remaining ingredients. Serves 4 or 5.

FRENCH DRESSING

1 teaspoon salt
½ teaspoon sugar
¼ teaspoon black pepper
½ teaspoon paprika

½ teaspoon dry mustard
¾ cup salad oil
¼ cup vinegar

HOT POTATO SALAD

10 medium sized potatoes
1 teaspoon salt
½ onion, diced
1 tablespoon flour
1 cup vinegar

½ cup water
½ cup sugar
10 bacon strips
1 tablespoon grease from bacon

Boil potatoes in salted water without peeling until tender. Slice. Combine with onion. Make dressing by combining hot bacon grease with flour. Stir. Mix together the sugar, water and vinegar. Add to the flour mixture and cook until it thickens. Pour over the onions and potatoes and let stand at least 6 hours at room temperature. Heat only slightly to serve. Crumble bacon over top and stir gently. Serves 10-12.

RICE SALAD

1¾ cups rice, uncooked
3 chicken bouillon cubes
¼ cup salad oil
2 tablespoons vinegar
1½ teaspoons salt
⅛ teaspoon pepper
2 hard boiled eggs, chopped

1½ cups celery, diced
¼ cup dill pickle, chopped
¼ cup pimento, chopped
½ cup onion, chopped
½ cup mayonnaise
2 tablespoons mustard

Cook rice with bouillon cubes in water. Drain well in a colander. While still in colander, pour a mixture of salad oil, vinegar, salt and pepper over rice and let it drain. Then toss rice with egg, celery, pickle, pimento and onion. Stir dressing of mayonnaise and mustard into salad. Chill until time to serve. Serves 8 to 10.

MRS. WALTER SCOTT III

SUPER SALAD GARNISH

1 can hearts of palm, drained
1 large can stems and pieces of mushrooms, drained
1 can heart of artichoke, drained (marinated in brine, not oil)

Slivered green bell pepper for color (optional)
Onion slices (optional)
Italian dressing
½ cup vinegar

Pour bottled Italian dressing (with ½ cup vinegar added) over above. Store in tightly closed jar in refrigerator. Pour over a lettuce salad for a super salad.

MRS. D. LACY KEESLER

MARINATED VEGETABLE SALAD

1 can Le Seur peas
1 can limas
2 cans French style green beans
1 can shoe peg corn
1 can water chestnuts, drained

1 2-ounce jar pimentos, drained
½ medium green pepper
1 cup chopped celery
Salt to taste

Drain all vegetables. Slice water chestnuts, pimentos, green pepper and celery. Alternate vegetables. Pour mixed marinade dressing over all. Refrigerate 24 hours. Makes 3 quarts.

DRESSING

¾ cup Wesson Oil
¾ cup white vinegar

½ cup sugar

MRS. WALTER RAY CUNNINGHAM

VEGETABLE MARINADE

2 15-ounce cans French style
green beans
2 15-ounce cans small green peas
1 small jar pimentos
1 medium onion, chopped fine

2 to 3 stalks celery, chopped fine
1 green pepper, chopped fine
¼ pound American cheese, cubed
Salt to taste

Drain beans, peas and pimentos. Combine all ingredients. Add more cheese if desired, or use sharp if preferred. Proportions of beans and peas may be used to suit own taste. Prepare the marinade described below. Pour over vegetables and let set several hours, preferably overnight. Just as good days later. Serves about 10-12.

MARINADE

1 cup sugar
1 cup vinegar

½ cup Wesson Oil

Bring sugar and vinegar to boil. Add oil. Cool and add to vegetables.

MRS. TERRY YOUNG

Salad Dressings

BLEU CHEESE SALAD DRESSING

¼ pound bleu cheese
½ pint sour cream
¼ cup mayonnaise
½ teaspoon salt

1 tablespoon vinegar
¼ teaspoon garlic salt
Dash of pepper
Dash of celery salt

Crumble cheese and mix with sour cream. Add rest of ingredients and mix well.

MRS. EVERETTE L. WOHLBRUCK

FRENCH SALAD DRESSING I

1 tablespoon grated onion
Dash of cayenne pepper
½ cup Mazola (or any salad oil)
⅓ cup catsup

1 teaspoon salt
¼ cup sugar
¼ cup vinegar
Juice of one lemon

Combine ingredients in blender. Good on almost any salad, especially fruit.

MRS. JOHN DABBS

FRENCH SALAD DRESSING II

1½ cups salad oil
1 can tomato soup
2 tablespoons Worcestershire sauce
½ cup sugar

¾ cup vinegar
1 teaspoon dry mustard
1 teaspoon salt
1 teaspoon pepper

Mix thoroughly; keep in refrigerator. Great with lettuce, chopped bacon, tomatoes and croutons! Lasts forever in the refrigerator.

MRS. C. F. CLARK, JR.

FRENCH DRESSING FOR SALAD III

¼ cup vinegar
¾ cup oil
1 teaspoon salt
1 teaspoon sugar

¼ teaspoon dry mustard
¼ teaspoon black pepper
Chopped parsley or a pinch of chervil

Put into jar and shake until blended. Makes 1 cup.

CROUTONS
Cut stale bread into small squares. Toast slowly (about 200°) until hard. Fry in olive oil. Sprinkle with salt and garlic salt. Keep in air-tight jar.

MRS. ALEX R. JOSEPHS

CAESAR SALAD DRESSING

2 egg yolks
8 ounces olive oil
2 tablespoons prepared mustard
2 tablespoons wine vinegar
½ small onion, quartered
1 small stalk celery cut in 1-inch bites

1 2-ounce can fillet anchovies, drained
½ teaspoon fresh ground pepper
Accent to taste
Few drops Tabasco
Croutons
Romano cheese, grated

Beat egg yolks until thick and lemon colored. Add olive oil very slowly, beating at high speed while adding (as for making mayonnaise). Thin with wine vinegar and add mustard. Put mixture in blender. Add remaining ingredients except croutons and cheese. Serve over large cut Romaine lettuce. Top with croutons and cheese. This can be doubled and stored in the refrigerator as it keeps well. If too thick, thin by adding vinegar. The dressing should be only slightly thinner than mayonnaise.

MRS. JOHN ALEXANDER STEWMAN III

DRESSING FOR FRUIT SALAD—ESPECIALLY GRAPEFRUIT

½ cup sugar
Juice of 1 lemon
Grated rind of 1 lemon
2 tablespoons vinegar

1 egg, well beaten
½ pint whipping cream (approximately)

Cook above ingredients, except whipping cream, until thick—stirring constantly. Fold in enough whipped cream to make desired consistency. Add lemon flavor if you desire.

MRS. SAMUEL R. SLOAN

SALAD DRESSING FOR GRAPEFRUIT

½ pint cream (whipped) or substitute Dream Whip
½ cup mayonnaise

½ cup chili sauce
¼ cup currant jelly

Mix together. Serve over fresh grapefruit sections and crisp lettuce. Makes approximately 2 cups.

FRUIT SALAD DRESSING

⅓ cup honey
⅓ cup lemonade concentrate
⅓ cup salad oil

1 teaspoon celery seed or poppy seed

Mix all ingredients well. Pour over a salad of melon chunks or balls (cantaloupe, honeydew, watermelon). Also, grapes, blueberries, peaches, strawberries, bananas, and avocado may be used.

MRS. HENRY PIERCE

GREEN GODDESS DRESSING A LA BLENDER

1 cup mayonnaise
1 clove garlic
2 tablespoons anchovy paste
3 tablespoons minced chives
1 tablespoon lemon juice

Salt
Pepper
3 tablespoons tarragon vinegar
¼ cup chopped parsley
½ cup heavy cream

Put all ingredients into a blender and run on high speed for 20 seconds. Chill before using. Approximately 2 cups.

MRS. PHILIP G. CONNER

HORSERADISH DRESSING

½ pint sour cream
½ pint mayonnaise
1 tablespoon chopped parsley
1 tablespoon Worcestershire

1 tablespoon prepared mustard
1 bottle ground drained
   horseradish
Salt to taste

Blend ingredients. Thin with 1 tablespoon wine or garlic vinegar. I serve this dressing on tomato aspic salad, vegetables and meats.

MRS. KEMP DUNAWAY*

PIQUANTE DRESSING

½ cup vinegar
2 teaspoons salt
1 teaspoon sugar
½ teaspoon pepper
1 teaspoon paprika

1 teaspoon dry mustard
1½ cups salad oil
2 teaspoons prepared mustard
1 teaspoon Worcestershire
8 drops Tabasco

Combine first six ingredients. Shake well, then add last four. Shake again. Put ¼ of a cut onion in jar with dressing to season. Do not pour onion out on salad. This is *particularly* good on all green—spinach or lettuce—salad.

MRS. JOHN J. HANES

POPPY SEED SALAD DRESSSING

1½ cups salad oil
⅔ cup sugar
½ cup vinegar
¼ cup poppy seeds

1 teaspoon salt
1½ teaspoons dry mustard
1 small onion, grated

Mix sugar, salt and mustard. Add vinegar slowly, beat in salad oil, add grated onion, then poppy seeds. Use with any fresh fruit salad or mixture of fresh and canned fruit. Good with grapefruit.

MRS. FRANCIS O. CLARKSON, JR.

ROQUEFORT DRESSING I

1 cup mayonnaise
¼ cup wine vinegar
¼ cup catsup (scant)

¼ teaspoon salt
1 cup half and half cream
8 ounces Roquefort cheese

Break up cheese and blend in blender with above ingredients. Store in refrigerator. Makes approximately 2 cups dressing.

MRS. WALTER SUMMERVILLE, JR.

ROQUEFORT DRESSING II

½ pound roquefort cheese
2 tablespoons lemon juice
¼ cup mayonnaise
2 tablespoons chopped chives

Dash of Worcestershire
Dash of Tabasco
Salt to taste
½ pint sour cream

Mash cheese until softened. Add remaining ingredients. Beat until fluffy. Yields 1½ cups. Will keep for a week in closed container in refrigerator.

MRS. MILTON C. GEE, JR.

SHRIMP SALAD DRESSING

¼ cup salad oil
2 tablespoons red wine vinegar
¼ teaspoon dry mustard
¼ teaspoon salt

¼ teaspoon paprika
¼ teaspoon garlic or onion salt
(optional)

Combine all ingredients and mix well. Pour over shrimp salad or other seafood.

MRS. TORRENCE E. HEMBY, JR.

SOUR CREAM DRESSING

1 quart jar Kraft mayonnaise
1 carton sour cream
1 cup buttermilk

2 teaspoons garlic salt
6-8 ounces Roquefort cheese

Mix well. Refrigerate.

MRS. JOSEPH K. HALL

SUZANNE'S SOUR DRESSING

Juice of 8-10 lemons
Equal portion of Mazola oil
2 teaspoons Lawry's salt
Pepper

Worcestershire sauce to taste
Dash of Tabasco
1 teaspoon celery salt
1 teaspoon white salt

Shake well the above ingredients in a quart bottle. Refrigerate. This keeps indefinitely and is better the day after it is made. I use this for salad dressing, also to marinate whole fillet, or a dish of cooked shrimp with onion and mushrooms.

MRS. JOHN L. CRIST

Desserts

Cakes

ANGEL FOOD CAKE

1½ cups finely granulated
    powdered sugar
1 cup cake flour
½ teaspoon salt
12 egg whites

1 tablespoon water
1 tablespoon lemon juice
1 teaspoon cream of tartar
½ teaspoon vanilla
½ teaspoon almond extract

Sift powdered sugar at least twice. Sift cake flour before measuring 1 cup. Resift flour at least 3 times with ½ cup sifted powdered sugar and ½ teaspoon salt. Beat egg whites until foamy. Add water, lemon juice and cream of tartar. Increase speed with electric mixer and whip until whites are stiff. Gradually add 1 cup sifted sugar, 1 tablespoon at a time. Fold in vanilla and almond extract. By hand fold in ¼ cup of flour-sugar mixture with gentle but rapid strokes using rubber scraper. Gradually fold in remaining flour-sugar mixture. Pour batter into ungreased tube pan which is completely grease free. Bake in preheated 350° oven for 45 minutes. To cool, reverse pan and rest hanging on funnel for 1½ hours.

MRS. WILLIAM H. MCNAIR

FRESH APPLE CAKE WITH GLAZE

1¼ cups Wesson Oil
2 cups sugar
3 eggs
3 cups flour
1 teaspoon soda

1 teaspoon salt
1 teaspoon vanilla
3 cups apples, peeled and chopped
1 cup nuts, chopped

Mix oil and sugar. Add eggs one at a time. Sift flour, soda and salt together and add to egg mixture. Combine remaining ingredients and bake in greased and floured tube pan. Bake at 325° for 1½ hours. When cool, add glaze.

GLAZE

½ cup butter
1 cup brown sugar

¼ cup Pet milk

While cake is baking, combine butter, brown sugar and milk, bring to a full boil, and stir. Set aside and stir every 15 minutes. Pour over cooled cake.

MRS. WALTER SUMMERVILLE, JR.

APPLESAUCE CAKE

½ cup butter or margarine
½ cup white sugar
½ cup brown sugar
1 egg
1 cup applesauce
1¾ cups flour
½ teaspoon salt

2 teaspoons baking powder
½ teaspoon baking soda (scant)
1 teaspoon cinnamon
½ teaspoon ground cloves
1 cup raisins
¼ cup margarine
1 cup brown sugar

Cream ½-cup butter with ½-cup white and ½-cup brown sugar. Add egg. Sift flour, baking powder, salt, and soda and mix with egg mixture. Add applesauce, spices and raisins. Put in greased 9x12-inch pan. Melt the ¼-cup margarine and dribble on top of cake. Sprinkle 1 cup brown sugar on top (using more or less according to taste). Bake at 350° for 30 minutes or until done. Serve warm, topped with whipped cream if desired.

MRS. TERRY YOUNG

BLACKBERRY JAM CAKE

⅔ cup butter
1½ cups sugar
4 eggs (yolks and whites beaten separately)
⅔ cup buttermilk with 1 teaspoon baking soda dissolved in it

2 heaping cups flour
1 cup blackberry jam (with seeds)
1 teaspoon ground cloves
1 teaspoon nutmeg
1 teaspoon cinnamon

Cream butter and sugar together. Add egg yolks, mixing thoroughly. Sift flour; measure and sift again. Add spices. Add flour alternately with buttermilk (to which soda has been added). Stir in jam lightly (do not beat). Fold in stiffly beaten egg whites last. Bake in 3 layers (10-inch pans) at 350° for about 20 minutes. Turn out on wire racks to cool.

FILLING
2 eggs, lightly beaten
1 cup sugar
1 cup milk

1 tablespoon butter
1 tablespoon cornstarch
1 teaspoon vanilla

Mix cornstarch and sugar thoroughly. Add other ingredients and cook in double boiler until mixture thickens and coats spoon. Let cool completely before spreading.

MRS. S. H. MCDONALD

CARROT CAKE

2 cups sugar
1½ cups Mazola oil
4 eggs beaten
2 cups plain flour
1 teaspoon salt

2 teaspoons baking soda
2 teaspoons cinnamon
½ cup chopped nuts (optional)
3 cups grated carrots

Mix sugar, oil and beaten eggs together. Sift flour, salt, soda and cinnamon together. Add flour mixture to egg mixture in four portions and fold in nuts and carrots. Bake in slightly oiled tube pan at 350° for 55 to 60 minutes or in 13x9x2 pan at 300° for 60-70 minutes. Cool and ice.

ICING:

1 box powdered sugar
1 stick margarine
1 8 oz. package cream cheese

2 teaspoons vanilla
½ cup chopped nuts

Have butter and cream cheese at room temperature. Cream together well. Add powdered sugar and vanilla and beat well. Stir in nuts. Spread on carrot cake. Keep in refrigerator. Freezes well.

MRS. HENRY JAMES, JR.*

CHERRY SPONGE CAKE

5 eggs, separated (room temperature)
1 cup granulated sugar
1 tablespoon grated orange peel
¼ cup orange juice
1 8-ounce jar maraschino cherries, drained, finely chopped in blender, and drained again

1 cup sifted cake flour
¼ teaspoon salt
¼ teaspoon cream of tartar
Confectioners sugar

Beat egg yolks until thick and lemon colored. Gradually add ½-cup granulated sugar. Gradually beat in orange peel and juice. Gently stir in cherries. (If you prefer plain sponge cake, omit the cherries.) Add flour. Beat egg whites. When almost stiff, add salt, cream of tartar, and ½-cup sugar. Continue beating until stiff. Fold into cherry mixture. Bake in ungreased 9-inch tube pan at 350° for 40 to 45 minutes, or until done. Invert and cool. Remove from pan and sprinkle with confectioners sugar. Top with additional cherries. At serving time, slice and serve with orange sauce. (See Orange Sauce.)

MRS. BRUCE H. RINEHART

CHOCOLATE CAKE DELUXE

1 cup butter
2 cups sugar
2 eggs
2 squares chocolate
2 teaspoons vanilla

1 cup sour cream
2 teaspoons soda
2½ cups flour
¼ teaspoon salt
1 cup boiling water

Cream butter and sugar. Mix in eggs. Melt chocolate and add vanilla to it. Blend into butter mixture. In separate bowl, mix sour cream and soda. Sift flour and salt together. Alternate adding sour cream mixture and flour mixture to first ingredients. Add 1 cup boiling water last. Grease and flour round tube pan. Bake at 325° for 1 to 1¼ hours.

ICING

1 6-oz. pkg. of chocolate chips
⅓ cup canned milk

2 cups powdered sugar

Melt chocolate, add milk, then sugar. Add more milk if the icing needs to be thinner.

MRS. J. K. HALL III

FRESH COCONUT CAKE

1 cup Crisco or butter
2 cups sugar
4 egg yolks, unbeaten
1 teaspoon vanilla
½ teaspoon salt

1 teaspoon soda
2½ cups sifted cake flour
1 cup buttermilk
4 egg whites
2 cups fresh grated coconut

Cream shortening and sugar until light and fluffy. Add egg yolks, one at a time, beating after each addition. Combine dry ingredients and add alternately with buttermilk to creamed mixture. Beat egg whites until stiff peaks form. Add vanilla and fold into batter. Bake at 375° for 25 minutes in three 8-inch or 9-inch pans. (Or bake in 9x13-inch pan at 350° for about 40 minutes.) Ice with frosting and cover with 2 cups fresh grated coconut.

SEVEN MINUTE FROSTING
2¼ cups sugar
1½ tablespoons white corn syrup
7½ tablespoons water

3 egg whites
1½ teaspoons vanilla

Combine all ingredients except vanilla in double boiler. Cook over boiling water, beating constantly for 7 minutes. Occasionally scrape sides with rubber spatula. Remove from heat and add vanilla. Continue to beat if necessry for 1 more minute or until of right spreading consistency. Spread on three cake layers and cover with 2 cups fresh grated coconut.

MRS. WILLIAM A. WHITE, JR.

WONDER CHOCOLATE CAKE

1½ cups flour
1 cup sugar
3 tablespoons cocoa
1 teaspoon salt
1 teaspoon soda

1 tablespoon vinegar
6 tablespoons salad oil
3 teaspoons vanilla
1 cup cold water

Sift flour, sugar, cocoa, salt, and soda directly into 9-inch square ungreased pan. Make 3 holes in dry ingredients. Pour the vinegar, oil, and vanilla in the three holes so each hole gets the same amount. Pour 1 cup water over the cake. Stir *very well* with fork, making sure all lumps disappear. (This is important.) Bake at 350° for 30 minutes. Let cool in pan and frost with favorite icing. Cake keeps moist and good for a long time.

MRS. HALL M. JOHNSTON, JR.

HERSHEY'S CHOCOLATE SYRUP CAKE

1 stick butter
1 cup sugar
4 eggs
1 teaspoon vanilla

1 cup flour
1 teaspoon baking powder
1 large can Hershey's chocolate
   syrup

Cream butter and sugar. Add eggs, one at a time. Add vanilla, flour and baking powder, then chocolate syrup and beat well. Bake in 9x9-inch greased pan at 350° for 20 to 30 minutes. (1½ recipe makes 3-layer cake.) Ice with favorite butter or chocolate icing.

MRS. ARTHUR B. CULBERTSON

GERMAN CHOCOLATE CAKE WITH COCONUT-PECAN FROSTING

1 package German's sweet cooking chocolate
½ cup boiling water
1 cup butter, margarine, or other shortening
2 cups sugar
4 egg yolks, unbeaten

1 teaspoon vanilla
2½ cups sifted cake flour
1 teaspoon baking soda
1 cup buttermilk
½ teaspoon salt
4 egg whites, stiffly beaten

Melt chocolate in ½-cup boiling water and cool. Cream butter and sugar until light and fluffy. Add egg yolks, one at a time, beating after each. Add vanilla and melted chocolate, and mix until blended. Sift flour with soda and salt. Add sifted dry ingredients alternately with buttermilk, beating after each addition until batter is smooth. Fold in stiffly beaten egg whites. Pour batter into three 8-inch or 9-inch layer pans, which have been greased and floured. Bake in 350° oven for 35 to 40 minutes. Cool. Frost top and between layers with coconut-pecan frosting.

COCONUT-PECAN FROSTING

1 cup evaporated milk (or half and half)
1 cup sugar
3 egg yolks

¼ lb. margarine
1 teaspoon vanilla
1 can tender-flaked coconut
1 cup pecans, chopped

Combine milk, sugar, egg yolks, margarine and vanilla in a saucepan. Cook over medium heat for 12 minutes, stirring constantly until mixture thickens. Add coconut and pecans. Beat until cool and of spreading consistency. Spread between layers and on top of 3-layer cake. *Do not* frost sides of cake.

MRS. KEITH STONEMAN*

RED DEVILS FOOD CAKE

1½ cups sifted cake flour
1½ teaspoons baking powder
½ teaspoon salt
4 tablespoons butter
1 cup sugar
½ cup buttermilk

2 eggs, well beaten
½ cup boiling water
2 squares unsweetened chocolate
1 teaspoon soda
1 teaspoon vanilla

Sift flour, baking powder and salt three times. Cream butter and sugar. Add well-beaten eggs to creamed mixture. Then add the flour and milk alternately to the butter-sugar-egg mixture. Melt chocolate with boiling water over low heat; add soda and stir well. Cool chocolate before adding it to the batter. Then stir in vanilla. Grease cake pans and line them with waxed paper (two 9-inch pans). Bake at 350° for 25 minutes. (Batter will be thin.) Frost with vanilla icing.

MRS. WALTER SCOTT, JR.

QUICK DEVILS FOOD CAKE

1 cup water	2 eggs
1½ ounces chocolate	½ cup buttermilk
½ cup Crisco	1 teaspoon soda
1 stick margarine	1 teaspoon vanilla
2 cups flour	Pinch of salt
2 cups sugar (scant)	

In saucepan, melt and boil for 1 minute the water, chocolate, Crisco, and margarine. Mix flour and sugar in large mixing bowl. Pour hot chocolate mixture in with flour. Mix eggs, buttermilk and soda together; add to other mixture. Add vanilla and salt and mix well. Bake at 350° in ungreased 10x13-inch pan for 30 minutes. Pour icing over cake after it is cooked, but is still hot.

ICING

1½ ounces chocolate	1 box confectioners sugar
1 stick margarine	½ cup pecans, optional
6 tablespoons sweet milk	1 teaspoon vanilla

Five minutes before the cake is done, melt the chocolate and margarine. Add milk, and mix well on low heat. Pour in small bowl of electric mixer and add confectioners sugar, nuts, and vanilla. Mix until smooth. Add more milk if too thick. Pour over cake when you take cake from oven and let it cool in pan. The iced cake freezes well.

MRS. JAMES H. BARNHARDT

CHOO CHOO TRAIN CAKE

Yellow or white cake	White icing
Chocolate icing	Colored candies

Instructions: Use yellow or white cake. Make in oblong pan 11¼ x 7¼ x 1⅜ or any good size sheet cake pan. After cake is cooled, remove from pan. Cut one strip 5″ wide and 13″ long (adding 2″ to 11″ strip). Cut two squares 3x3-inches; (round off these squares to make wheels). Cut one piece 5-inches long x 3½-inches wide for cabin of train. Cut piece 2½ x 2½-inches for smoke stack. Secure all of this with toothpicks on serving tray. Ice with chocolate icing. Decorate with white icing and colored candies.

MRS. HALL M. JOHNSON

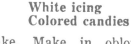

HOT MILK CAKE

1 cup milk
1 stick butter or margarine
4 eggs, well beaten
2 cups sugar

2 cups sifted flour
2 teaspoons baking powder
½ teaspoon salt
1 teaspoon vanilla

In small saucepan, bring the milk and margarine to a boil. Combine other ingredients and mix well. Mix the two mixtures together and bake immediately in tube pan for 35 to 40 minutes at 350° or in three 8-inch layer pans for 25 minutes. Serve warm or cold. Good served with Easy Hot Fudge Sauce.

MRS. LEE A. FOLGER III

DUMP CAKE

1 box powdered sugar
4 cups plain flour
6 eggs

1 stick margarine
2 sticks butter
¼ teaspoon mace

Mix all ingredients well in electric mixer for about 5 minutes. Bake in a greased and floured tube pan at 300° for 1¼ hours or until done. Ice with favorite icing, if desired.

MRS. WALTER B. MAYER

EASY LIGHT FRUIT CAKE

1 cup sugar
2 sticks butter
4 eggs
2 cups plain flour, sifted
1 teaspoon vanilla

1 teaspoon almond flavoring
1 cup candied pineapple
1 cup candied cherries
1 cup white raisins
1 cup pecans, chopped

Cream sugar and butter. Add eggs, one at a time, beating well after each addition. Add remaining ingredients and mix well. Bake in floured and well-greased tube pan at 275° for 1½ to 2 hours. Test with a straw. Cool well in pan before removing.

MRS. ROBERT FREEMAN

WHITE FRUIT CAKE

¾ pound butter
2½ cups sugar
6 eggs, separated
5 cups sifted flour
3 teaspoons baking powder
3 teaspoons vanilla

¾ cup liquid (whiskey)
¾ pound cherries, chopped
¾ pound pineapple, chopped
¾ pound citron, chopped
¾ pound nutmeats, chopped

Cream butter and sugar. Beat eggs separately. Add yolks to sugar mixture; then add flour which has been sifted with baking powder. Add liquid, then fold in egg whites. Dredge fruit in flour and add last, along with nuts and vanilla. Bake at 250° for 3¼ hours in tube pan.

MRS. MILTON C. GEE, JR.

MARCELLA'S ELEGANT DATE CAKE

1 package dates, chopped
1½ cups boiling water
1 teaspoon baking soda
1 cup sugar
½ cup butter
2 eggs, well beaten

1¼ cups plus 3 tablespoons flour
¼ teaspoon salt
¾ teaspoon soda
½ cup brown sugar
1 cup pecans, chopped
1 small package chocolate chips

Pour water over chopped dates. Add soda, let cool. Mash dates with hands when cool. Cream sugar and butter. Add eggs and blend well. Sift together flour, salt, and soda. Combine with sugar mixture. Add date mixture. Pour in oblong 8 x 12-inch pan.

Mix together brown sugar, pecans, and chocolate chips. Sprinkle on top of batter. Bake at 350° for 40 to 45 minutes. Serve with "spiked" whipped cream (2 tablespoons sugar and rum or bourbon to taste, added to whipped cream). Cake is good with or without added whipped cream.

MRS. J. FRANK TIMBERLAKE, JR.

FRUIT COCKTAIL CAKE

1½ cups sugar
2 eggs
½ cup Wesson Oil
2 cups flour

½ teaspoon salt
2 teaspoons soda
1 medium can fruit cocktail, not drained

Mix together sugar, eggs, and oil. Add flour, salt, and soda which have been sifted together. Add fruit cocktail and mix. Pour into greased 13 x 9 x 2-inch pan and bake at 350° for 45 minutes.

TOPPING

1 stick margarine
½ can Carnation milk (or 6½ oz.)
¾ cup sugar

½ cup nuts
½ cup coconut
1 teaspoon vanilla

Boil margarine, milk, and sugar for 10 minutes. Add nuts, coconut, and vanilla. Pour over hot cake.

MISS VIRGINIA KILROY

SOFT GINGERBREAD CAKE

½ cup shortening
½ cup brown sugar
½ cup milk
½ cup molasses
1 egg
2 cups flour

3 teaspoons baking powder
½ teaspoon ginger
½ teaspoon salt
¼ teaspoon soda
¼ teaspoon allspice
1 teaspoon cinnamon

Cream shortening and sugar. Mix milk and molasses; add the egg. Pour liquid mixture into creamed mixture. Sift dry ingredients together, then stir them into batter. Grease and flour 8-inch square pan, pour in batter and bake at 375° about 45 minutes or until tester inserted comes out clean. Serve with Butter Sauce.

MRS. WALTER SCOTT, JR.

OATMEAL CAKE

1¼ cups boiling water
1 cup quick cooking oats
½ cup shortening
1 cup white sugar
1 cup brown sugar
2 eggs

1⅓ cups sifted plain flour
1 teaspoon soda
½ teaspoon each salt,
  cinnamon, nutmeg
1 teaspoon vanilla

Pour water over oats. Set aside. Cream shortening and sugars. Add eggs, one at a time, beating well after each. Sift flour, salt, soda, and spices together. Set aside. Combine oatmeal and creamed mixture. Add flour and spices. Stir in vanilla. Pour into well-greased 9 x 13-inch pan and bake at 350° for 25 minutes. Pour topping mix on hot cake. Place under broiler for 1 to 2½ minutes, until just delicately browned. Serves about 16.

TOPPING
2 egg yolks
1 teaspoon milk
1 stick butter or margarine,
  melted

1 cup brown sugar
1 cup pecans, chopped
1 cup coconut

Beat egg yolks and milk until light. Add butter and sugar. Fold in nuts and coconut. Pour on hot cake.

MRS. WALTER RAY CUNNINGHAM

1-2-3-4 CAKE

1 cup butter
2 cups sugar
4 eggs, separated
3 cups flour

2 teaspoons baking powder
1 cup milk
1 teaspoon vanilla

Cream butter and sugar. Add egg yolks, then dry ingredients which have been sifted together and milk alternately, then vanilla. Fold in stiffly beaten egg whites. Bake at 375° 20 minutes for cupcakes. Can be used for layer cake.

MRS. WALTER SCOTT, JR.

PINEAPPLE UPSIDE DOWN CAKE

1 stick butter
1 cup brown sugar, packed
1 cup pecans (optional)
1 can pineapple rings
3 eggs, separated

1 cup white sugar
5 tablespoons pineapple juice
1 cup flour
1 teaspoon baking powder

Melt butter and brown sugar in large frying pan. Add pecans and cover with pineapple rings. Beat egg yolks until lemon-colored. Add white sugar and pineapple juice, then flour, which has been sifted with baking powder. Fold in stiffly beaten egg whites. Pour this mixture over mixture in frying pan. Bake at 350° for 35 to 45 minutes. When done, turn upside down on plate.

MRS. MOFFATT G. SHERARD, JR.

ORANGE CAKE WITH SAUCE

1 cup sugar
½ cup butter
2 eggs
2 cups flour
Pinch of salt
⅔ cup buttermilk

1 teaspoon soda
1 cup (or 1 package) dates, chopped
½ cup nuts, chopped
1 tablespoon grated orange rind
½ teaspoon orange extract

Cream sugar and butter. Add eggs one at a time and mix. Sift flour and salt together. Dissolve soda in buttermilk. Add flour and buttermilk alternately to sugar mixture. Fold in dates, nuts and rind. Bake at 350° for 25 to 30 minutes in 8 x 12-inch pan, or in tube pan at 325° for 45 minutes. (Or to make 2½ dozen miniature muffin-pan sized cakes bake at 325° for 35 minutes.) Combine icing ingredients and pour over the baked cake as soon as it comes from the oven, so that the liquid seeps into it.

ICING
⅔ cup sugar
½ cup orange juice

1 teaspoon grated orange rind (or rind from 2 oranges)

Combine above ingredients and spread on hot cake. Serve with whipped cream, warm or cold.

MRS. HUGH CAMPBELL
MRS. JOHN L. DABBS III
MRS. SAMUEL R. SLOAN

PRUNE CAKE

2 cups sugar
2 cups cake flour
2 teaspoons baking powder
1 teaspoon soda
1 teaspoon nutmeg
1 teaspoon cloves
1 teaspoon cinnamon
1 teaspoon allspice

1 cup corn oil or Wesson Oil
1 cup buttermilk
3 eggs
1 teaspoon vanilla
1 cup cooked prunes, pitted and chopped
1 cup pecans (optional)

Stir and mix first 8 ingredients. Add oil, buttermilk, then eggs one at a time, and vanilla. Mix well. Add chopped prunes and nuts, mixing well. Bake at 325° for 1 hour, or until done, in tube pan (or in 13x7-inch sheet pan for about 50 minutes). Pour hot icing over hot cake.

TOPPING
1 cup sugar
1 cup buttermilk
1 teaspoon soda

5 tablespoons margarine
2 teaspoons Log Cabin syrup

Mix soda with buttermilk. Combine all ingredients in heavy saucepan and boil slowly, stirring occasionally. Cook for about 30 minutes while the cake is baking. Remove cake from oven when cooked. Pour hot icing over cake in sheet pan, or take from tube pan and pour over it. (For a more moist cake, make tiny holes in the cake so the topping can seep through. Keep spooning the topping on it.) This is a moist cake and keeps well. Good served warm or cold.

MRS. E. OSBORNE AYSCUE, JR.

FESTIVE HOLIDAY SPICE CAKE

2 cups flour
1 teaspoon soda
2 teaspoons baking powder
½ teaspoon salt
1 teaspoon cinnamon
1 teaspoon powdered cloves

½ teaspoon allspice
2 eggs
1 cup white sugar
2 tablespoons molasses
1 cup buttermilk
⅔ cup melted shortening

Sift flour, soda, baking powder, salt, and spices together. Beat eggs until thick. Beat in sugar and molasses until very well blended and then add flour mixture alternately with buttermilk. Stir in cooled melted shortening. Pour into two well-greased and floured 9-inch cake pans. Bake at 375° for about 25 minutes. Do not overcook. Top with frosting.

FROSTING

1 medium-sized jar red cherries, drained and sliced into halves
1 medium-sized jar green cherries, drained and sliced into halves

1½ cups pecans, chopped
2 cartons heavy cream, whipped and seasoned to taste with powdered sugar and vanilla

Frost first layer of cooled cake with part of the whipped cream. Sprinkle with half of cherries and nuts. Then place second layer of cake on top, pressing gently into place. Frost the top and sides in same manner.

Frost immediately before serving and place in refrigerator until time to serve, or make ahead and freeze, allowing at least 4 hours to thaw. When cream gets soft, put cake in refrigerator for 1 hour or until serving time.

MRS. AMOS BUMGARDNER, JR.

SUGAR CAKE

3 eggs, beaten until lemony
1½ cups sugar
1½ cups self-rising flour
½ pint heavy cream

1 tablespoon lemon juice
1 teaspoon grated lemon rind
Powdered sugar

Beat eggs; add sugar gradually. Add flour, then cream. Add flavoring last. Bake for 1 hour at 350° in buttered and floured 9x5-inch loaf pan. Sprinkle powdered sugar on top before serving.

MRS. STEPHEN K. URNER, JR.

SPECIAL TIP

Try: A light sprinkling of sugar on the cake plate to keep
a freshly baked cake from sticking.

MRS. JOHN A. STEWMAN

Pound Cakes

BLACK WALNUT CHOCOLATE POUND CAKE

2 sticks butter
½ cup vegetable shortening
3 cups sugar
5 eggs
3 cups plain flour
½ teaspoon baking powder
½ teaspoon salt

5 tablespoons cocoa
1 cup sweet milk
1 teaspoon black walnut flavoring
1 square unsweetened chocolate, melted
½ cup chopped black walnuts

Cream well butter, shortening, and sugar. Beat in eggs one at a time. Sift together three times flour, baking powder, salt and cocoa. Add to creamed mixture alternately with milk, starting with flour, etc. Add flavoring and chocolate. Fold in nuts. Bake in well-greased tube pan at 325° for 1 hour and 20 minutes. Do not open oven during baking.

MRS. BEN C. ASHCRAFT

BUTTERMILK POUND CAKE

1 cup butter
2 cups sugar
3 eggs
3 cups flour

½ teaspoon soda
½ teaspoon salt
1 cup buttermilk
1 teaspoon vanilla

Cream sugar and butter. Add eggs one at a time, mixing well. Stir together flour, soda and salt. Add alternately with buttermilk to creamed mixture. Add vanilla and pour into greased, floured tube pan. Bake at 325° for 1¼ hours.

MRS. JULIUS JOSLIN CHAMBERLAIN

CHOCOLATE POUND CAKE

2 sticks butter or margarine
½ cup Crisco
3 cups sugar
½ cup cocoa
5 eggs

Dash of salt
1 teaspoon vanilla
3 cups flour
1 teaspoon baking powder
1 cup milk

Cream butter and shortening. Add sugar and beat well. Add eggs one at a time. Add salt and vanilla. Sift flour, measure it, and sift again with baking powder. Add cocoa (using more cocoa, if you like a dark chocolate.) Add dry ingredients alternately with milk. Blend thoroughly. Turn into tube pan. Bake at 325° for 1½ hours. Cool and ice.

CHOCOLATE ICING

2 cups sugar
¼ cup cocoa
1 stick butter

½ cup milk
½ teaspoon vanilla

Mix all ingredients except vanilla. Put over medium heat. Cook, stirring, until mixture boils. Boil for 3 minutes. Remove from heat. Add vanilla and beat until cool. Spread over cooled cake.

MRS. NORMAN S. RICHARDS

GERMAN CHOCOLATE POUND CAKE

1 package German chocolate
2 sticks margarine
3 cups sugar
½ cup shortening
5 eggs
3 cups flour

1 teaspoon baking powder
½ teaspoon salt
1 cup milk
1 teaspoon lemon extract
1 teaspoon vanilla
1 cup chopped nuts (optional)

Melt chocolate and margarine together. Cream sugar and shortening and add to chocolate mixture. Add the eggs and mix well. Sift flour, baking powder and salt, and add alternately with milk. Add lemon, vanilla and nuts, and mix well. Bake in a tube pan at 350° for 1¼ to 1½ hours. When cool, add the chocolate icing.

CHOCOLATE ICING
1 stick margarine
1 box powdered sugar
6 tablespoons cocoa

1 egg, slightly beaten
1 teaspoon vanilla
2 teaspoons lemon juice

Melt margarine. Add ½ box powdered sugar and cocoa. Mix. Add other ½ box powdered sugar and remaining ingredients and mix well. If too thick to spread, add a little milk. Spread on cake.

MRS. THOMAS N. MASSEY

COCONUT POUND CAKE

3 sticks butter
3 cups white sugar
6 eggs
1 13-ounce can evaporated milk
1 tablespoon lemon flavoring

3 cups plain flour
1 teaspoon baking powder
¼ teaspoon salt
1 3½-ounce can Angel Flake coconut

Have all ingredients at room temperature. Cream butter and sugar. Add eggs one at a time. Add remaining ingredients. Bake in tube pan in 325-350° oven for about one hour. As soon as cake is done, frost while still warm.

FROSTING
1½ cups confectioners sugar, sifted

Juice of 1 large lemon

Mix together and frost warm cake.

MRS. C. DIXON SPANGLER, JR.

OLD FASHIONED POUND CAKE

1 cup butter
3 cups sugar (scant)
6 eggs, separated
3½ cups flour

¼ teaspoon salt
2 teaspoons baking powder
1 cup milk
1 teaspoon vanilla

Cream butter and sugar. Add egg yolks, well beaten. Add sifted flour, salt, and baking powder alternately with milk. Add vanilla and stiffly beaten egg whites. Bake in greased tube pan at 350° until done (about 1 hour).

MRS. WALLACE B. BRADFORD

RUM POUND CAKE

2 sticks butter (no substitute)
3 cups sugar
½ pint (1 carton) sour cream
6 eggs

3 cups plain flour
¼ teaspoon soda
2 tablespoons rum flavoring
or 4 tablespoons light rum

Cream together butter and sugar until light and fluffy. Add sour cream all at one time. Then add eggs, one at a time, and beat well after each. Sift flour and soda together and gradually add to batter. When all ingredients are well blended, add flavoring. (Orange or vanilla can be substituted for rum.) Pour into a well greased and floured tube pan. Bake at 325° for 1 to 1¼ hours. If desired, add the following icing to the cooled cake.

ICING
1 stick butter or margarine
1 box confectioners sugar

1 egg white
Almond flavoring to taste

Beat softened butter with other ingredients. Pour on cold cake. Cake is very moist and keeps well.

MRS. BEN C. ASHCRAFT
MRS. MILTON C. GEE, JR.

Cake Mixes

APRICOT LEMON CAKE

4 eggs
1 box yellow supreme cake mix
¾ cup cooking oil
¾ cup canned apricot nectar

2 teaspoons lemon extract
1½ cups confectioners sugar
4 tablespoons lemon juice or
apricot nectar

Beat eggs, cake mix, oil and ¾ cup nectar together for 5 minutes. Bake at 325° for 45 to 50 minutes in greased tube pan. Cool in pan for 5 minutes. Place cake on plate while still warm and punch holes in it with ice pick. Mix remaining ingredients together and pour over cake, letting it run into holes. (Moist cake, which stays fresh many days.)

MRS. NATHANIEL HOWARD

LEMON CAKE

1 package Betty Crocker yellow cake mix
1 package lemon Jello
¾ cup Mazola Oil

¾ cup water or milk
4 eggs
1 teaspoon lemon extract

Beat all ingredients for 5 minutes. Pour into greased and floured tube pan. Bake at 325° for 50 to 60 minutes. Remove from oven and spread with the following icing while warm.

ICING
1½ cups powdered sugar
Juice of 1 lemon

1 tablespoon melted butter

Mix the above together and spread.

MRS. RUSSELL M. ROBINSON II
MRS. C. E. WILLIAMS, JR.

WEE LEMON CAKES

1 package Betty Crocker yellow cake mix
1½ pounds confectioners sugar
Strained juice of 2 lemons

Grated rind of 2 lemons
Strained juice of 2 oranges
Grated rind of 2 oranges

Mix cake according to directions except OMIT 3 tablespoons water. Drop by teaspoons into greased, floured miniature cup cake pans. Bake at 375° for 10 to 12 minutes. Combine remaining ingredients thoroughly. Remove cakes when cooked and immediately drop cakes into mixture. When cakes are coated, remove from mixture with slotted spoon and place on waxed paper. Makes 4 to 5 dozen. Serve warm or cold.

MRS. ALFRED H. MURRELL

PINK LEMONADE CAKE

1 package yellow cake mix
1 quart vanilla ice cream
6 drops red food coloring

1 6-ounce can frozen pink lemonade concentrate
1 cup whipping cream
2 tablespoons sugar

Prepare cake according to directions for two 9-inch layers. Cool. Stir ice cream to soften. Quickly stir in food coloring and ½-cup of the thawed lemonade concentrate. Spread evenly in 9-inch round foil-lined cake pan. Freeze for 2 or 3 hours, or until firm.

Place one cake layer on serving plate. Add ice cream layer, and top with second layer. Whip cream with sugar and the remaining lemonade concentrate until stiff. Frost sides and top of cake; decorate if desired. Return to freezer for at least 1 hour, or until serving time.

MRS. JOHN R. CAMPBELL

HAZELNUT BUTTER CAKE

1 package all-butter cake mix
1 cup finely ground hazelnuts
 (filberts)
12-ounce jar apricot preserves

¼ teaspoon rum (or brandy)
 flavoring
Sweetened whipped cream

Prepare cake mix as directed on package. Stir in nuts. Pour batter into 9 or 10-cup turban mold or 10-inch tube pan, generously greased and floured. Bake at 350° for 45 to 50 minutes. Test with toothpick. Cool cake for 15 minutes, then remove from pan and cool completely. In saucepan, warm preserves until of glaze consistency. Stir in flavoring. Spoon glaze over cooled cake. Let glaze cool. Serve with whipped cream.

MRS. ROBERT W. BRADSHAW, JR.

LAZY MAN'S DESSERT

1 cup chocolate syrup
1 cup cold water

1 package miniature
 marshmallows
½ package fudge cake mix

In a 6x10-inch pan, pour in the syrup, then the water. Do not mix the two together. Cover the surface with as many marshmallows are as needed. Mix half the cake mix according to directions on the package. Pour over marshmallows. Bake at 350° for 55 minutes. Serve while warm, topped with whipped cream if desired.

MRS. WALTER SCOTT, III

STRAWBERRY MERINGUE CAKE

1 package yellow cake mix
 (2-layer size)
1 cup orange juice
⅓ cup water
4 egg yolks
1 teaspoon grated orange peel

4 egg whites
¼ teaspoon cream of tartar
1 cup sugar
1 quart fresh strawberries
2 cups whipping cream
¼ cup sugar

Combine cake mix, orange juice, water, egg yolks and orange peel. Beat for 4 minutes in mixer. Pour into two greased and floured 9-inch round cake pans. Beat egg whites with tartar to soft peaks. Gradually add 1 cup sugar, beating until stiff. Spread meringue evenly over batter. Bake at 350° for 35 to 40 minutes. Cool completely. With flexible spatulas carefully remove layers from pans, keeping meringue side up.

Set aside a few berries for garnish. Slice remainder. Whip cream with ¼ cup sugar. Spread ⅔ of the whipped cream over meringue on bottom cake layer. Arrange berries on whipped cream. Add top layer, meringue side up. Top with remaining whipped cream and whole berries.

MRS. JOHN CAMPBELL

MOCHA MYSTERY CAKE

1 box chocolate cake mix
1 cup milk
¼ cup salad oil
1 cup brown sugar
1 cup granulated sugar

½ cup cocoa
¼ teaspoon cinnamon
2 cups cold strong coffee
2 ounces brandy

Add milk and salad oil to cake mix in large bowl of electric mixer. Beat for 4 minutes and spread in greased and floured 9x13 pan. Mix brown sugar, sugar, cocoa and cinnamon. Sprinkle evenly over cake batter. Add brandy to coffee and pour over top. The cake now looks terrible, but cooks up into its own sauce. Bake at 350° for 35 to 40 minutes, or until thoroughly done. Cool and serve.

MRS. RICHARD BILGER

SPECIAL TIP

Add milk instead of water in all cake mixes (and most other mixes, such as corn muffins, etc.) for a more moist and richer product.

Icings

THE EASIEST CHOCOLATE ICING (UNCOOKED)

1 package (6-ounces)
    semi-sweet chocolate bits
3 tablespoons butter
⅓ cup hot milk

2¼ cups sifted powdered sugar
¼ teaspoon salt
½ teaspoon vanilla

Melt chocolate and butter over hot water. Stir hot milk into salt and sugar. Add vanilla, then chocolate mixture, and beat until smooth. Makes icing for 2 layers.

MRS. ERVIN JACKSON, JR.

CHOCOLATE ICING FOR SHEET CAKE

1 stick margarine
4 tablespoons cocoa
6 tablespoons milk
1 cup small marshmallows

1 box powdered sugar
1 teaspoon vanilla
1 cup chopped pecans
(optional)

Start icing five minutes before cake is done. Mix together and bring to a boil the margarine, cocoa, milk and marshmallows. Remove from heat and add powdered sugar, vanilla and nuts. Beat well and spread on a hot cake. (Use your favorite recipe for a 13x9x2 size cake.) Leave in pan to cool.

MRS. DOUGLAS BOOTH

EXACTLY ONE MINUTE CHOCOLATE ICING

2 cups sugar
3 tablespoons cocoa
1 stick butter

⅓ cup milk
Pinch of salt

Mix all ingredients well, place over heat and when mixture comes to full boil, boil exactly one minute by the clock, stirring often. Remove from heat and beat until cool with electric mixer. It hardens as it cools. Will ice 2 layers or one sheet cake.

MRS. DOUGLAS BOOTH

CHOCOLATE-COFFEE ICING

1 box confectioners sugar
4 to 5 tablespoons hot coffee,
  drinking strength

4 tablespoons cocoa
¾ stick of margarine (very soft)
1 teaspoon vanilla

Put sugar in electric mixer bowl. Make a hole in the sugar, put softened margarine in this, and pour hot coffee over. Add vanilla and cocoa. Beat until smooth and of spreading consistency. Will ice a 9-inch 2 layer cake.

MRS. DOUGLAS BOOTH

CHOCOLATE LEMON ICING

1 box confectioners sugar
½ cup (1 stick) margarine
2 bags Choco-bake (or 2 squares
  melted chocolate)
2 teaspoons lemon juice

1 egg
1 teaspoon vanilla
¼ teaspoon salt
½ cup nuts (optional)

Mix sugar, butter and chocolate. Add lemon juice and egg, which has been thoroughly beaten. Add vanilla, salt and nuts. Beat until smooth, then spread. Will ice an 8-inch 2 layer cake or sheet cake.

MRS. DOUGLAS BOOTH

LAPLANDER FROSTING (CHOCOLATE)

2 whole eggs or 4 yolks
4½ tablespoons cream
3 tablespoons butter or margarine
1½ cups sugar
3 squares unsweetened chocolate
1 teaspoon vanilla

Beat eggs until light. Add other ingredients, except vanilla, and cook in 2-quart heavy saucepan on high heat until mixture boils. Stir constantly and watch carefully to prevent burning. Remove from heat. Pour in electric mixer, or beat by hand, until mixture is cold. Add vanilla and continue beating until thick enough to spread. Will ice a 2-layer 8-inch cake. Double recipe for larger cake. For good fudge sauce: substitute ¾ cup whole milk for the cream.

MRS. P. M. SMITH, JR.

PENUCHE ICING (COOKED—CARAMEL)

½ cup butter
1 cup brown sugar (packed)
¼ cup milk
1¾ to 2 cups sifted 4x sugar

Melt butter in large saucepan. Add 1 cup brown sugar. Boil over low heat 2 minutes, stirring constantly. Add milk and bring to boil, stirring constantly. Take off heat and beat about 5 minutes. Gradually add the sifted 4x sugar. Beat until thick enough to spread. If too thick, add milk. Wonderful on honey spice cake. Ices 2-layer 8-inch cake or one 13x9-inch sheet cake.

MRS. ERVIN JACKSON, JR.
MRS. WILLIAM D. THOMAS

SEVEN MINUTE SEA FOAM ICING

2 egg whites, room temperature
1½ cups firmly packed brown sugar
⅛ teaspoon salt
5 tablespoons water
1 teaspoon vanilla

Place all ingredients except vanilla in top of double boiler, which is over boiling water. Beat constantly for 5 minutes. Occasionally scrape sides with rubber spatula. Remove from fire, but leave over boiling water. Beat 2 minutes longer. Add vanilla. Place icing in cold water and beat 2 minutes. Frosts 2 9-inch cake layers. (Good with spiced or chocolate cake.)

SEVEN MINUTE WHITE ICING

2 egg whites, room temperature
1½ cups sugar
5 tablespoons cold water
¼ teaspoon cream of tartar
1 to 2 teaspoons vanilla

Place all ingredients except vanilla in top of double boiler, which is over boiling water. Beat constantly for 7 minutes. Occasionally scrape sides with rubber spatula. Remove from fire and add vanilla. Continue beating until icing is right consistency to spread — about 1 minute. Spread immediately on two 9-inch cake layers.

QUICK MILE HIGH WHITE ICING

2 egg whites
1 cup white corn syrup
  or 1 cup of tart red jelly

2 teaspoons vanilla

Into large mixing bowl, put 2 egg whites and syrup or jelly. Start beating on low speed, then increase to high. Add vanilla and beat until mixture will hold shape. Spread on 9-inch layer cake or sheet cake.

MRS. P. M. SMITH, JR.

Cookies

APRICOT BALLS

2 boxes dried apricots
2 large cans Angel Flake coconut
1 can Eagle Brand condensed
  milk

½ cup pecans, chopped
  (optional)
Sifted confectioners sugar

Grind apricots, add coconut and nuts and mix with fork. Add milk gradually and mix with hands until large pinch will roll into ball. (This uses about ¾-can of milk, but add small amount at a time.) Roll mixture into balls, then roll in sifted confectioners sugar. Put in tight can with waxed paper between layers, refrigerate, and roll in sugar again before serving. Makes 12 to 14 dozen. Make marble-sized for tea. Excellent for sherry parties because of tartness.

MRS. JULIAN WRIGHT CLARKSON

APRICOT BROWNIES

½ cup butter
2 cups light brown sugar, firmly
  packed
2 eggs
1¾ cups flour
2 teaspoons baking powder

½ teaspoon salt (scant)
1½ teaspoons vanilla
½ cup pecans, chopped
  (optional)
¾ cup dried apricots, chopped
  and patted with flour

Cream butter and sugar. Add eggs, one at a time. Add flour, sifted with baking powder and salt. Add remaining ingredients and mix well. Pour into greased oblong 2-quart Pyrex dish. Batter should be ¾-inch thick. Bake at 350° for 25 to 30 minutes. Turn down heat to 275° and continue baking for 18 to 20 minutes or until golden brown. Do not overcook. Makes 32 to 40 squares.

MRS. RICHARD D. GILLESPIE

BILLY GOAT COOKIES

1 cup butter or margarine
2 cups sugar
3 eggs
4 cups flour
4 teaspoons baking powder
½ teaspoon soda

2 teaspoons cinnamon
½ teaspoon ground cloves
½ cup sour cream
1 teaspoon vanilla
2 7-ounce packages pitted dates,
  chopped

Cream butter or margarine with sugar. Add eggs. Sift flour, baking powder, soda, cinnamon and cloves. Add to sugar mixture along with sour cream. Add vanilla and dates. Drop by heaping teaspoonfuls on cookie sheet and bake at 350° for 10 to 12 minutes. Makes 7 to 8 dozen.

MRS. MOFFATT G. SHERARD, JR.

ICED BLONDIES

⅔ cup butter
2 cups light brown sugar
2 cups flour
1 teaspoon baking powder
1 teaspoon salt

2 whole eggs
2 egg yolks
1 teaspoon vanilla
1 cup chopped nuts (optional)

Melt butter and brown sugar over low heat. Mix remaining ingredients together. Combine both mixtures and pour into greased 9x12-inch pan. Bake at 350° for 25 to 30 minutes. Ice while warm. Cool and cut into squares.

ICING

4 tablespoons butter
4 tablespoons milk

⅔ cup brown sugar
1½ cups powdered sugar

Boil the butter, milk and brown sugar for 2 minutes. Beat the powdered sugar in after removing from heat. Use to ice the brownies as soon as they are taken from oven.

MRS. JOHN R. CAMPBELL

"GRANNY" WELLON'S BLONDE BROWNIES

2 cups light brown sugar
2 eggs
1 stick margarine
½ teaspoon salt

1 cup flour
1 cup chopped pecans
1 teaspoon vanilla
½ teaspoon baking soda

Cream butter and sugar; add eggs one at a time, beating well. Add all other ingredients. Beat. Grease a 9x12-inch pan and pour in mixture. Cook at 350° for 25 minutes. Do not overcook.

MRS. HARLEY GASTON, JR.

BLUE RIBBON FUDGE BROWNIES

2 ounces unsweetened chocolate
½ cup butter
2 eggs
1 cup sugar
1 cup flour
½ teaspoon baking powder

½ teaspoon salt
1 cup apple sauce
1 cup chopped nuts (optional)
½ cup raisins (optional)
1 teaspoon vanilla

Combine chocolate and butter and melt. Beat eggs until light and lemon-colored. Gradually add sugar. Stir in chocolate mixture. Beat for 1 minute. Sift together flour, baking powder, and salt and stir into mixture. Add apple sauce, nuts, raisins, and vanilla. Put in greased 9x13x2-inch pan. Bake at 350° for 20 to 30 minutes. Makes 2 dozen.

MRS. DONALD S. MCMILLAN

ICED FUDGY BROWNIES

2 sticks margarine
4 ounces unsweetened chocolate
4 eggs, beaten
2 cups sugar

½ cup flour
1 tablespoon vanilla
1¼ cups nuts (optional)

Melt chocolate and margarine over low heat. In mixing bowl, beat eggs slightly and add sugar. Pour in chocolate mixture. Add flour, vanilla and nuts and mix well. Bake at 325° for approximately 25 minutes, or until fudgy, in 13x7-inch pan. Cool. Spread with the following icing.

ICING
¼ pound margarine
2 cups confectioners sugar
4 tablespoons cream

3 tablespoons cocoa
1 teaspoon vanilla

Mix all together in electric mixer. Spread on cooled brownies. Cut into squares. Makes about 36 to 40 brownies. (These are very moist and stay fresh for days.)

MRS. TERRY YOUNG

FUDGE CAKE (BROWNIES)

3 eggs
1½ cups sugar
1 stick real butter
3 squares unsweetened
chocolate

1½ teaspoons vanilla
¼ teaspoon salt
¾ cup flour
1 cup chopped nuts

Beat eggs until light. Add sugar and half of butter. Melt chocolate with rest of butter and pour into egg mixture; then add rest of ingredients and mix well. Bake in greased 8-inch square pan at 350° for 25 to 35 minutes. Cut into squares while warm, but allow to cool before taking from pan.

MRS. GEORGE B. ADAMS, JR.

CHOCOLATE MINT BROWNIES

½ cup butter
1 cup sugar
2 eggs
1 teaspoon vanilla
2 squares chocolate, melted
½ cup flour
½ cup nuts (optional)

1 cup confectioners sugar
2 tablespoons butter
1 tablespoon light cream
¼ to ½ teaspoon peppermint extract
Melted chocolate

Cream butter and sugar. Beat in eggs and vanilla. Blend in chocolate. Stir in flour and nuts. Bake in 8x8-inch greased pan for 25 minutes in 325° oven. Cool. Combine remaining ingredients and spread on top of cooled brownies. Drizzle with desired amount of melted chocolate. (You can use chocolate chips or sweetened chocolate squares.)

MRS. THOMAS N. MASSEY

BROWNIE CUP CAKES

4 squares unsweetened
chocolate
2 sticks margarine
1½ cups broken pecans (optional)

1¾ cups sugar
1 cup flour
4 large eggs
1 teaspoon vanilla

Melt chocolate and margarine over low heat in heavy saucepan. Add nuts and stir to coat. Remove from heat. Combine sugar, flour, eggs and vanilla. Mix only to blend (do not beat). Add chocolate-nut mixture and mix carefully. Put into 20 baking cups. Fill almost to the top as they don't rise much. Bake at 325° for 30 to 35 minutes.

MRS. DENNIS MYERS
MISS FRANCES WADDILL

CHRISTMAS BOURBON BALLS

1 6-ounce package chocolate chips
¼ cup bourbon
2 tablespoons white corn syrup
¼ cup water
1 cup chopped pecans
2½ cups vanilla wafers, crushed fine
Powdered sugar (about ½ cup)

Melt chocolate in ¼ cup water. Stir in syrup and bourbon. (Add more bourbon if you like stronger flavor.) Add nuts and wafer crumbs. Mix well and let stand for 20 minutes. Make into small balls. Roll in powdered sugar. Makes about 40.

MRS. FRANK H. CONNER, JR.

CHEWY COOKIES

1⅓ sticks margarine
2 cups light brown sugar, packed
2 eggs, beaten slightly
1 cup coconut
1 cup flour
1 teaspoon vanilla

Cream margarine and sugar slightly. Add eggs, then remaining ingredients. Bake in greased 12x7-inch pan at 325° for 40 to 45 minutes, or until done. Cut while warm, but leave in pan until cool. These are chewy and delicious. Makes about 28.

MRS. TERRY YOUNG

CHOCOLATE CRISPIES

4 squares unsweetened chocolate, melted
1 cup butter or margarine
2 cups sugar
4 eggs, unbeaten
1 cup flour, sifted
1 teaspoon vanilla
½ to 1 cup pecans, finely chopped

Melt chocolate in ¼-cup butter. Cool slightly. Cream sugar with the rest of butter; add eggs and then melted chocolate, mixing all well. Stir in flour and vanilla. Spread evenly on ungreased cookie sheet with sides. Sprinkle chopped nuts evenly on top of batter. Bake at 375° for 15 to 17 minutes. Cut in small squares and take out of pan while warm or they will stick. Keep in tin or other tight container.

MRS. CHARLES L. WICKHAM, JR.

CHRISTMAS COOKIES

1 cup margarine
1½ cups dark brown sugar
3 cups plain flour
1 teaspoon soda, dissolved in small amount warm water
2 teaspoons cinnamon
3 eggs
1 teaspoon allspice
1 teaspoon vanilla
1 teaspoon salt
1 pound large seeded raisins
1 pound chopped pecans (4 cups)

Cream margarine, sugar and eggs. Add remaining ingredients. Drop by teaspoons on greased cookie sheet. Bake at 300° for 20 minutes. Makes about 12 dozen.

MRS. THORNWELL G. GUTHERY

CORNFLAKE-OATMEAL DROP COOKIES

1 cup shortening (Crisco is best)
1 cup brown sugar
1 cup granulated sugar
2 eggs
1½ cups flour, sifted
1 teaspoon soda
½ teaspoon salt
½ teaspoon vanilla
2 cups oatmeal
1 cup cornflakes
1 cup pecans, chopped
1 6-ounce package chocolate chips

Cream shortening and sugar; add beaten eggs. Sift flour, soda, and salt together and add to shortening and sugar. Add vanilla, oatmeal, cornflakes, pecans, and chocolate chips, and mix. Drop by spoonfuls onto cookie sheet and bake at 350° for 10 minutes, or until lightly browned. Makes 6 to 7 dozen.

MRS. C. E. WILLIAMS, JR.

COWBOY COOKIES

1 cup granulated sugar
1 cup brown sugar
1 cup shortening (Crisco)
2 eggs, unbeaten
1 teaspoon vanilla
2 cups sifted flour
½ teaspoon baking powder
1 teaspoon baking soda
½ teaspoon salt
2 cups rolled oats (old-fashioned, not quick-cooking)
1 small package chocolate chips
1 cup chopped pecans

Cream sugar and shortening; add eggs and vanilla. Sift together flour, salt, baking powder and baking soda, and add. Mix well. Add oatmeal, chopped nuts and chocolate chips. Spoon in small amounts on greased cookie sheet and bake at 350° for 12 to 15 minutes. Makes 7 to 8 dozen cookies.

MRS. EVERETT L. WOHLBRUCK

CREAM CHEESE COOKIES

1 stick real butter
1 3-ounce package cream cheese
1 cup sugar
1 cup plain flour
½ teaspoon vanilla
9 English walnuts, chopped

Cream butter and cheese. Add sugar and mix well. Add flour, vanilla and nuts. Drop by teaspoons on ungreased cookie sheet. Bake at 375° until brown. (These burn easily, so watch them.) Makes approximately 3 dozen.

MRS. RUFUS S. PLONK, JR.

CZECHOSLOVAKIAN COOKIES

½ pound butter
1 cup sugar
2 egg yolks
2 cups flour
1 cup walnuts, chopped
½ cup apricot jam

Cream butter and sugar. Add egg yolks, then flour and nuts. Divide batter in half, putting half in 8x8-inch greased pan with sides. Spread with jam. (You can substitute any jam.) Put other half of batter on top. Bake at 325° for 1 hour.

MRS. JOHN R. CAMPBELL

DANISH PASTRY COOKIES

3 egg yolks
1 cup sugar
1 stick butter

1 cup nuts, chopped
1 cup dates, chopped
1 cup coconut
1 pie crust

Combine and cream together yolks, sugar and butter. Add dates, nuts, and coconut and mix well. Roll pie crust to a 9x12 size. With your hands, spread the date mixture thinly over the pie crust on a flat pan, making sure the edges are the same thickness. Bake at 350° for 20 minutes. Remove from oven and immediately spread the icing on top. (If icing doesn't melt enough, put back in oven for a minute.) Cool slightly and cut into very small squares. These are very rich. Makes about 50 small squares.

ICING

2 cups confectioners sugar
½ stick butter

2 tablespoons lemon juice and grated rind

Mix together and spread on cookies. If necessary, add 1 or 2 teaspoons hot water to thin for spreading.

MRS. ELLEN G. GOODE

DATE BARS

2 cups brown sugar
2 cups flour
4 eggs
2 teaspoons baking powder
1 package dates, chopped fine

1 cup pecans, chopped
¼ teaspoon cinnamon
¼ teaspoon ground cloves
2 tablespoons melted butter
½ teaspoon vanilla

Mix as for a cake. Spread in a shallow 9x13-inch pan. Bake in 375° oven about 20 minutes. Cool slightly. Cut in squares.

OLD NORTH STATE COOKBOOK

DATE ROLLS

1 cup sugar
1 egg
1 stick butter
1 package dates (ground in
   blender)

2 cups Rice Krispies
1 cup pecans (finely chopped)
1 cup Angel Flake coconut

Place sugar and butter over low heat. Stir and let come to bubble. Beat egg and add a little melted mixture to it, then add all to hot mixture. Stir in dates, nuts, and Rice Krispies. Mix well and cool. Shape in crescents and roll in coconut. Put in waxed paper and refrigerate. These keep well. Makes 4 to 5 dozen.

MRS. THOMAS W. BAKER

"DEADLYS" (DESSERT COOKIES)

1 stick butter
1½ squares bitter chocolate
1 cup sugar
⅔ cup flour, not sifted

1 teaspoon vanilla
2 eggs, well beaten
1 cup chopped nuts

Melt chocolate and butter over low heat. Remove from heat and mix in all other ingredients. Pour into paper baking cups, filling half full. Bake for 15 minutes in 350° oven on a cookie sheet. Makes about 18 to 20 standard cupcake size, 35 to 40 tiny cups.

ICING

2 tablespoons butter
1 square bitter chocolate

2 cups 4x sugar
½ cup cold liquid coffee

While "deadlys" are cooking, melt butter with chocolate. Remove from heat. Add powdered sugar and enough cold coffee to make mix smooth. Put icing on cakes while hot. Refrigerate at least 3 hours. Freeze if you desire; thaw for 1 hour.

MRS. ERVIN JACKSON, JR.

DROP FRUIT CAKE COOKIES

1 stick butter
1 cup light brown sugar, firmly
  packed
4 eggs
2 ounces brandy or bourbon
3 teaspoons soda dissolved in
  3 tablespoons milk
1 pound dates, chopped

1 pound cherries, chopped
1 pound pineapple, chopped
1½ pounds white raisins
2½ (or more) cups nuts, chopped
3 cups flour
¾ teaspoon nutmeg
¾ teaspoon mace

Roll candied, chopped fruit in one cup of the flour. Put aside. Cream butter and sugar. Add one egg at a time, beating well after each. Add bourbon, milk, spices, and flour. Last, add the fruit and nuts. (This batter is so thick that I have to mix it with my hands.) Drop by teaspoons onto well-greased cookie sheets. Bake at 300° for 15 to 18 minutes. Remove from pans immediately to cool. Makes about 200 cookies. These freeze well.

MRS. DONALD S. MCMILLAN

HERSHEY BAR COOKIES

½ cup butter
½ cup brown sugar
1 cup flour

½ teaspoon vanilla
4-5 small Hershey bars
Pecans, finely chopped

Mix softened butter, sugar, vanilla and flour together. Press into a 9-inch pan and bake for 10 to 15 minutes in 350° oven. While hot, place Hershey bars on top and add nuts over chocolate. If necessary, put back in oven with heat turned off to completely melt chocolate.

MRS. TERRY YOUNG

ICE BOX COOKIES

½ cup white sugar
½ cup brown sugar
1 cup butter
1 egg, unbeaten
2½ cups flour

½ teaspoon soda
½ teaspoon cinnamon
½ cup chopped blanched almonds
    or coconut
Pinch of salt

Mix, knead, and make into a roll (or two rolls) about as big around as a water glass. Let stand in refrigerator overnight or longer. Slice as thin as possible, and bake until lightly browned in a 375° oven. Do not grease cookie sheet. Remove soon after taking from oven, or they stick and may break.

MRS. RICHARD K. SIMS*

JAM COOKIES

3 sticks butter
1 cup sugar
2 egg yolks

3 cups flour
1 teaspoon vanilla
1 small jar raspberry jam

Soften butter. Add sugar and cream. Add egg yolks, then flour and vanilla, mixing thoroughly. Pinch off small pieces and roll into a ball in palm of hand. Make identation in center of each with finger. Put in wee bit of raspberry jam. Bake at 375° to 400° for 10 to 12 minutes. If batter becomes sticky, lightly dust hands with flour. These freeze beautifully.

MRS. GEORGE IVEY, JR.

KISSES

3 egg whites
1 cup sugar
Pinch of salt

1 cup chopped dates
1 cup chopped pecans

Put egg whites, sugar and salt into mixing bowl of electric mixer. Set at medium. Beat until very stiff. Add dates and pecans. Drop by teaspoons on waxed paper on cookie sheet. Bake at 200° for 25 to 30 minutes. Do not allow to brown. Makes 40 to 42.

MRS. WALTER SCOTT, JR.

LEMON BARS

2 sticks butter
½ cup powdered sugar
2 cups flour
4 eggs, beaten well
½ teaspoon salt

2 cups sugar
8 tablespoons lemon juice
½ tablespoon grated lemon rind
4 tablespoons flour
1 teaspoon baking powder

Cream first three ingredients together. Spread evenly on ungreased cookie sheet with sides. Cook at 350° for 15 minutes or until brown. Beat eggs and mix with remaining ingredients. Add on top of cooked pastry. Bake at 325° for 30 minutes. Sprinkle with powdered sugar. Cool for 15 minutes, then cut in oblong "finger" shapes. Makes about 32. Store in refrigerator. Can be made several days ahead.

MRS. JOHN HILLHOUSE

M & M COOKIES

1 cup shortening
1 cup brown sugar
1 cup granulated sugar
2 teaspoons vanilla
2 eggs

2¼ cups sifted all-purpose flour
1 teaspoon soda
1 teaspoon salt
1 cup plain M&M candies

Blend shortening and sugars. Beat in vanilla and eggs. Sift remaining dry ingredients together; add to the sugar and egg mixture. Mix well. Stir in M & M's. Drop from teaspoon onto greased cookie sheet. Bake at 375° for 10 to 12 minutes, until golden brown. Makes about 100 cookies.

MISS CRAIG MASON

MINCE MEAT COOKIES

3¼ cups sifted flour
½ teaspoon salt
1 teaspoon baking soda
1 cup shortening

1½ cups sugar
3 eggs, well beaten
1 9-ounce package mince meat

Sift together flour, salt and soda. Cream shortening and gradually add sugar, creaming until fluffy. Add eggs and beat until smooth. Add flour mixture and mince meat, mixing well. Drop by teaspoonfuls on greased cookie sheet. Bake at 400° for about 10-12 minutes. Makes 4 dozen cookies.

MRS. RALPH H. ALEXANDER, JR.

NAMAIMO BARS

½ cup butter
5 teaspoons cocoa
2 teaspoons vanilla
¼ cup sugar

2 cups graham cracker crumbs
½ cup nuts, chopped
1 cup grated coconut

Mix butter, cocoa, vanilla and sugar and heat until slightly thick. Stir in graham cracker crumbs, nuts and coconut. Pack in greased pan and chill. When cool, top with mixtures below.

TOPPING #1

½ cup margarine
2 tablespoons milk
2 teaspoons vanilla

2 cups powdered sugar
2 teaspoons Jello vanilla pudding mix

Melt butter and stir in rest of ingredients, mixing well. Spread on first mixture. Chill, and cover with the following:

TOPPING #2

1 teaspoon butter

4 or 5 squares semi-sweet chocolate

Melt butter and chocolate together. Spread on as final topping.

Use 13x9x2 pan for single batch. Cut in squares like brownies. Keep in refrigerator.

MRS. HUGH CAMPBELL

NUTTY FINGERS

1¼ sticks butter
4 tablespoons powdered sugar
1 tablespoon ice water

1 tablespoon vanilla
2 cups sifted flour
1 cup nuts, chopped fine

Cream butter and sifted sugar and add water. Add vanilla, flour and nuts, mixing well. Roll out in shape of fingers or in small balls. Place on greased or Teflon cookie sheet. Bake in 350° oven for 15 to 20 minutes. When cool, roll in powdered sugar. These keep for days.

MRS. JOHN W. MCALISTER III*

OATMEAL COOKIES

¾ cup Crisco
1 cup brown sugar
½ cup granulated sugar
1 egg
¼ cup water

1 teaspoon vanilla
1 cup sifted flour
1 teaspoon salt
½ teaspoon soda
3 cups oats, uncooked

Place Crisco, sugar, egg, water and vanilla in bowl. Beat thoroughly. Sift together flour, salt and soda. Add to first mixture, mixing well. Blend in oats and drop by teaspoons on greased cookie sheets. Bake at 350° for 12 to 15 minutes. Makes about 4 dozen. (For variety, add butterscotch chips, nuts, or raisins to dough.)

MISS COURTNEY DICK

PEANUT BUTTER SQUARES

½ cup margarine
½ cup white sugar
¼ cup brown sugar
1 egg
⅓ cup peanut butter
½ teaspoon soda

¼ teaspoon salt
½ teaspoon vanilla
1 cup all purpose flour
1 cup quick-cooking oatmeal
1 cup chocolate chips (or more)

Cream butter and sugars well. Blend in egg, peanut butter, soda, salt, and vanilla. Add flour and oatmeal and mix well. Spread in greased 13x9-inch pan. Bake at 350° for 20 to 25 minutes. While hot, sprinkle with 1 cup chocolate chips. Spread evenly over top. Cool. Spread with following frosting.

FROSTING

½ cup sifted confectioners sugar
¼ cup peanut butter

4 tablespoons evaporated milk
or 4 tablespoons whole milk

Mix together and drizzle over peanut butter squares. Makes about 36.

MRS. CHARLES POLLARD

PECAN SLICES

1 cup plain flour
½ cup butter
2 eggs, beaten
1½ cups brown sugar
1 cup chopped pecans
2 tablespoons flour

½ teaspoon baking powder
½ teaspoon salt
1 teaspoon vanilla
1½ cups confectioners sugar
Juice of 1 small lemon

Sift 1 cup flour and mix with butter until it is a smooth paste. Spread in a 9x12-inch pan and bake at 350° for 12 minutes. Combine eggs, brown sugar, pecans, 2 tablespoons flour, baking powder, salt and vanilla. Spread on flour and butter cake. Bake at 350° for 25 minutes. When cool, spread with confectioners sugar thinned to spreading consistency with lemon juice. Cut in oblongs.

MRS. FRANCES K. AKERS

POUND CAKE WAFERS

2½ sticks real butter
1 cup sugar
2 egg yolks

3 cups flour, sifted
1 teaspoon vanilla
Cherry halves or pecans

Cream butter and add sugar gradually. Add egg yolks one at a time. Add flour gradually. Add flavoring last. Drop by teaspoonfuls on ungreased cookie sheet and bake at 350° for 12 to 15 minutes. Garnish before baking with cherry halves or pecans. Makes 5 to 6 dozen cookies.

MRS. VAN L. WEATHERSPOON*

PUMPKIN COOKIES

2 cups flour
1 teaspoon baking powder
1 teaspoon soda
1 teaspoon cinnamon
½ teaspoon salt
1 cup shortening

1 cup sugar
1 egg
1 cup canned pumpkin
1 teaspoon vanilla
½ cup chopped nuts
½ cup dates or raisins

Sift dry ingredients together. Cream shortening, sugar and egg together. Add remaining ingredients and flour mixture. Drop by teaspoons on cookie sheet and bake at 350° for 10 to 12 minutes.

MRS. JOHN R. CAMPBELL

SHORTBREAD

2 sticks butter
½ cup sugar

2½ cups unsifted regular flour
Pinch of salt

Soften butter; add dry ingredients; mix with fork or hand. Press into 9x9-inch pan. Cook 30 to 35 minutes in 325° oven. This is a good base for strawberry shortcake. Also, good as cookie or brownie.

MRS. JAMES WARD WELLER*

ROCKS

1 cup sugar
⅔ cup butter
2 whole eggs
1 teaspoon soda
1 teaspoon warm water
2 cups flour

Dash of salt
2 teaspoons cinnamon
1 teaspoon cloves
½ teaspoon allspice
¾ to 1 pound seedless raisins
½ to 1 pound pecans, chopped

Cream sugar and butter. Add eggs and mix well. Dissolve soda in warm water. Sift dry ingredients together and add to egg mixture. Combine all ingredients with pecans and raisins, blending well in electric mixer. The dough must be stiff. Drop from a teaspoon on well buttered cookie sheet and bake at 350° for about 12 minutes. Take them from the pan immediately or they will stick and crumble.

MRS. CHARLES L. WICKHAM, JR.

OLD FASHIONED SUGAR COOKIES

1 cup real butter
1 cup sugar
2 small eggs or 1 large egg
1 teaspoon vanilla

2½ to 3 cups flour
½ scant teaspoon salt
½ scant teaspoon soda

Cream butter and sugar until fluffy. Add egg and blend well. Add vanilla and blend. Sift dry ingredients and add to mixture. Refrigerate several hours or overnight, covered. Roll small portion at a time. Cut into shapes, sprinkle with sugar, and bake at 350° for 10 to 12 minutes on greased cookie sheet. Better when rolled thin. Richer when only 2½ cups flour are used. Makes about 8 dozen.

MRS. JOHN C. MARKEY

SWEDISH CAKES

½ cup butter
½ cup brown sugar
1 egg, slightly beaten
1 cup flour

1 small jar red or green currant jelly
1½ cups pecans, chopped in blender

Cream butter, sugar, and egg. Add flour and mix. Form into small balls and roll in finely chopped nuts. Bake at 300° for 15 minutes. Remove and press down centers and fill with jelly. Cool.

MRS. JOHN R. CAMPBELL

SPECIAL TIP

To make chocolate brownies different: ice each one with a thick layer of sour cream and eat it with a spoon.

MRS. JAMES S. WILCOX, JR.

$\mathcal{D}$esserts

ANGEL BAVARIAN

2 cups milk
1 cup sugar
4 eggs
2 tablespoons flour
Pinch of salt
1 tablespoon plain gelatin

½ cup cold water or cream
  sherry
1½ pints whipping cream
1 large angel food cake
Coconut and maraschino cherries

Make a custard of the sugar, flour, egg yolks, milk, and salt. Cook in a double boiler until thick. Dissolve gelatin in water or sherry and put into custard while hot. Let cool. Fold in 1 pint of the cream, whipped, and 4 stiffly beaten egg whites. Break up the cake in a tube pan and pour in custard. Let this stand 6 hours or overnight.

After the cake is turned out on a plate, ice with remaining half-pint of cream, whipped. Sprinkle with coconut and cherries. (Fresh strawberries may also be used as a topping.) Serves 12 to 14.

MRS. THOMAS M. BARNHARDT III

ANGEL KISS CAKE

4 egg whites
1½ cups sugar
2 teaspoons baking powder
1 teaspoon vanilla

4 cups whipped cream (or
  Smooth Whip)
Green food coloring

Beat egg whites stiff, gradually adding 1 cup sugar. Sift ½-cup sugar with baking powder and fold lightly into egg whites by hand. Fold in vanilla. Spread in well-greased and floured 9x12-inch pan. Bake at 250° for 1 hour. Cool. Leave in pan.

Whip cream. Tint light green. Spread 2 cups whipped cream over cooled meringue. Make lemon filling and spread over whipped cream. Spread remaining cream on top. Chill in refrigerator at least 3 hours. Serves 12.

LEMON FILLING

1 15-ounce can Eagle Brand
  condensed milk
½ cup lemon juice

2 teaspoons grated lemon rind
  or ¼ teaspoon lemon extract
2 egg yolks

Combine ingredients and stir until mixture is well blended. Pour over meringue with whipped cream layer.

MRS. TERRY YOUNG

INSTANT APPLE COBBLER

¾ stick butter
1 tablespoon lemon juice
6 cups sliced apples
2 cups sugar

1 cup flour
3 teaspoons baking powder
Dash of salt
½ cup milk

Melt butter in 7x11-inch pan. Mix lemon juice and half the sugar with apples. Add to butter. Mix dry ingredients with milk and pour over apples. Sprinkle with cinnamon. Bake at 375° for 45 minutes. Serves 6 to 8.

MRS. NORMAN S. RICHARDS

APPLE CRISP

8 apples
1 teaspoon cinnamon
¼ teaspoon salt
½ cup water

7 tablespoons butter
1½ cups brown sugar
¾ cup flour

Grease oblong Pyrex dish with butter. Peel and slice apples. Sprinkle with cinnamon and salt. Add water. Mix butter, sugar, and flour, but do not cream until smooth. Sprinkle mixture over apples and bake for 1 hour at 325°. Serve hot or cold, topped with whipped cream or ice cream. Serves 6 to 8.

MRS. GENE W. McGARITY

APPLE CRUNCH

6 tart apples, pared and sliced
thin
¾ cup Quaker oats
¾ cup sugar (half white and
half brown)

¼ cup flour
1 stick butter or margarine
½ cup water

Slice apples into 8-inch square greased casserole. Mix oats, sugars, and flour together. Add melted butter and spread over apples. Add ½-cup water. Cook at 375° for 45 to 60 minutes. Serve warm. Top with whipped cream or vanilla ice cream if desired. Serves 4 to 6.

MRS. JOHN A. BRABSON

YUMMY APPLE DESSERT

4 cups cut up, peeled apples
½ cup water
1 teaspoon cinnamon
1 stick butter

1 cup sugar
¾ cup sifted flour
½ cup chopped pecans

Put apples, water, and cinnamon together in oblong Pyrex dish. Mix together butter, sugar, and flour until creamy. Pat on top of apple mixture. Sprinkle with nuts. Cook, uncovered, for 1 hour in 300° oven.

MRS. KEMP DUNAWAY

APPLE SAUCE DANDY

¼ cup margarine
10 graham crackers, crushed
2 tablespoons brown sugar

½ teaspoon cinnamon
⅛ teaspoon salt
2 cans apple sauce

Melt margarine in skillet; add graham cracker crumbs, sugar and cinnamon; brown slightly. Pour half the crumb mixture in 8″ square baking dish, then pour in 2 cans apple sauce. Cover with remainder of crumb mixture. Bake at 375° for 15 minutes. Top with whipped cream or ice cream and serve, preferably slightly warm. (Nuts may be added to crumb mixture if desired.) Serves 6.

MISS VIRGINIA KILROY

BLACKBERRY COBBLER

CRUST
1½ cups flour
½ cup shortening
Dash of salt
½ cup ice water

FILLING
1 quart blackberries
1 cup sugar
Pinch of cinnamon
¼ cup butter

Combine crust ingredients and roll out thin. Grease 2-quart baking dish. Put three-fourths of the dough on bottom of baking dish (leave one-fourth for top crust). Combine blackberries, sugar, and cinnamon. Pour half of berry mixture into dish. Dot with butter. Pour other half of berry mixture in. Place rest of dough on top in strips. Cook at 350° for 1 hour, or until crust is browned. (Excellent with vanilla ice cream or a hard sauce.) Serves 6 to 8.

MRS. SAM H. McDONALD

BLUEBERRY TORTE

16 double graham crackers, rolled into crumbs
½ cup butter
2 cups sugar
2 eggs
1 package cream cheese (8 ounces)

5 tablespoons cornstarch
2 tablespoons lemon juice
1 can Thank You blueberries
½ pint whipping cream, whipped

Combine crumbs, ½ cup sugar, and butter. Mix and line a 10-inch square pan. Beat eggs, ½-cup sugar, and cream cheese until smooth. Pour over crumb mixture and bake for 20 minutes at 350°.

While this bakes, make topping. Blend cornstarch, 1 cup sugar, lemon juice and juice of blueberries. Cook until thick. Cool and add blueberries. Pour over baked mixture. When ready to serve, spread with whipped cream. Serves 10 to 12. Can be made a day ahead.

MRS. LARRY J. DAGENHART*

BISCUIT TORTONI

2 egg whites
¼ cup granulated sugar
1 cup heavy cream, whipped
½ cup macaroon crumbs

2 tablespoons brandy or rum
2 tablespoons maraschino cherry
liqueur

Beat egg whites until stiff. Beat in sugar, a bit at a time. Fold egg whites into whipped cream *gently* but thoroughly. Fold in all but six teaspoons of crumbs. Add flavoring and cherry liqueur. Spoon into paper baking cups. Sprinkle with crumbs. Top with rosette or cherry. Freeze. Serves 6.

MISS VIRGINIA KILROY

QUICK CHEESE CAKE

2 large packages cream cheese
3 eggs
¾ cup sugar
½ teaspoon almond extract

1 cup sour cream
3 tablespoons sugar
1 teaspoon vanilla

Beat cream cheese, eggs, sugar and almond extract for 20 minutes at medium speed, until smooth. Pour into a well-greased 9-inch pie pan. Bake at 350° for 25 minutes. Allow to cool for 20 minutes.

Mix a topping of sour cream, sugar and vanilla. Pour over cooled pie. Bake *only* 10 minutes at 350° (no longer, or the sour cream will curdle). Refrigerate at least 5 hours before serving. Serve plain or topped with frozen or fresh strawberries. Serves 6 to 8. (For variety, pour into 9-inch graham cracker shell.)

MRS. JACQUES BROURMAN

CHERRIES JUBILEE

1 can dark Bing Pitted Cherries,
not drained

1 quart vanilla ice cream
1 cup brandy

Heat cherries at table in chafing dish. (It is best to first preheat cherries on stove in kitchen.) Add brandy and blaze immediately. Spoon over ice cream.

MR. O. D. BAXTER, JR.

CHERRY PIE SQUARES

1 can cherry pie filling
1 box Ann Page butter pecan
cake mix (14-ounces)

¼ pound butter

Butter pan; put in pie filling. Sprinkle cake mix over top of cherry filling. Dot top with butter. Bake in 9-inch square pan at 375° for 30 minutes. Turn off oven and leave 10 minutes more. Serves 6 to 8.

MRS. JOHN STEDMAN

CHOCOLATE ANGEL FANCY

2 6-ounce packages chocolate
  chips
2 tablespoons water
3 beaten egg yolks
1 teaspoon vanilla

½ teaspoon salt
1 tablespoon sugar
1 cup cream, whipped
3 egg whites, beaten stiff
1 angel food cake, loaf or round

Tear cake into bite-sized pieces and place in 2-quart casserole dish. Melt chocolate in water over low heat. Blend in beaten egg yolks. Add vanilla and salt. Cool. Whip the cream, gradually adding sugar as you beat. Fold chocolate mixture into cream, then fold in stiffly beaten egg whites. Pour over cake pieces. Chill overnight. Serve with additional whipped cream. (If you like more chocolate, don't use all the cake.) Serves 8.

Mrs. Charles E. Warner

CHOCOLATE CHARLOTTE RUSSE CAKE

4 squares unsweetened
  chocolate
¾ cup granulated sugar
⅓ cup milk
6 eggs, separated
1½ cups unsalted butter

1½ cups confectioners sugar
⅛ teaspoon salt
1½ teaspoons vanilla
2 dozen lady fingers, split
1 cup heavy cream, whipped
Shaved unsweetened chocolate

Melt chocolate squares in top of double boiler over hot water. Mix granulated sugar, milk, and egg yolks and add to chocolate; cook until smooth and thick, stirring constantly. Cool. Cream butter, add ¾-cup confectioners sugar, and cream the two together. Add chocolate mixture and beat well. Beat egg whites with salt until stiff; gradually beat in remaining ¾-cup sugar and fold into chocolate mixture. Add vanilla. Line deep 9-inch spring-form or loose-bottomed pan with split lady fingers. Put in alternate layers of ⅓ of mixture and remaining lady fingers. Chill overnight (or it may be frozen). Remove to cake plate and garnish with whipped cream and shaved chocolate. Makes 12 servings.

Mrs. Edgar A. Terrell, Jr.*

CHOCOLATE DELIGHT DESSERT

½ box chocolate cookie wafers
1½ cups confectioners sugar
½ cup butter
2 egg yolks, well beaten

1 teaspoon vanilla
1 can crushed pineapple, drained
½ pint whipping cream
1 teaspoon vanilla

Cream butter and sugar well. Add beaten egg yolks and 1 teaspoon vanilla. Whip cream until stiff and add second teaspoon of vanilla. Fold cream into pineapple. Crush wafers very fine and spread part over bottom of 9-inch square pan. Next, spread butter mixture, then cream and pineapple, then cover with crumbs. Refrigerate. Serves 8.

Mrs. John Campbell

CHOCOLATE MOUSSE

2 bars German sweet chocolate
6 eggs
6 tablespoons sugar
½ teaspoon vanilla extract

¼ teaspoon almond extract
Lady fingers
Whipped cream

Melt chocolate in top of double boiler. Separate eggs. Beat yolks with sugar with rotary beater. When thoroughly beaten, add chocolate and beat until smooth. Place in bowl. Beat egg whites until fluffy but not dry. Add this to chocolate mixture and stir well. Add vanilla and almond extract and stir again. Place in refrigerator and leave for 8 to 10 hours, or overnight if possible. Serve on lady fingers and top with whipped cream. Serves 4 to 6.

MRS. JAMES CRAIG

CHOCOLATE ROLL

5 eggs, separated
1 cup confectioners sugar
2 tablespoons cocoa

½ teaspoon vanilla
2 cups heavy cream
1 cup chopped nuts

Beat egg yolks until lemon-colored. Continue to beat while gradually adding sugar and cocoa. Add vanilla and fold mixture into beaten egg whites. Bake in greased jelly roll pan, lined with waxed paper. Bake at 350° for 15 minutes. Turn out on damp towel. Remove paper and roll up like jelly roll in damp towel and let cool. Whip cream, sweeten and flavor. Add chopped nuts to cream. Unroll cake, spread cream mixture on it and re-roll. Ice with Chocolate Roll Icing and sprinkle with nuts. Let set in refrigerator for 7 hours.

CHOCOLATE ROLL ICING

1 tablespoon cocoa
1 tablespoon butter

3 tablespoons boiling water
1½ cups confectioners sugar

Put butter and boiling water in mixing bowl. Add cocoa and sugar. Beat thoroughly.

MRS. JAMES J. HARRIS

ALVENA'S BAKED CUSTARD

4 eggs
1 cup sugar
4 tablespoons butter, melted
3 cups whole milk

½ teaspoon freshly grated
nutmeg
Pinch of salt

Beat eggs well and add sugar. Stir warmed (not boiling) milk into eggs and sugar. Add a pinch of salt and nutmeg. Add melted butter and pour into 1½ quart long casserole. Place casserole in a shallow pan containing a little water (enough to cover bottom) and bake in preheated 400° oven for 25 to 30 minutes. *Do not overcook;* it will become watery. (This may also be poured into two 9-inch pie crusts and baked at the same temperature.)

MRS. VERNER E. STANLEY, JR.

BOILED CUSTARD

1 cup sugar
4 eggs

1 quart milk
1 teaspoon vanilla

Beat eggs with sugar. Heat milk in a double boiler. When hot, add a little milk to the eggs and sugar. Then add all to the milk in the double boiler. Cook until thickened slightly. Remove from heat and stir in vanilla. Refrigerate. It will thicken more as it cools. (This is delicious as is, or served over fresh fruit. I also use it as the base for peach ice cream.)

MRS. GEORGE IVEY, JR.

CUP CUSTARD

3 large eggs
½ cup sugar
Dash of salt

Whole milk (about 2¼ cups)
1 teaspoon vanilla flavoring

Put eggs, sugar and salt into 1 quart measure. Whip one minute with electric beater. Fill container to quart line with whole milk. Add 1 teaspoon vanilla and stir. Pour into custard cups and place cups in a pan half-full of warm water. Bake in 300° oven until knife inserted will come out clean, approximately 1 hour.

Gourmet suggestion: After custard is done, cool. Spread a layer of light brown sugar over the top of the custards and place under broiler until sugar begins to melt. Place in refrigerator to get cold and serve with heavy cream.

MRS. JAMES J. ELLIOTT

BAVARIAN CUSTARD CAKE

1 cup sugar
2 tablespoons flour
4 eggs, separated
1 teaspoon vanilla
2 cups milk
1 package unflavored gelatin
¼ cup cold water

1 cup heavy cream, whipped
1 large angel food cake, broken
  into bite-sized pieces
1 cup heavy cream, whipped
  (for frosting)
2 or 3 cups sliced, sweetened fresh
  strawberries (or frozen)

Mix 1 cup sugar, flour and egg yolks; add vanilla and blend well. Stir milk into mixture and blend thoroughly; cook over low heat, stirring constantly, until thickened (about 10 or 12 minutes). Stir in gelatin that has been soaked in cold water; blend until gelatin is thoroughly dissolved; set aside to cool. When cool, fold in the first cup of whipped cream and the stiffly beaten egg whites.

In large tube pan, alternate layers of broken cake pieces and sauce, ending with a layer of sauce. Chill in refrigerator for at least 24 hours. When ready to serve, turn out onto serving platter and frost with second cup of heavy whipped cream (slightly sweetened if desired). Garnish generously with strawberries. Serves 12 to 14.

MRS. ALEX MCMILLAN

QUICK DESSERT OR SALAD

½ pint sour cream
1 cup miniature marshmallows
1 #2 can pineapple chunks,
    drained

1 can mandarin oranges, drained
½ can coconut

Mix all together and chill. Serves 6 to 8. (Add 1 can Queen Anne cherries, pitted and drained for variety.)

MRS. FRANCIS M. PINCKNEY, JR.
MRS. O. D. BAXTER, JR.*

ANDREW JACKSON'S FLOATING ISLAND

1 cup blanched almonds, chopped
2 tablespoons sherry
1 sponge cake

1 quart plain boiled custard
1 cup whipped cream
½ jar currant jelly

Cover the bottom of a large bowl with sponge cake, whole or broken into pieces. Sprinkle over this the almonds and then the sherry. Pour over all the boiled custard (using favorite recipe for this). Put on top a generous amount of whipped cream and dab bits of currant jelly over it. Serve chilled from the bowl. This is good with angel food cake, too.

OLD NORTH STATE COOKBOOK

SPRING FLOWER DESSERT

1 large round angel food cake,
    broken into pieces
6 eggs
¾ cup sugar (twice)
½ cup lemon juice

Grated rind of 2 lemons
¼ cup cold water
1 envelope gelatin
½ pint whipping cream
Coconut, grated

Separate eggs and put whites aside. Beat yolks and put in double boiler. Add ¾ cup sugar, lemon juice, and grated rind. Cook until thick, stirring frequently. Remove from heat and add gelatin, which has been softened in cold water. Cool. Beat egg whites until stiff, gradually adding ¾ cup sugar. Fold egg whites into lemon mixture. Add pieces of cake. Pour into 10-inch tube pan or 9½x13-inch pan. Put in freezer overnight.

Next day take dessert from freezer and leave at room temperature for 20 minutes. Dip pan in hot water to loosen dessert. Turn onto plate and place back in freezer for 20 minutes. Whip cream with touch of sugar. Ice cake and sprinkle with coconut. Cover and put back in freezer. Bring out 30 minutes before cutting. Serves 12 to 14.

Decorate with fresh flowers that have been washed thoroughly, or with grapes that have been washed, dipped in egg white and rolled in sugar.

MRS. SAMUEL R. SLOAN

FORGOTTEN DESSERT

10 egg whites
½ teaspoon salt
1 teaspoon cream of tartar

3 cups sugar
2 teaspoons vanilla

Beat egg whites until foamy. Add salt and cream of tartar. Beat until whites stand in peaks. Add sugar gradually, beating until stiff. Add vanilla. Grease and flour two pie pans. Spread meringue in pie pans so it is high around edge and scooped out in center. Have oven preheated to 400°. Place meringue in oven and turn off heat completely. Leave in oven overnight. Don't peek. Fill with Silver Lake Filling.

SILVER LAKE FILLING

1½ cups sugar
⅔ cup flour
Pinch of salt

4 eggs
4 cups light cream
3 teaspoons vanilla

Mix flour, sugar and salt. Add eggs to cream and beat together. Combine this mixture with dry ingredients gradually, and beat well. Cook in top of double boiler, stirring constantly, until mixture is thick and smooth. Cool and add vanilla. Pour into meringue. Chill until very cold.

MRS. W. KENT WALKER

BRANDIED FRUIT

1 cup chunk pineapple
1 cup sliced canned peaches
1 cup sliced canned apricots

1 cup sliced cherries
 (canned or fresh)
1 cup sugar
Brandy

Drain juice. Mix fruits with sugar and any amount of brandy. Keep covered at room temperature. Stir twice each week. Every three weeks add 1 cup sugar plus 1 cup of either of the fruits above. Delicious served over ice cream or broiled grapefruit. Always keep minimum of 1 cup to build upon. Keeps indefinitely. Makes nice and attractive gift, especially when put in an apothecary jar.

MRS. HENRY F. WELFARE

LIME CREAM WITH STRAWBERRIES

1 tablespoon gelatin
¼ cup cold water
⅓ cup sugar
¼ cup white wine
¼ cup white creme de cocoa
¼ cup green creme de menthe

¼ cup lime juice
2 egg whites, stiffly beaten
½ cup cream, whipped
Pistachio nuts
Strawberries
Red currant jelly

Soften gelatin in cold water. In saucepan, combine gelatin, sugar, wines and lime juice. Stir over low heat until dissolved. Place pan in bowl of crushed ice and stir until thick. Then beat until foamy. Fold in egg whites and cream. Pour into oiled mold and chill. Garnish with chopped pistachio nuts and whole strawberries that have been dipped in red currant jelly. Serves 4 to 6.

MRS. GEORGE LILES

CHAMPAGNE FRUIT

1 box frozen strawberries
1 box frozen peaches
1 box frozen raspberries
1 box frozen pineapple chunks

½ cup brandy
1 bottle champagne (or pink champagne), chilled

Place all fruit, partially thawed, in bowl. Pour brandy over fruit, stirring it well for flavor to reach all fruit. Let stand in refrigerator at least 2 hours (maximum of 12 hours). At serving time, spoon fruit halfway to top of chilled champagne glasses. Pour enough chilled champagne over fruit to fill glasses. Serves 10.

CURRIED FRUIT

1 large jar mixed fruit
1 large can pears
1 large can peaches or pineapple

¾ cup light brown sugar, packed
1 stick butter
1 to 2 teaspoons curry powder

Drain fruit well. Dry it with a paper towel. Melt butter, add sugar, and curry powder. Mix well. Arrange the drained fruit in a 9x12-inch pan. (Any fruits may be substituted.) Pour sugar mixture over fruit. Bake at 325° for 1 hour in covered dish. Serve hot. Serves 6 to 8.

MRS. MARSHALL WARE

LEMON ICE CREAM DESSERT

1 6-ounce can frozen lemonade, undiluted

½ gallon vanilla ice cream
1 package lady fingers

Pour can of lemonade in softened ice cream. Split lady fingers and line tube pan. Pour in ice cream mixture. Refreeze. The lemonade changes the consistency of the ice cream. Unmold at serving time. (If you want plain lemon ice cream, omit the lady fingers.) Serves approximately 10.

MRS. WALTER RAY CUNNINGHAM

LEMON SOUFFLE

2 eggs
1 cup sugar
⅓ cup flour

1 cup milk
2 tablespoons melted butter
1 lemon (grated rind and juice)

Separate eggs. Beat yolks, sugar and flour. Add milk, butter, lemon juice and rind, then stiffly beaten egg whites. Put in buttered 1½-quart dish. Bake at 300° in pan of hot water for 30 to 40 minutes. Serves 4 to 6.

MRS. WALTER SCOTT, JR.

LEMON SPONGE

8 eggs, separated
1½ cups sugar
Juice and rind of 2 lemons
1½ tablespoons gelatin

½ cup orange juice
½ cup boiling water
1½ dozen lady fingers
½ pint whipping cream

Beat egg yolks well. Add ½-cup sugar, juice and rind of lemons. Cook in double boiler until thick. Soak gelatin in orange juice. Add ½-cup boiling water, and pour into yolks. Let cool. Beat egg whites, and add one cup sugar. Fold into yolks. Line a 9-inch spring form pan, bottom and sides, with split lady fingers. Pour in mixture. Chill at least 8 hours. Release mold and top dessert with whipped cream. Serves 15.

MRS. RICHARD N. BLYTHE*
MISS FRANCES WADDILL

MACAROON DESSERT

1 package plain gelatin
1 pint cold milk
2 egg yolks, well beaten
3 tablespoons sugar
1 teaspoon vanilla

2 egg whites, stiffly beaten
1 dozen almond macaroons, crushed
Whipped cream (optional)

Soak gelatin in cold milk. Place milk over heat and bring to scalding point, then add egg yolks and sugar. When mixture begins to thicken, remove from heat. Add vanilla and egg whites. Fold in macaroons. Pour into individual molds or 1 large one. Refrigerate until firm. Serve with whipped cream if desired. Serves 6 to 8.

MRS. JAMES M. TROTTER

MAPLE MOUSSE

3 cups pure maple syrup
1 dozen eggs
1 cup milk

2 quarts heavy cream, whipped
White grapes, peeled

Put maple syrup in double boiler and heat to boiling point. Whip eggs until lemon colored. Stir eggs into maple syrup over boiling water, stirring constantly, until it coats a spoon. Remove and let cool. Pour whipped cream into egg mixture and stir until well mixed. Freeze mixture in ice cream freezer and then put into 4 large grape molds or large ring molds. Refrigerate. Unmold and decorate with white, peeled grapes. Serves 20.

MRS. JAMES J. HARRIS

MOCHA CAKE DESSERT

¾ cup sugar
1 cup sifted flour
2 teaspoons baking powder
⅛ teaspoon salt
2 tablespoons butter
1 square unsweetened chocolate (1 ounce)

½ cup milk
1 teaspoon vanilla
½ cup brown sugar
½ cup white sugar
4 tablespoons cocoa
1 cup cold double-strength coffee

Mix and sift first 4 ingredients. Melt chocolate and butter. Add to first mixture; blend well. Add milk and vanilla. Mix well. Pour into greased 8-inch oblong dish. Combine sugars and cocoa (this will be fairly lumpy). Sprinkle over batter. Pour 1 cup cold black coffee over top. Bake at 350° about 50 minutes. Serve hot or cold with whipped cream or ice cream. Serves 6.

MRS. PHILLIP G. CONNER

MACAROON CHARLOTTE RUSSE WITH BUTTERSCOTCH SAUCE

1 pint whipping cream
½ tablespoon almond extract
½ tablespoon vanilla
½ pound macaroons, crumbled

1 large beaten egg white
1/16 teaspoon salt
Lady fingers

Whip cream, but not hard. Blend flavorings into whipped cream. Fold in macaroons. Beat egg white and salt and fold into cream mixture. Arrange lady fingers around sides of sherbet or dessert dishes and fill with mixture. Chill and serve with butterscotch sauce. Serves 6.

BUTTERSCOTCH SAUCE

1 pound brown sugar
1 can (14½-ounces) evaporated
    milk

4 tablespoons butter or margarine

Put all ingredients in saucepan and cook very slowly until mixture thickens. Cut this recipe in half if you don't want any sauce left. However, it is excellent over ice cream and keeps well in the refrigerator.

MRS. RICHARD BILGER

MOUSSE A L'ORANGE

3 tablespoons orange liqueur
3 or 4 oranges
½ lemon
 Orange juice
6 egg yolks
½ cup granulated sugar
2 teaspoons cornstarch

6 egg whites
Pinch of salt
1 tablespoon granulated sugar
½ cup chilled whipping cream
6 orange shell cups or dessert
 cups

Pour the liqueur into a quart measuring cup. Grate the skins of 3 oranges and the half-lemon into the cup. Strain enough orange juice so liquid measures 2 cups. Beat egg yolks and sugar in large mixing bowl until mixture is pale yellow. Beat in cornstarch and orange juice mixture. Pour into 2½-quart heavy saucepan. Stir over moderate heat with wooden spoon until mixture heats through and thickens, but does not simmer or come to more than 170°. (It should coat the spoon lightly.) Remove from heat and beat a moment to stop the cooking.

Beat the egg whites and salt in a separate bowl until soft peaks are formed. Sprinkle in the sugar and beat until stiff peaks are formed. Fold egg whites into hot orange mixture. Refrigerate until thoroughly chilled, folding occasionally so custard will not separate. Beat cream until stiff and fold into the chilled mousse. Turn into orange shell cups or dessert cups. Chill at least 2 hours. May be garnished with whipped cream or mint leaves when served. Serves 6.

MRS. RODDEY DOWD

ORANGE CHARLOTTE

1½ tablespoons gelatin
⅓ cup cold water
⅓ cup boiling water
1 cup sugar
3 tablespoons lemon juice

1 cup orange juice
3 egg whites
½ pint whipping cream
4 to 5 large oranges, sections cut and drained

Soak gelatin in cold water. Dissolve in boiling water. Stir in sugar, lemon, and orange juice. Chill in refrigerator. When thick, beat with mixer until fluffy. Fold in stiffly beaten egg whites and whipped cream. Line mold or 8-inch square dish with orange sections and pour in mixture. Chill thoroughly in refrigerator. Serves 8 to 10.

MRS. GEORGE IVEY, JR.

FRESH PEACH CUSTARD MOUSSE

1 envelope gelatin
½ cup orange juice
¼ cup lemon juice
1 cup sugar
¼ cup flour
¼ teaspoon salt
1 cup milk
3 egg yolks, slightly beaten

1 tablespoon grated lemon rind
5 or 6 medium fresh peaches, crushed
3 egg whites
3 tablespoons sugar
18 lady fingers, split in half
1 cup whipping cream

Soften gelatin in orange and lemon juice. Mix sugar and flour and salt in pan. Gradually add milk. Cook over medium heat, stirring constantly, until thickened. Cook 2 more minutes. Blend small amount of hot mixture into egg yolks; return all to pan and cook 1 minute. (Do not boil.) Stir in softened gelatin until dissolved. Add lemon rind. Cool.

Crush peaches and add custard. Beat egg whites until frothy; beat in sugar 1 tablespoon at a time; beat until mixture forms stiff peaks. Fold into cooled custard. Line bottom and sides of 7x11-inch pan with lady fingers. Pour in peach mixture. Cover, refrigerate for 2 to 3 hours. Spread with whipped cream just before serving.

MRS. JOHN P. MAYNARD

PEACH OR APPLE COBBLER

6 cups fruit (2 #303 cans prepared fruit or fresh peaches or apples)
½ stick margarine

1 cup sugar
¾ cup self-rising flour
¾ cup milk

Melt butter in a 2-quart oblong Pyrex dish. Add fruit. (If apples are used, use 1½ to 2 cups sugar.) Mix sugar, flour and milk and pour over fruit. Bake in 300° oven for 1½ hours. Serves 6 to 8. (Extra: Sprinkle with sugared cinnamon and pecans before cooking.)

MRS. JOHN STEDMAN
MRS. J. ALEXANDER STEWMAN III

EASY ORANGE-PINEAPPLE CAKE

1 orange chiffon cake
2 small packages instant Jello
  vanilla pudding

1 #2 can crushed pineapple, not
  drained
1 large Cool Whip

Cut cake in 3 layers. Mix instant pudding directly from package into pineapple. Fold in Cool Whip. Put between layers and on top.

MRS. HENRY MIDDLETON

PINEAPPLE CREAM ROYALE

1½ cups uncooked rolled oats
  (quick or old-fashioned)
1 cup brown sugar
2 tablespoons flour
½ teaspoon salt

½ cup soft butter or margarine
1 #2 can crushed pineapple,
  drained
½ pint heavy cream whipped
½ cup nuts, chopped

Place rolled oats, sugar, flour, salt and butter in 8x8-inch pan. Place in moderate (350°) oven for 10 minutes. Remove from oven and stir to moisten all ingredients. Cool. Remove 1 cup of oats mixture from pan. Spread remainder of oats mixture evenly in bottom of pan. Next, spread well-drained pineapple over oats in pan. Sprinkle ½-cup of remaining oats mixture over pineapple. Combine whipped cream and chopped nuts. Spread over oats. Sprinkle remaining oats over top. Chill several hours before serving or make it a day ahead. Makes 9 servings.

MRS. WALTER SUMMERVILLE, JR.

MOTHER'S POTS DE CREME

6 ounces semi-sweet chocolate
2½ cups tiny marshmallows
2 cups half and half cream
5 egg yolks

1 tablespoon cognac
Whipped cream and grated nuts
(garnish)

Mix chocolate, marshmallows, and half and half in top of double boiler. Place this over simmering, *not* boiling water and stir continuously until mixture has completely melted. Remove from heat and cool for 10 minutes, stirring frequently. Beat the egg yolks and pour the chocolate mixture very slowly over the egg yolks, beating after each addition and until mixed thoroughly.

Return mixture to double boiler and cook over water just under boiling point. Stir constantly and allow to thicken to custard consistency (about 10 to 12 minutes). Remove from heat, beat well, and add 1 tablespoon cognac. Mix and pour into little pots. Cover immediately and allow to chill for 2 hours. (May be made the day before.) Top before serving with scant spoon of sweetened whipped cream and grated nuts on top. Serves 8.

MRS. AMOS BUMGARDNER, JR.

BREAD PUDDING

5 thick slices bread
2 tablespoons soft butter
½ cup moist raisins
3 cups scalded milk
3 eggs

¹₂ teaspoon salt
¾ cup sugar
1 teaspoon vanilla
1 teaspoon cinnamon
¼ teaspoon allspice

Butter a 7x11 inch casserole. Adjust rack 6 to 7 inches from bottom of oven. Preheat oven to 350°. Toast bread and butter it while hot. Cut slices in quarters. Fit in prepared dish with raisins sprinkled between slices.

Beat eggs slightly in 2-quart bowl. Stir in salt and all but 2 tablespoons sugar, the scalded (hot) milk, and vanilla. Pour over toast and let stand for 10 minutes. Press down toast to soak up milk. Blend cinnamon and allspice and remaining sugar and sprinkle over top. Bake about 40 minutes, until inserted knife comes out clean. Serve hot or cold, plain or with cream or hard sauce. Serves 8 to 10. MRS. PHIL VAN EVERY

OLD FASHIONED CHOCOLATE BREAD PUDDING

1½ squares unsweetened
   chocolate
3 cups milk
1 cup sugar
½ teaspoon salt

3 eggs, slightly beaten
1 teaspoon vanilla
3 slices bread, toasted and cut in
   ¼-inch squares

Break chocolate in pieces and add to 1 cup milk; melt over low heat. Add remaining milk, mixing well. Combine sugar, salt and eggs in mixer or blender and mix. Add chocolate mixture and vanilla and blend well. Place toasted cubes in buttered 2-quart baking dish. Pour mixture over it. Place dish in pan of hot water and bake in 350° oven for 1 hour, or until pudding is firm. Serve with whipped cream or hard sauce. Top with cherry. Serves 6 to 8. MRS. JOHN MILTON ARCHER

MOTHER'S CHERRY PUDDING

1 egg
1 tablespoon melted butter
1¼ cups sugar
2 cups drained red sour pitted
   cherries
1 cup flour

¼ teaspoon salt
½ teaspoon soda
1 teaspoon cinnamon
1 teaspoon almond extract
½ cup pecans (chopped)

Beat egg; add butter and sugar. Cream. Fold in cherries. Add rest of ingredients. Bake in loaf pan at 350° for 45 minutes.

SAUCE FOR PUDDING

1 cup cherry juice
2 tablespoons cornstarch
2 drops almond extract

½ cup sugar
1 tablespoon butter

Cook until slightly thickened. Pour sauce over pudding and top with whipped cream, if desired. Serves 8 to 10. MRS. THOMAS W. DAVIS

FRENCH PUDDING

½ pound vanilla wafers, crushed
½ cup melted butter
2 eggs (whole)
1½ cups sugar

2 packages frozen strawberries (drained)
1 pint whipping cream
1 cup pecans, broken

Line greased 8x8-inch dish with ¾ of the crumbs. Combine butter, sugar and eggs. Mix well. Pour egg mixture over crumbs. (Should penetrate into crumbs.) Top with strawberries, then whipped cream. Add remaining crumbs and pecans on top. Freeze. Serves 6.

MRS. SAMUEL R. SLOAN

OZARK PUDDING

1 egg
¾ cup sugar
½ cup flour
¼ teaspoon salt

1¼ teaspoons baking powder
½ cup chopped nuts
½ cup chopped apple
¼ teaspoon vanilla

Beat egg and sugar. Stir in flour, salt, and baking powder. Add nuts, apple, and vanilla. Bake at 350° for 35 minutes in 8-inch square pan. Top with whipped cream. Serves 6.

MRS. VIRGINIA GRIFFIN

RASPBERRY FLUFF

1 cup sugar
1 envelope unflavored gelatin
½ teaspoon salt
1¼ cups milk

1 teaspoon vanilla
1 3½-ounce can coconut
2 cups heavy cream, whipped

Thoroughly mix sugar, gelatin, and salt. Add milk and stir over medium heat until gelatin and sugar dissolve. Chill until partially set. Add vanilla and fold in coconut, then whipped cream. Pile into 1½-quart greased mold and chill until firm (at least 4 hours). Unmold and serve with sauce.

SAUCE

1 10-ounce package frozen red raspberries

1½ teaspoons cornstarch
½ cup red currant jelly

Thaw and crush berries. Combine with cornstarch and jelly. Cook, stirring constantly, until it is clear and slightly thick. Strain and chill. Makes 1⅓ cups. Serves 8.

MRS. ROBERT LYNN III

SCOTCH IRISH COFFEE

Several hours before serving, make as many cups of strong coffee as needed and sweeten (1½ teaspoons granulated sugar per cup). Chill in refrigerator—then chill silver julep cups. At serving time, put 1½ ounces Irish whiskey into each frosted cup, add coffee, 1 scoop of coffee ice cream, and garnish with whipped cream. Serve with brownies as dessert.

MRS. ALEX McMILLAN III*

SHERRY ALMANDRADO

1 heaping tablespoon gelatin (1 tablespoon plus 1 teaspoon)
¼ cup cold water
¾ cup boiling water
1 cup sugar

6 egg whites
¼ teaspoon almond extract
⅓ cup sherry
⅓ cup chopped almonds (CHOPPED FINE)

Put gelatin in cold water for 5 minutes. Add boiling water and stir until gelatin dissolves. Add sugar and stir. Chill the mixture until it begins to stiffen. (*Watch this carefully.*) Then, beat until frothy. Beat egg whites until stiff, then add to beaten gelatin. Beat until mixture is completely blended, then add flavoring and sherry. Pour into mold, alternating a layer of mixture with a layer of chopped almonds. I always chill overnight. (Cover with Saran wrap.)

SHERRY CUSTARD SAUCE

6 egg yolks
1 pint milk
¼ cup sugar
⅛ teaspoon salt

½ teaspoon vanilla
½ pint whipping cream
3 tablespoons sherry

Put milk in double boiler and scald. Beat eggs lightly. Add sugar and salt. Pour milk *slowly* into egg mixture. Return to double boiler. Cook until mixture coats spoon. Strain, if you have to (I always do. It makes for smoother sauce.) When cool, add vanilla, whipping cream (do not whip it) and sherry. Chill. Make one day ahead. Cover.

Before guests arrive, unmold on silver tray, garnish with mint leaves and cherries (cut into quarters to make a flower). Serve sauce in separate bowl. Serves 8.

MRS. WALTER SUMMERVILLE, JR.

WHITE GRAPES DIVINE

Seedless white grapes
Brown sugar

Rum
Sour cream

Cover grapes with brown sugar and let stand a short while. Marinate with rum and chill overnight.

Just before serving, add a generous spoonful of sour cream to each individual serving. The amount used of each ingredient is up to the cook.

MRS. JOHN SCOTT CRAMER

MOTHER'S TIPSY DESSERT

1 box Duncan Hines yellow cake mix
2 tablespoons vanilla
2 cups milk
2 or 3 eggs, separated
3 tablespoons flour (or cornstarch)

1 teaspoon salt
½ cup sugar (sweeten to taste)
1 cup sherry wine
1 cup crushed almonds
1 pint sweetened whipped cream

Make cake according to directions, adding 2 tablespoons vanilla. Bake in two 10-inch round pans. Scald the milk. Add to egg yolks, flour, salt and sugar. Cook over low heat about 10 minutes, or until mixture coats spoon. Pour carefully over stiffly beaten egg whites. Add sherry and mix well. Cover 1 layer of the cake with half the almonds, custard and small amount of whipped cream. Add second layer of cake, topping with remaining almonds and custard. Cover entire cake with whipped cream. Custard soaks into cake. Serves 10 to 12.

MRS. E. OSBORNE AYSCUE, JR.

ENGLISH TOFFEE SQUARES

16 vanilla wafers (1 cup crumbs)
3 eggs, separated
1 cup nuts, chopped
1 cup powdered sugar

¼ pound butter
1½ squares bitter chocolate
2 tablespoons vanilla

Roll wafers into crumbs and mix with nuts. Using half of mixture, cover bottom of buttered 9x9-inch pan. Cream butter and sugar. Add beaten egg yolks, melted chocolate, and vanilla. Fold in stiffly beaten egg whites. Pour over wafers and spread remaining crumbs on with spoon. Put in refrigerator overnight. Cut in squares and serve with whipped cream or coffee ice cream. Serves 6.

MRS. ROBERT KNOX MORROW*
MRS. WILLIAM S. PIERCE

Pies

EASY AS PIE PASTRY

½ cup shortening (Crisco)
2 cups flour

½ teaspoon salt
¼ cup ice water

Sift flour and salt together. Cut shortening into flour with pastry blender or two knives. (Do not use hands.) Gradually add ice water, a little at a time, using just enough to make it hold together. The less water, the tenderer the pastry. Knead two or three times to make a ball. Chill for 20 minutes. Knead lightly on floured board. Roll thin. Place dough loosely in pan and pat over surface to eliminate any air pockets. Cut edge ½-inch larger than pan. Turn under so folded edge is even with rim of pan. Flute edge. Prick pastry with fork. Bake at 450° for 12 to 15 minutes. Makes two 8-inch pie shells or one double-crust pie.

PLAIN PASTRY

2 cups flour, unsifted
⅔ cup shortening (Crisco);
(Measure by packing into measuring cup;
Do NOT use water method)

1 teaspoon salt
⅔ cup milk (approximately)

Stir flour and salt together. Cut in shortening with pastry blender or two knives until the particles are the size of small peas. Add liquid just until particles stick together, forming a ball of dough which can be handled. Divide dough in half, lightly press each part into a flat disc shape and place on floured pastry cloth. (The beginner should roll the pastry between two sheets of floured waxed paper.) Gently roll with a floured rolling pin from center to edge, rolling in every direction so that every part of the dough is even and it remains circular in shape. Roll to about ⅛-inch thickness. Never turn the pastry over during the rolling process. (You may turn it over if you are using wax paper.)

To lift the pastry, roll it onto the rolling pin and unroll onto an ungreased pie pan. Press the pastry lightly into the pan so that it fits snugly but is not stretched. Roll edges under to make an even rim. Flute with fingers. (If using wax paper, peel one side of the paper off and fit the pastry into the pan. Then peel off top paper.) Bake at 450° for 12 to 15 minutes. Makes one double-crust pie or two single-crust pies.

MRS. LARRY J. DAGENHART

GRAHAM CRACKER CRUST

1 packet (1½ cups) graham
  crackers

¼ cup sugar
¼ cup melted butter

Roll graham crackers to fine crumbs, or pulverize in blender. Mix crumbs, sugar, and melted butter in 9-inch pie pan. Blend well with fingers or fork. Pat the crumbs evenly and firmly against bottom and sides of pan, forming the pie shell. Bake in 375° oven for 8 minutes, or chill until ready to fill.

MERINGUE SHELLS

3 egg whites
⅛ teaspoon salt
½ teaspoon baking powder
1 teaspoon vanilla

1 teaspoon vinegar
1 teaspoon water
1 cup granulated sugar

Combine all ingredients except sugar in mixing bowl. Using high speed, whip the mixture until stiff peaks form. Add the sifted sugar, one table-spoon at a time. Continue beating until very stiff peaks form and the sugar is well blended. Make desired sized shells. Heap in lightly greased platter, or on well-greased unglazed brown paper on cookie sheet. Use a spatula or knife to make an edge or rim. Bake in 275° oven for 1 hour or longer. When the shells are cool, remove from pan and paper. If de-sired, fill centers with fruit or ice cream. Serves 6.

ALMOND PASTRY SHELLS WITH FRUIT PRESERVE FILLING

¾ cup butter
¾ cup sugar
1 egg yolk
⅓ cup finely ground canned
  almonds

1¾ cups sifted flour
Fruit preserves (damson, apricot
  or strawberry)
Sour cream

Cream butter and sugar well with mixer (4 to 5 minutes). Grind al-monds on middle grinder setting and then measure 1/3 cup. Add egg yolk and almonds to creamed mixture. Add flour and stir well. Work mixture with hands to form dough. Shape into roll and wrap with wax paper. Chill dough 3 hours or overnight.

Roll out only part of dough at a time, keeping rest in refrigerator. Lightly flour rolling pin and dough board, then roll out dough to 1/4-inch thickness. Cut in 2-inch circles and fit into greased muffin tins. Bake at 350° for 15 to 18 minutes (on the middle rack in oven) until delicately brown. Loosen edges carefully as soon as you take shells out of oven. Then allow to cool several minutes before removing from tins. (Shells may be frozen after baking. If frozen, thaw for 30 minutes, then heat in low oven for 20 minutes.) Fill *after* baking with fruit preserves — damson, apricot or strawberry. Top with sour cream. Makes 3½ dozen.

MRS. JOHN HARVEY RODDEY, JR.

GRACE'S MERINGUES

1 teaspoon vanilla
1 box powdered sugar
1 teaspoon vinegar

1 teaspoon cream of tartar
6 egg whites

Combine vanilla, vinegar and cream of tartar. Whip egg whites until almost stiff. Add the sifted sugar slowly, alternately with a few drops of the combined liquids. Beat constantly until very stiff peaks form. Shape desired shell sizes on greased brown paper on a cookie sheet. Bake at 200° for 10 minutes, then at 250° for 20 more minutes. Makes 12 to 15 meringue shells, depending on size.

MRS. HERBERT H. BROWNE, JR.

APPLE PIE

1 9-inch unbaked pie shell
5 or 6 apples
1 cup sugar
½ stick butter
Juice of ½ lemon

1 tablespoon flour
1 teaspoon cinnamon
½ teaspoon nutmeg
Dash of salt

Peel apples, cut in quarters, and slice thin. Heap apples in 9-inch unbaked pie shell, as it will bake down. Dot with butter. Squeeze juice of ½ lemon over apples. Mix other ingredients in with apples, sprinkling the nutmeg on top. Cook at 450° in preheated oven for 15 minutes. (Set pan underneath to catch drippings.) Turn down oven to 300° and cook for one hour or until done. Serve hot or cold with butter and brown sugar or ice cream.

MRS. RICHARD D. GILLESPIE
MRS. PAUL B. GUTHERY

FROZEN BAKED ALASKA PIE

1 graham cracker crust

1½ pints ice cream (any flavor)

Make crust according to package directions. Bake 8 to 10 minutes in 9-inch pie pan. Freeze immediately. Melt 1½ pints ice cream until mushy. (I add crushed peppermint candy, red coloring and a few drops oil of peppermint to vanilla ice cream.) Pour in crust and refreeze. (This will keep in the freezer at least a week.) The day before serving, make meringue and refreeze after baking.

MERINGUE
3 egg whites
Pinch of salt

6 tablespoons sugar

Beat egg whites with salt until stiff. Gradually add sugar. Put on frozen pie and bake 5 minutes at 425°. Refreeze immediately. Take out of freezer about 10 minutes before serving. Serves 7. (For variety, drip chocolate sauce over slices.)

MRS. JOHN A. BRABSON

BLACK BOTTOM PIE

½ cup sugar
1 tablespoon cornstarch
2 cups milk, scalded
4 beaten egg yolks
1 6-ounce package chocolate bits
1 teaspoon vanilla

1 cup heavy cream, whipped
1 baked 9-inch pie shell
1 envelope unflavored gelatin
¼ cup cold water
4 egg whites
½ cup sugar

Combine sugar and cornstarch. Slowly add scalded milk to beaten egg yolks. Stir in sugar mixture. Cook in top of double boiler until custard coats spoon. To 1 cup custard, add the chocolate bits and stir until melted. Add vanilla, stir, and pour into baked pie shell. Chill.

Soften gelatin in cold water, add to remaining hot custard. Stir until dissolved, then chill until slightly thickened. Beat egg whites, adding sugar gradually, until stiff peaks hold. Fold in gelatin-custard mixture and pour over chocolate layer in pie shell. Chill until set. Garnish with shaved chocolate.

MRS. JAMES J. ELLIOTT

BLACK BOTTOM PIE WITH GINGERSNAP CRUST

1 tablespoon unflavored gelatin
4 tablespoons cold water
2 cups milk
½ cup sugar
1 tablespoon cornstarch

¼ teaspoon salt
4 egg yolks, beaten
2 ounces (squares) unsweetened chocolate, melted
1 teaspoon vanilla

Soften gelatin in cold water. Scald milk in double boiler. Mix sugar, cornstarch and salt together, stir slowly into milk, and cook until thick. Add gradually to beaten egg yolks. Return to double boiler and cook 3 minutes longer. Stir in gelatin to dissolve. Divide in half. Add melted chocolate and vanilla to one half of the mixture to make chocolate layer. Pour carefully into gingersnap crust.

CREAM LAYER

4 egg whites
⅛ teaspoon cream of tartar
½ cup sugar
1 tablespoon rum

1 teaspoon sherry
¾ cup heavy cream
1 tablespoon shaved unsweetened chocolate

Let remaining half of custard cool. Beat egg whites until frothy. Add cream of tartar. Continue beating to a soft peak and gradually add sugar. Fold meringue into cooled custard. Add flavorings. Pour carefully over chocolate layer. Chill in refrigerator until set. When ready to serve, whip cream, spread on top of pie and sprinkle with shaved chocolate.

GINGERSNAP CRUST

35 gingersnaps
¼ pound butter, melted

1 tablespoon confectioners sugar

Roll gingersnaps with rolling pin to make fine crumbs. Add melted butter and sugar. Press firmly into a 9-inch pie pan. Bake at 300° for 5 minutes.

MRS. RAY CUNNINGHAM
MRS. LARRY DAGENHART

BUTTERMILK PIE

3 eggs
2 cups sugar
1 tablespoon flour
⅔ cup buttermilk

½ cup melted butter
1½ teaspoons vanilla
Pinch of salt
2 unbaked pie shells

Beat eggs and combine with buttermilk. Stir in rest of ingredients. Pour into 2 unbaked pie shells. Bake at 275° for 10 minutes, then increase temperature to 300° and bake for 50 minutes.

MRS. DOUGLAS BOOTH

BUTTERSCOTCH PIE WITH SEA FOAM MERINGUE

1 9-inch baked pie shell
⅓ cup butter or margarine
1 cup brown sugar, firmly packed
1 cup boiling water
6 tablespoons cornstarch

¼ teaspoon salt
1½ cups milk
3 eggs, separated
2 teaspoons vanilla
¼ teaspoon cream of tartar
½ cup light brown sugar

Heat butter in skillet over low heat until it foams and becomes amber brown. Add 1 cup brown sugar. Cook, stirring constantly, until mixture liquefies slightly and just begins to bubble. Add boiling water slowly and carefully. Cook, stirring constantly, until sugar mixture is dissolved. Blend cornstarch, salt, and 1/4-cup milk in saucepan until smooth. Add remaining milk and brown-sugar syrup. Cook over medium heat, stirring constantly, until mixture becomes thick and comes to a boil. Boil for 1 minute. Be sure it is thick. Blend half of the mixture into egg yolks, then stir it all into saucepan mixture. Cook for 1 minute. Remove from heat; stir in vanilla. Cool slightly.

Beat egg whites and cream of tartar until foamy. Add brown sugar a small amount at a time, beating well until it forms stiff, glossy peaks. Fill pie crust with filling. Spread meringue over filling, making sure it seals the crust. Bake at 350° for 15 minutes, or until meringue is tipped with brown. Cool to room temperature. Refrigerate until serving time.

MRS. TERRY YOUNG

NO CRUST EGG CUSTARD PIE

3 tablespoons flour
3 eggs
1 cup sugar
2 tablespoons butter

1 tall can evaporated milk (1⅔ cups)
1 teaspoon vanilla

Mix in blender for 18 seconds. Pour into greased 9-inch glass pie plate. Bake at 325° for 35-40 minutes.

MRS. GEORGE LILES

CHEESE CAKE

1 graham cracker crust (1 cup
  crumbs mixed with ¼ cup
  melted butter)
1 pound cream cheese
1 cup sugar

5 eggs
1 pint sour cream
3 tablespoons lemon juice
1 teaspoon vanilla

Press cracker crumbs, mixed with butter, into a 9-inch pie pan. Cream sugar and cream cheese. Add eggs, one at a time. Add sour cream, lemon juice, and vanilla. Beat at high speed on electric mixer for 15 to 20 minutes. Pour into graham cracker crust and bake at 325° for 1 hour. Turn heat off and leave in oven for 1 more hour. Be sure cake is completely cool before removing from pan.   MRS. WALLACE B. BRADFORD

CREAM CHEESE PIE

1¼ cups graham cracker crumbs
1 teaspoon cinnamon
⅓ cup butter, melted
3 3-ounce packages cream
  cheese
2 eggs

¾ cup sugar
1 teaspoon vanilla
⅓ cup milk
½ cup sour cream
½ teaspoon vanilla
¼ cup sugar

Combine cracker crumbs, butter, and cinnamon and mix well. Press into a 9-inch pie pan. Soften cream cheese to room temperature. Add eggs, sugar, and vanilla, mixing well. Slowly add milk and stir until smooth. Pour filling into pie shell. Bake at 350° for 20 minutes. Make topping by mixing sour cream, vanilla, and sugar. Spread over filling and continue baking pie for 5 more minutes. Cool and chill. Serves 8.

MRS. WALTER SCOTT III
MRS. GEORGE MACBAIN III

REFRIGERATOR CHERRY PIE

1 can Eagle Brand milk
¼ cup lemon juice
1 can sour pitted cherries,
  drained

1 cup chopped pecans
½ pint cream, whipped
1 10-inch graham cracker pie
  shell or 2 8-inch shells

Mix first four ingredients, then fold in cream. Pour into a 10-inch (or two 8-inch) graham cracker pie shell. Chill for 8 hours before serving. May be frozen ahead. Serves 8.   MRS. THORNWELL G. GUTHERY

EASY CHESS PIE OR TARTS

1 8-inch unbaked pie shell
3 eggs
2 cups brown sugar

½ cup butter
Nutmeg to taste

Cream butter and sugar; add eggs and nutmeg. Pour into uncooked pie crust or individual uncooked shells. Bake in very slow oven (275°) until firm (about 50 minutes). Makes one pie or 10 individual tarts.

MRS. WALTER SCOTT, JR.

CHESS PIE OR TARTS

1½ cups brown sugar
1½ cups white sugar
1½ sticks margarine
3 eggs, whole
½ cup water

1 teaspoon vanilla
1 tablespoon flour
1 tablespoon cornmeal
½ teaspoon nutmeg
2 8-inch unbaked pie shells

Mix flour, sugar, cornmeal, and nutmeg together. Add well-beaten eggs. Melt margarine and add to egg mixture. Put water in last. Do not beat —Stir. Pour into pie shells and bake at 325° for 50 to 60 minutes, or until done. It takes less time for tarts. Makes two pies or 24 tarts.

MRS. MOFFATT G. SHERARD, JR.

CHOCOLATE CHESS PIE

1 unbaked pie crust
1 stick butter
1 square chocolate
1 cup sugar

2 eggs
Dash of salt
1 teaspoon vanilla

Melt butter and chocolate. Mix with other ingredients, which have been blended together. Pour into unbaked crust and bake at 350° for 25 to 30 minutes. Top with whipped cream and serve.

MRS. JOHN PURDIE

CHOCOLATE PEPPERMINT PIE

1 cup sugar
⅔ cup butter or margarine
3 eggs, beaten
2 1-ounce squares unsweetened chocolate
⅓ cup semi-sweet chocolate pieces
1 8-inch or 9-inch graham cracker crust

1 cup heavy cream, whipped
4 tablespoons sugar
1 teaspoon vanilla
⅓ cup crushed peppermint stick candy

Cream butter and sugar together until light. Blend in eggs. Melt both chocolates and mix thoroughly with sugar mixtures. Pour into chilled graham cracker crust. Chill 3 to 4 hours or overnight. Before serving, spread with whipped cream, to which sugar and vanilla have been added. Sprinkle crushed peppermint candy on top.

MRS. TERRY YOUNG

CHOCOLATE SILK PIE

¾ cup sugar
1 stick real butter
1 ounce unsweetened chocolate
1 teaspoon vanilla

Pinch of salt
2 eggs
1 8-inch baked pie shell

Cream sugar and butter. Melt chocolate. Cool and add to first mixture. Add vanilla and salt. Add 1 egg and beat 5 minutes. Add other egg and beat 5 minutes. Pour into 8-inch baked pie shell and chill at least 4 hours. Top with whipped cream if desired.

MRS. MARSHALL T. WARE

BROWNIE PIE

¾ cup crushed chocolate Nabisco
  wafers (1 box makes 2 pies)
Pinch of salt
½ cup chopped walnuts

3 egg whites
¾ cup sugar
1 teaspoon vanilla

Have egg whites at room temperature. Beat until soft peaks form. Gradually add sugar and beat until stiff peaks form. Add vanilla and salt. Fold in crumbs and nuts. Pour into greased 9-inch pie pan. Bake at 325° for 35 minutes. (This is best done the day before.) With ice cream, it serves 8; with whipped topping, 6.

MRS. A. L. CHASON, JR.

GERMAN CHOCOLATE PIES

3½ cups sugar
1½ teaspoons flour
1 teaspoon cornstarch
2 eggs
1 stick butter or margarine,
  melted
2 ounces bitter chocolate,
  melted

1 pint evaporated milk
Pinch of salt
1 teaspoon vanilla
1 cup coconut
1 cup chopped pecans
2 10-inch unbaked pie shells

Mix sugar, flour, and cornstarch together, blending well. Add eggs, mixing well; add melted margarine and chocolate, mixing only until blended and smooth. Gradually add evaporated milk, mixing and keeping bowl scraped well. Stir in vanilla (more than 1 teaspoon, if desired) and salt.

Sprinkle flaked coconut over bottom of two 10-inch unbaked pie shells. Sprinkle chopped pecans on top of coconut. Turn chocolate mixture into shells, and bake about 40 minutes in 350° oven. (This pie gets better each day after it is made.)

MRS. JOHN P. MAYNARD

GRASSHOPPER PIE

18 chocolate wafers
½ cup melted butter
½ cup milk
20 marshmallows

1 cup whipping cream
1½ ounces creme de menthe
1½ ounces creme de cocoa

Crush chocolate wafers and combine with melted butter. Press firmly around sides and bottom of 8-inch pie plate. In double boiler, put ½-cup milk and the marshmallows and cook until marshmallows are melted. Cool mixture by setting the pan in a large pan of ice; stir. Whip cream and fold in creme de menthe and creme de cocoa. Add to cooled mixture and pour into chocolate crust. Chill in refrigerator for 24 hours or store in freezer.

MRS. JOHN DABBS
MRS. KEMP R. DUNAWAY*
MISS FRANCES WADDILL

FUDGE PIE

¼ pound margarine
2 squares unsweetened chocolate
2 eggs
1 cup sugar

¼ cup flour
¼ teaspoon salt
1 teaspoon vanilla
⅓ cup chopped pecans

Melt margarine and chocolate over low heat. Combine eggs and sugar. Add chocolate mixture, flour, salt, nuts and vanilla, mixing well. Bake in greased 9-inch pie pan at 350° for 30 minutes. Just before serving, top with vanilla or coffee ice cream or whipped cream. This is a very rich pie. Serves 6 to 8. Freezes well. Can be made ahead of time.

MRS. JOSEPH DULANEY

HEAVENLY PIE

6 egg whites
¼ teaspoon salt
2 cups sugar
1 teaspoon vanilla
1 tablespoon vinegar

1 cup cream
Almond extract
Strawberries, raspberries, or
peaches

Grease well a 9-inch pie plate. Sprinkle on a complete coating of flour, then shake off. Beat egg whites with salt until stiff but not too dry. Gradually add 1 cup sugar and beat. Add vanilla and remaining 1 cup of sugar alternately with vinegar, beating continuously. Put meringue into pie plate, heaping it in the center. Bake for 1 hour (30 minutes at 275° and 30 minutes at 300°). Cool.

Whip cream stiff. Sweeten to taste and flavor with almond extract. Spread cream on pie. Cut up desired fruit and arrange on the cream. Do not put in the refrigerator. Serve at once.

OLD NORTH STATE COOKBOOK

HERSHEY BAR PIE

20 graham crackers
2 tablespoons sugar
1½ tablespoons melted butter
16 whole marshmallows
6 Hershey bars, plain or almond
(more if desired)

½ cup milk
1 teaspoon vanilla
Dash of salt
½ pint whipped cream

Combine graham crackers, sugar and butter, and press into 9-inch pie pan. Place in freezer until pie is made, or heat 5 minutes in 350° oven and cool. Melt remaining ingredients (except whipped cream) over very low heat. Cool completely. Fold in whipped cream. Place in graham cracker crust and refrigerate. Serve with small amount of whipped cream. Serves 6 to 7. Just as good fixed a day ahead.

MRS. HARRY NICHOLAS*

ICE BOX ANGEL PIE

MERINGUE SHELL

4 egg whites
1 cup sugar

¼ teaspoon cream of tartar

Beat egg whites until stiff. Add cream of tartar. Gradually add sugar, beating until mixture stands in peaks. Pour into well-greased pie pan. Bake at 300° for 1 hour and 15 minutes. Chill thoroughly and add filling. which has also been chilled.

FILLING

4 egg yolks
½ cup sugar
½ pint cream, whipped

3 teaspoons lemon rind, grated
3 tablespoons lemon juice

Cook eggs, sugar, rind and lemon juice in double boiler until thick. Whip cream and spread half over the meringue. Spread lemon filling over cream and top with remaining whipped cream. Place in ice box for 24 hours.

MRS. W. KENT WALKER

ICE CREAM PIE WITH SAUCE

3 egg whites
1 teaspoon baking powder
¼ teaspoon salt
1 cup sugar

1 cup graham cracker crumbs
½ cup pecans, chopped
1 quart coffee ice cream

Beat egg whites stiff. Add baking powder and salt. Slowly add sugar, beating constantly. Fold in graham cracker crumbs and pecans. Pour into well greased and floured 10-inch pie pan. Bake for 30 minutes at 350°. Cool and fill with 1 quart of coffee ice cream. Serve with chocolate sauce. Serves 8.

CHOCOLATE SAUCE

4 squares unsweetened chocolate
2 cups sugar
1 13-ounce can Carnation milk

1 tablespoon butter
Pinch of salt
2 teaspoons vanilla

Put all ingredients in a saucepan and cook over low heat. Stir occasionally and cook until thick. Do not boil. This makes more sauce than is needed. Leftover sauce good on future ice cream snacks.

MRS. W. KENT WALKER

ICE CREAM PIE (CHOCOLATE CRUST)

2 squares chocolate
2 tablespoons butter or
   margarine
2 tablespoons milk
⅔ cup sifted confectioners sugar

1½ scant cups coconut
1 quart coffee, peppermint, or
   any flavor ice cream
Whipped cream

Melt chocolate and butter over low heat. Add milk and confectioners sugar. Add coconut and mix well. Press into bottom and sides of well-greased 9-inch pie pan. Refrigerate. Just before serving, fill shell with slightly softened ice cream. (Can use several kinds of ice cream or sherbet, putting in layers.) Serve topped with whipped cream or chocolate sauce. Serves 6 to 7.

MRS. WILLIAM A. WHITE, JR.

JAPANESE FRUIT PIE

1 stick butter, warmed
1 cup sugar
2 eggs
1 tablespoon vinegar
1 teaspoon vanilla

½ cup frozen coconut
½ cup pecans
½ cup white raisins
Pinch of salt
1 unbaked pie shell

Mix butter and sugar. Add eggs and beat well. Add remaining ingredients and pour into unbaked pie shell. Bake at 350° for 30 to 35 minutes.

MRS. ROBERT CHERRY

LEMON PIE

3 eggs
1 cup sugar
Juice of 2 or 3 lemons

1 tablespoon corn meal
½ stick margarine, melted
1 9-inch unbaked pie shell

Beat eggs and sugar together. Add other ingredients and pour into unbaked pie shell. Bake at 350° until crust and filling have browned. Quick and easy pie.

MRS. ELLEN G. GOODE

LEMON CHESS PIE I

1 unbaked 9-inch pie crust
2 cups sugar
1 tablespoon flour
1 tablespoon corn meal
4 eggs

¼ cup butter
¼ cup milk
4 tablespoons grated lemon rind
¼ cup fresh lemon juice

Mix sugar, flour and corn meal with a fork. Beat eggs well and blend into sugar mixture. Melt butter. Add milk, lemon rind and juice to it. Combine all ingredients, mixing thoroughly. Pour into unbaked 9-inch crust. Bake at 375° for 30 to 40 minutes.

MRS. THOMAS W. BAKER

LEMON CHESS PIE II

½ cup butter or margarine
2 cups sugar
1 tablespoon flour
5 eggs, well beaten

Juice of 3 lemons
1 teaspoon lemon rind, grated
2 9-inch unbaked pie shells

Cream butter and sugar. Add flour, then well-beaten eggs. Add lemon juice and rind. Mix well and pour into 2 pie shells. Bake at 325° for 30 to 40 minutes, until golden brown and set. (One half of this recipe is enough for 1 pie if using frozen Pet Ritz pie shells. If using larger pie shell, you can pour entire recipe into it.)

MRS. RUSSELL M. ROBINSON II

MINIATURE LEMON CHESS TARTS

Pie crust (for 4 dozen tarts)
Grated rind from 2 medium
  lemons
½ cup lemon juice

2 cups sugar
1 cup butter or margarine
4 eggs, well beaten

Use favorite recipe for crust. Cut into 2½-inch rounds and fit into muffin pans. Prick and bake until light, golden brown. Cool. (Make 4 dozen.)

Combine lemon rind, lemon juice, and sugar in top of double boiler. Add butter. Heat over boiling water, stirring until butter is melted. Stir in beaten eggs. Continue cooking, stirring constantly, until mixture is thick enough to pile slightly (about 15 minutes). Cool thoroughly. Spoon filling into cooled tart shells. Fills 4 dozen miniature tart shells.

MRS. JOHN J. HANES

LEMON AND ORANGE TASSIES

PASTRY

1 stick butter
1 3-ounce package cream cheese
1 cup sifted flour

½ teaspoon grated orange rind
½ teaspoon grated lemon rind

Blend softened butter and cheese together until creamy. Add flour, one-fourth at a time, blending well each time. Blend in lemon and orange rind. Take pastry and make little round balls, putting each ball into a tiny muffin tin. Take your thumb and spread in muffin tin to make it cup-like. Mix the filling together and spread it in pastry shells. Sprinkle nuts on top. Bake in ungreased muffin tins for 25 minutes at 325°. Makes about 3 dozen small ones.

FILLING

1 egg, beaten
¼ cup light brown sugar
1 tablespoon butter

Pinch of salt
1 teaspoon vanilla
Few nuts, broken up

Mix together and fill pastry shells.

MRS. LOUIS ROSE, JR.

IDA'S LEMON CHIFFON PIE

3 eggs, separated
1 cup sugar plus 3 tablespoons
Pinch of salt
½ cup milk

1 package gelatin
¼ cup cold water
½ cup lemon juice
1 graham cracker crust

Combine egg yolks, 1 cup sugar, salt and milk. Cook in double boiler until mixture thickens. Add gelatin, which has been dissolved in water. Let mixture cool. Add lemon juice. Beat egg whites stiff and gradually add 3 tablespoons sugar. Fold lemon mixture into egg whites. Pour into graham cracker crust. Sprinkle a few crumbs on top and chill. Serves 6.

MRS. SAM H. MACDONALD

LEMON CUSTARD PIE

1 package graham crackers (rolled to fine crumbs)
6 tablespoons butter, softened
4 eggs, separated
Juice of 3 lemons (about ½ cup)

1 teaspoon lemon rind, grated
1 15-ounce can Eagle Brand condensed milk
5 tablespoons sugar

Mix graham cracker crumbs with softened butter and fit into 8 or 9-inch pie pan. In large mixing bowl, slightly beat 4 egg yolks. Blend in milk, lemon juice and rind, and mix until it thickens. Pour filling into cooled pie shell. Beat 4 egg whites until stiff, adding sugar gradually. Seal meringue on top and sides of custard. Sprinkle a few graham cracker crumbs on top. Bake at 325° about 15 minutes, until golden brown on top. (or: You can add whipped cream on top instead of meringue and freeze pie. Take out of freezer 30 minutes or less before serving.)

MRS. LOUIS ROSE, JR.

LEMON LUSCIOUS PIE

1 cup sugar
3 tablespoons cornstarch
¼ cup butter
1 tablespoon grated lemon rind
¼ cup lemon juice

3 unbeaten egg yolks
1 cup milk
1 cup sour cream
1 baked pie shell

Combine sugar and cornstarch in saucepan. Add butter, lemon rind, lemon juice and egg yolks. Stir in milk. Cook over medium heat, stirring constantly until thick. Cool. Fold in sour cream. Spoon into baked pie shell. Chill at least 2 hours. Serve with whipped cream and chopped walnuts sprinkled over the top, or top with meringue.

MRS. GENE W. McGARITY
MRS. JOHN PURDIE

LIME ANGEL PIE

4 eggs, separated
¼ teaspoon cream of tartar
¾ teaspoon vanilla
½ teaspoon salt
1⅓ cups sugar
¼ cup lime juice

2 teaspoons grated lime rind
¼ cup sugar
1 cup heavy cream, whipped
Green food coloring
Toasted slivered almonds

Beat egg whites with cream of tartar, vanilla and salt until soft peaks form. Gradually add 1⅓ cups sugar, beating until very stiff. Lightly grease 9-inch glass pie plate. Spread meringue in plate, covering bottom and building up around sides. Bake in very slow oven (275°) for 1½ hours. Turn off heat and let stand another hour. Cool.

Filling: Mix egg yolks well with ¼ cup sugar in top part of double boiler. Add lime juice and rind and beat well. Cook over simmering water until thickened, stirring constantly. Chill. Fold into whipped cream and tint with a few drops of color. Pile in center of shell and sprinkle with almonds. Chill several hours or overnight.

MRS. JOHN L. McCANN, JR.

LIME PIE

1 cup milk
1 egg
⅔ cup sugar
Pinch of salt
1 package Knox gelatin

¼ cup cold water
¼ cup Key lime juice
Green coloring
½ pint cream, whipped
2 8-inch or 1 10-inch pie shell

Make a custard of the first four ingredients over low heat. Soften the gelatin in cold water and add to the hot mixture. Add the lime juice and a few drops of food coloring. Let it begin to congeal and fold in whipped cream. Pour into pie shell and chill for at least 1 hour.

MRS. DONALD GRAHAM

CHRISTMAS MACAROON PIE

2 dozen macaroons (dried thoroughly)
½ cup soft butter
½ cup milk
2 slightly beaten eggs
⅓ cup sugar
Pinch of salt
½ envelope unflavored gelatin

¼ cup cold water
1 cup heavy cream, whipped
¼ cup finely chopped pecans
4 regular size marshmallows, cut fine
1 slice canned pineapple, cut fine
2 ounces candied cherries

Make a crust from crushed macaroons and butter. Press into a 9-inch pie plate. Make a custard of next 5 ingredients over low heat. Soak gelatin in cold water and add to hot custard, stirring until gelatin dissolves. Allow to cool, then fold in fruits, nuts and marshmallows. Pour in pie shell and chill.

MRS. PERRIN Q. HENDERSON

LUSCIOUS PEACH PIE

6 to 8 fresh peaches
1 cup sugar
4 tablespoons flour
Dash of cinnamon

Dash of nutmeg
1 cup heavy cream, not whipped
1 unbaked pie shell

Fill unbaked pie shell with sliced peaches. Mix sugar, flour, spices and cream together and pour over peaches. Bake at 350° for 1 to 1½ hours. Place a pan under the pie to catch the drippings.

MRS. PHIL VAN EVERY

PECAN PIE I

½ cup granulated sugar
½ stick margarine or butter
1 cup light corn syrup
3 eggs

¼ teaspoon salt
1 cup chopped pecans (not too fine)
1 uncooked pie shell

Cream sugar and butter. Add syrup and salt. Beat in eggs, one at a time. Add pecans. Pour in pie shell. Bake at 350° for 50 minutes.

MRS. JOHN L. DABBS III
MISS CRAIG MASON

PECAN PIE II

3 eggs
1 cup dark brown sugar
¼ cup corn syrup
3 tablespoons butter, melted

1 teaspoon vanilla
½ cup pecans (broken)
1 unbaked pie shell

Beat eggs; add brown sugar, corn syrup, melted butter, vanilla, and pecans. Pour in pie shell which has been lightly browned in oven. Cook for 45 minutes in 350° oven.

MRS. GEORGE K. SELDEN, JR.

PUMPKIN PIE OR PUDDING

3 eggs, slightly beaten
2 cups cooked pumpkin
1½ cups milk
1 cup sugar
½ teaspoon salt

1½ teaspoons cinnamon
½ teaspoon cloves
½ teaspoon ginger
½ teaspoon nutmeg
2 unbaked 8-inch pie shells

Mix all ingredients. Pour into 8-inch square dish for pudding, or 2 unbaked 8-inch pie shells. Bake at 400° for 45 minutes, or until knife in center comes out clean. (I usually use fresh pumpkin cut in large pieces. Cook in pressure cooker for about 10 minutes with 1-1/4 cups water at 15 pounds pressure. When cool, remove pulp and mash.) If you desire a more highly seasoned pie, add more seasonings.

MRS. IRA NATHANIEL HOWARD

PUMPKIN PIE

1 pound canned pumpkin
⅔ cup brown sugar, packed
1 tablespoon cinnamon
1 teaspoon ginger
½ teaspoon salt
1 teaspoon nutmeg

1 teaspoon allspice
3 eggs
1½ cups milk
½ cup cream
2 8-inch unbaked pie crusts

Mix ingredients in order given, adding one egg at a time and beating after each. Bake at 425° for 10 minutes. Reduce temperature to 325° and bake 45 to 50 minutes longer, or until knife inserted in center comes out clean.

MRS. BREVARD S. MYERS

SHERRY PIE

1 10-ounce package
  marshmallows
½ cup sherry

½ pint whipping cream
1 graham cracker crust

Melt marshmallows. Stir in sherry. Fold in whipped cream and pour into crust. Grate bitter chocolate over top. Chill.

MRS. HARRY BURKE
MRS. THOMAS CUMMINGS

RUM CREAM PIE

1 9-inch graham cracker pie shell	½ cup cold water
6 egg yolks	1 pint whipping cream
1 cup sugar	½ cup rum
1 envelope gelatin	Bitter sweet chocolate curls

Make a crumb pie shell. Beat yolks until light and add 1 cup sugar. Soak gelatin in ½ cup cold water. Put the gelatin and water over low heat and bring to boil. Pour this over the sugar-egg mixture, stirring briskly. Whip cream until stiff; fold it in egg mixture. Add rum. Cool until mixture begins to set and pour into pie shell. Chill until firm. Sprinkle top of pie generously with chocolate curls, and garnish with whipped cream if desired.

MRS. J. NORMAN PEASE, JR.*

STRAWBERRY PIE

1 baked 9-inch pie shell	3 tablespoons cornstarch
1 quart fresh strawberries	½ cup water
1 cup sugar	1 tablespoon butter

Mash enough strawberries to make 1 cup of pulp (about 1 pint). Combine sugar and cornstarch. Mix well. Add water. Stir and add pulp. Cook, stirring constantly, until thick and translucent (about 10 minutes). Stir in butter and cool. Place remaining uncooked berries in bottom of cooled pie shell. Cover with cooked mixture. Place in refrigerator for two hours. Serve with "Cool Whip" or whipped cream. (The same recipe can be used with peaches, with only ½ cup sugar.)

MRS. J. R. ADAMS

STRAWBERRY GLAZE PIE

6 cups fresh strawberries	3 tablespoons cornstarch
1 cup water	Red food coloring
¾ cup sugar	1 9-inch baked pie shell

Wash and remove hulls from berries. Crush 1 cup of smaller berries and cook with the water for about 2 minutes. Put in sieve. Blend sugar and cornstarch and stir in berry juice. Cook and stir over medium heat until glaze is thickened and clear. Stir in about 5 drops of food coloring. Spread about 1/4 cup of glaze on bottom and sides of baked pie shell.

Arrange half of the remaining whole berries, (some stem-end down and some sliced lengthwise) on the glaze in shell. Spoon half the remaining glaze carefully over the berries, coating each well. Arrange remaining sliced and whole berries on first layer. Spoon remaining glaze, coating all berries. Chill 3 to 4 hours. If desired, top with whipped cream and a few additional whole strawberries.

MRS. JOHN R. CAMPBELL

STRAWBERRY RHUBARB PIE

1½ cups sugar
3 tablespoons quick cooking tapioca
¼ teaspoon salt
¼ teaspoon nutmeg

1 pound rhubarb (3 cups)
1 cup sliced fresh strawberries
1 9-inch unbaked pie shell
1 tablespoon butter
1 top crust, cut for lattice strips

In large bowl, combine sugar, tapioca, salt and nutmeg. Add rhubarb that is cut in ½-inch pieces and sliced strawberries. Mix well to coat fruit. Let stand about 20 minutes. Spoon fruit mixture into unbaked pie shell. Dot with butter. Top with lattice crust. Flute edges. Bake at 400° for 35 to 40 minutes. (If desired, decorate lattice top with additional sliced fresh strawberries, dipped in melted currant jelly.)

MRS. BRUCE R. RINEHART

Ice Creams

BASIC ICE CREAM
(For Crank or Electric Freezer)

3 eggs, well beaten
2 cups sugar
1 tablespoon flour
1 13-ounce can evaporated milk

Dash of salt
3 tablespoons vanilla
Enough milk to make 1 gallon
(2 cups peaches or other fruit)

Add sugar, flour, and salt to beaten eggs. Add this to canned milk and part of the whole milk, mixing thoroughly. Pour into freezer can, adding vanilla and enough milk to fill container, leaving 2 inches at top for ice cream to expand.

For peach or other fruit ice cream, mash about 2 cups of fruit in blender with ½ to ¾ cup more sugar. Add only 1 tablespoon vanilla if using fruit. Add fruit mixture last to ice cream.

For richer ice cream, use another can of evaporated milk and less whole milk. Cook part of the milk, eggs, flour, and sugar on low heat until it coats the spoon, making a custard.

Makes 1 gallon.

MRS. WARREN W. DENBY

EASY COFFEE ICE CREAM

½ gallon vanilla ice cream (or ice milk)
½ cup instant coffee (in powder form)

1 tablespoon vanilla
2 tablespoons rum flavoring

Soften ice cream slightly in large mixer bowl. Add remaining ingredients. (Add more or less according to personal taste.) Mix with beaters until well blended, doing it as quickly as possible. Put in tight-fitting container and freeze until ready to use. Serves approximately 10.

MRS. WILLIAM A. WHITE, JR.

CRANBERRY SHERBET

1 package (4 cups) cranberries
2 cups water
2 cups sugar

½ cup lemon juice
2 egg whites, beaten

Simmer cranberries in water about 8 minutes. Strain through colander and press out all pulp. Add sugar and cool. Stir in lemon juice and beaten egg whites. Pour into ice trays. When partially frozen, put in mixer and beat. Return to freezer until serving time. Place in sherbet glasses and serve with turkey or chicken in place of salad, or serve as dessert. Serves 8 to 10.

MRS. JOHN H. RODDEY, JR.

FRUIT SHERBET

1 large can crushed pineapple
3 pints water
3 cups sugar

3 lemons (juice)
3 oranges (juice)
3 bananas, crushed

Boil sugar and water together for 5 minutes. Add can of undrained crushed pineapple, then add the juices and bananas. Freeze in refrigerator tray, stirring well after it begins to freeze. (Can be taken out when partially frozen, beaten with electric mixer, and returned to freezer.)

MRS. PAUL B. GUTHERY
OLD NORTH STATE COOKBOOK

LUSH MUSH

1 cup sugar
3 tablespoons water
1 egg white

1 pint strawberries, crushed and strained
½ pint whipping cream

In top of double boiler, over boiling water, beat sugar, egg white and water until thickened and peaks form. Cool. Fold strained fruit into cooled mixture. Whip cream and fold in. Spoon into tray or mold and freeze. Serves 6. (This can be eaten freshly made, but if frozen let soften in refrigerator before serving. Can also be made with crushed ripe peaches.)

MRS. DONALD W. GRAHAM

PACIFIC FREEZE

⅔ cup fresh orange juice
¼ cup fresh lemon juice
¼ cup pineapple juice

1 teaspoon grated orange rind
1 cup sugar
1 cup whipping cream

Mix together first 5 ingredients. Stir until sugar is dissolved. Whip cream and fold into juice mixture. Put in refrigerator and freeze. During next 2 hours, remove tray 2 times and whip mixture with egg beater. Serves 4 generously.

MRS. RUSSELL M. ROBINSON, II*

FRESH PEACH ICE CREAM

2 cups peach pulp
¾ cup sugar
Juice of 1 lemon

1 or 2 drops almond extract
2 cups whipped cream
2 tablespoons sugar

After mashing peaches to 2 cups pulp, add 3/4 cup of sugar, lemon juice and almond extract and freeze in ice tray to a mush. Add cream, whipped with 2 tablespoons of sugar, and return to freezer. Whip mixture after a half hour in electric mixer. Serves 6.

MRS. ROBERT P. BAYNARD

PEPPERMINT ICE CREAM

1 package Bob's peppermint
  stick candy
1 pint milk

1 heaping teaspoon flour
½ pint whipping cream

Crush candy and let stand in milk in refrigerator several hours. Bring to scalding point. Add flour that has been mixed with a little cold milk. Mix well. Chill. Add unwhipped cream and stir. Freeze in tray, stirring occasionally. Serves 4 to 6.

MRS. WALTER SCOTT III

STRAWBERRY ICE CREAM

5 pints strawberries
1½ cups sugar
1 pint half and half

1 pint whipping cream
  (not whipped)
Juice of 3 lemons

Hull and wash berries, then strain through sieve. In large bowl, add sugar to strawberries. Add more sugar if desired and be sure it's plenty sweet. Add 2 pints cream and lemon juice, mixing thoroughly. Let this stand in refrigerator overnight for better flavor. Churn in ice cream freezer. Makes 4 quarts of ice cream. (Peaches may be substituted for berries. Adjust sugar accordingly.)

MRS. CARROLL F. TOMLINSON*

Candy

CHEWY CARAMELS

1 cup sugar
1 cup light corn syrup
1 cup light cream

¼ cup butter
1 cup chopped pecans
1 teaspoon vanilla

Place sugar, syrup, cream and butter in large, heavy saucepan. Cook over moderate heat, stirring occasionally. When mixture starts to caramelize, lower the heat and cook, stirring constantly, to 244° on a candy thermometer or until a teaspoonful dropped into a cup of very cold water forms a firm ball. (The ball should not flatten when removed from the water.)

Stir in nuts and vanilla. Pour into lightly buttered cake pan (8x8x2) and allow to stand until cold. Turn the block of candy on a cutting board. Mark off 3/4-inch squares. Cut with a sharp knife. Wrap caramels individually in wax paper. Makes 1-¼ pounds.

MRS. GEORGE IVEY, JR.

VANILLA CARAMELS

2 sticks butter or margarine
1 box (1 pound) light brown sugar
1 can Eagle Brand condensed
   milk

2 cups dark Karo syrup (1 bottle)
1 or 2 cups broken walnuts or
   pecans
1 teaspoon vanilla

Mix ingredients together in heavy saucepan (2½-quart size). Let them boil, stirring to keep from sticking, until it will form a ball (caramel likeness) when tried in ice water. The ball should make a "click" sound against the cup. Take from heat and add vanilla and nuts. Pour into two separate pans (8x8-inches) or one large pan equivalent to this size. Let stand until thoroughly cooled. Cut into squares with a sharp knife and wrap in waxed paper. Makes 4 pounds or around 180 to 200 pieces if you use two cups of nuts.

MISS ELIZABETH GAY GLOVER*

EASY CHOCOLATE FUDGE

1 pound confectioners sugar
   (10X)
½ cup cocoa
¼ teaspoon salt

6 tablespoons butter
4 tablespoons milk
1 tablespoon vanilla
1 cup chopped pecans

Combine all ingredients except nuts in saucepan over very low heat. Stir until smooth. Mix in nuts. Spread quickly into buttered ice tray. Cool and cut into squares. Makes about 24 pieces.

MRS. FRANK H. CONNER, JR.

CHOCOLATE FUDGE

2 squares unsweetened chocolate,
  cut in pieces
⅔ cup cold milk
2 cups sugar

Dash of salt
2 tablespoons butter
1 teaspoon vanilla

Add chocolate to milk and place over low heat. Cook until mixture is smooth and blended, stirring constantly. Add sugar and salt, and stir until sugar is dissolved and mixture boils. Continue cooking, without stirring, until a small amount of mixture forms a very soft ball in cold water (232° F.) Remove from fire. Add butter and vanilla. Cool to luke-warm (110° F), then beat until mixture begins to thicken and loses its gloss. Pour at once into greased 8x4-inch pan. When cold, cut in squares. Makes 18 pieces.

MRS. WALTER RAY CUNNINGHAM

CAN'T FAIL CHOCOLATE FUDGE

2 cups sugar
¼ cup butter
¾ cup evaporated milk
1 cup marshmallow creme or 1
  cup miniature marshmallows

1 12-ounce package semi-sweet
  chocolate bits
1½ teaspoons vanilla
1½ cups broken pecans (optional)

Combine sugar, butter and milk in saucepan. Bring to boil and cook until syrup forms a soft ball when dropped in cold water. Make sure you cook it long enough. Pour over creme (or marshmallows) and chocolate chips. Beat with electric beater until smooth. Fold in vanilla and nuts. Pour into buttered 8-inch square dish. Cut in squares.

MRS. WILLIAM A. WHITE, JR.

CHOCOLATE COVERED GOODIES

2 sticks butter (or margarine)
1 package graham cracker, rolled
  very fine
1 cup nuts, chopped very fine

1 cup Angel Flake coconut
½ cup crunchy peanut butter
1 pound confectioners sugar
1 teaspoon vanilla

COATING
⅓ stick paraffin wax

1 6-ounce package chocolate
  or butterscotch bits

Melt butter in large skillet; add all ingredients (except paraffin and chocolate bits) and mix very thoroughly. Roll into balls and dip into mixture of chocolate bits (or butterscotch bits) and paraffin heated to a syrup in double boiler. Keeping the mixture over the heat while dipping makes it easier. Remove and allow to dry on waxed paper.

MRS. JAMES H. GLENN, JR.
MRS. WALTER SUMMERVILLE

CHRISTMAS MINTS (AFTER DINNER)

2 cups sugar
1 cup water
1 stick butter

6 drops of oil of peppermint
Food coloring

Combine ingredients in saucepan. Bring to a boil and boil over medium heat to 262° on candy thermometer. Do not stir. Turn out on greased marble slab. Add 6 drops of oil of peppermint and desired food coloring for colored mints. (Be careful not to add more than 6 drops of peppermint or the flavor will be too strong.) Work in extract and coloring with hands. Pull as taffy. Cut with scissors into desired lengths. Cool and store in airtight container until creamed.

MRS. NORMAN S. RICHARDS

COCONUT CANDY BALLS

½ cup Eagle Brand milk
1 box confectioners sugar (10X)
1 stick butter (or margarine), melted

½ cup Angel Flake coconut
1 cup nuts, chopped very fine

Mix all ingredients together well and chill. Roll into balls and dip in coating mixture.

COATING

⅓ stick paraffin wax

1 6-ounce package chocolate chips (or butterscotch)

Melt in double boiler until mixture becomes syrupy. Keep the double boiler over the heat while coating the balls. Place on waxed paper.

MRS. JAMES H. GLENN, JR.

CRYSTALLIZED GRAPEFRUIT PEEL

2½ pink grapefruit
2 cups sugar

½ cup water (scant)

Cut skin of grapefruit into strips 1/4-inch wide. Cover with cold water and bring to a boil. Cover and cook 15 minutes. Drain through colander. Repeat 3 times. Mix sugar and water. Add drained, cooked peel and boil slowly until grapefruit peel becomes transparent and all syrup is absorbed (about 1 hour). Dip each piece in granulated sugar and place on waxed paper to dry.

MRS. GEORGE IVEY, JR.

DATE NUT CANDY BALLS

1 8-ounce box chopped dates
1 stick butter (or margaraine), melted
1 cup brown sugar, packed

2 cups Rice Krispies (not crushed)
1 cup pecans, chopped
Confectioners sugar

Cook dates, butter and brown sugar over low heat, stirring, until dates melt or are very soft. Add Rice Krispies and nuts. Form into balls when cool enough to touch. Put on waxed paper. When completely cool, sprinkle with confectioners sugar.

MRS. WALTER SCOTT III

DIVINITY

2⅓ cups sugar
½ cup water
⅔ cup light corn syrup

¼ teaspoon salt
2 egg whites, beaten stiff
1 teaspoon vanilla

In saucepan, combine sugar, water, corn syrup and salt. Cook over low heat stirring constantly until mixture boils. Continue cooking without stirring until mixture forms a very hard ball when dropped in cold water (266 degrees). Beat egg whites very stiff. Slowly pour mixture over egg whites, beating constantly. Continue beating until candy is very stiff and mixture will hold its shape when dropped from a spoon. Add vanilla. Pour into 8x8 buttered pan and let stand until firm. Candy may be topped with half of nut or piece of candied cherry. Makes about 30 pieces.

SEAFOAM DIVINITY:

1 cup light brown sugar
1 cup granulated sugar
¼ teaspoon salt
1 tablespoon corn syrup

¾ cup water
2 egg whites, beaten stiff
1 teaspoon vanilla

Combine ingredients in same order and follow directions as for making divinity candy.

MARTHA WASHINGTON CANDY

2 pounds confectioners sugar
1 stick butter
1 small can evaporated milk

Vanilla to taste
Cherries
Pecans

COATING

1 square unsweetened chocolate, shaved

1 square paraffin

Cream butter, adding sugar gradually. Add milk and about 1 teaspoon vanilla, mixing together. (Must not be too soft.) Pinch off small bits, press flat, and insert cherry. Roll into small balls.

Over low heat, heat shaved chocolate and paraffin until rather dark. Dip candy balls into hot chocolate mixture, using a hat pin. Coat the chocolate evenly over it. Cover the pinhole with a pecan.

MRS. PAUL B. GUTHERY

PEANUT BRITTLE

2 cups sugar
1 cup light corn syrup
½ cup water
2 cups peanuts, broken

1 tablespoon butter
1 teaspoon vanilla
1 teaspoon soda
½ teaspoon salt

In large saucepan, cook sugar, syrup, and water until it reaches soft ball stage (236°) when dropped in cup of cold water. Add peanuts and cook until mixture is golden brown. Add butter and vanilla, cooking and stirring, to hard ball stage (294°). Add soda and salt, stirring well. Do not stir too long after adding soda (This is the secret.). Pour into buttered jelly roll pan or cookie sheet with sides. Makes 2 to 2½ pounds.

MRS. BRUCE RINEHART

PEANUT BUTTER FUDGE

3 cups sugar
1 cup milk
2 tablespoons margarine or butter
   butter

½ cup peanut butter (plain or crunchy)

Mix sugar, milk and butter (or margarine). Cook to soft ball stage (about 10 minutes). Remove from heat for a very few minutes until mixture stops boiling. Add the peanut butter. Beat until it starts to lose its glaze and get thick. Pour in buttered pan. Cut in squares. Makes 16 to 32 pieces.

MRS. LARRY J. DAGENHART

PRALINES

½ cup milk
½ stick real butter
2 cups sugar

2 cups whole pecans
1 teaspoon vanilla

Mix milk, butter and sugar and cook until soft ball stage. Remove from heat. Add whole or half pecans and vanilla. Beat with a spoon until creamy and shiny. Drop on waxed paper, greased platter, or marble slab in desired shapes.

MRS. WILLIAM A. NICHOLS

Beverages

Drinks

CAFE AU LAIT

1 gallon strong coffee
10 level tablespoons sugar
1 quart whipping cream

1½ teaspoons almond flavoring
or 3 tablespoons cocoa
1 quart vanilla ice cream

Make 1 gallon very strong coffee and sweeten with 10 level tablespoons sugar. Cool and place in refrigerator overnight. It must be *very* cold. Just before serving time, whip 1 quart whipping cream, which has been flavored with 1½ teaspoons almond flavoring. Put coffee and whipped cream in chilled punch bowl and stir together. Add 1 quart vanilla ice cream that has been broken into a dozen pieces. Stir all together. Makes approximately 65 punch cups full. NOTE: May be made with half Sanka and half coffee for less caffein. Also, chocolate ice cream gives mocha flavor.

MRS. HOWARD M. WADE
MRS. DAVID TOWNSEND

VIENNESE CHOCOLATE

4 ounces semi-sweet chocolate
⅓ cup sugar
⅓ teaspoon salt
1⅓ cups boiling water

4 cups scalded whole milk
1 teaspoon vanilla
½ pint heavy cream, whipped

In the top of a double boiler, over hot water, melt the chocolate. Stir in sugar and salt. Slowly add boiling water, blend, then add scalded milk. Simmer the chocolate for a few minutes and beat with a wire whisk until frothy. Add the vanilla. Serve in a heated pitcher and pass the whipped cream separately. Makes 6 cups.

MRS. VERNER STANLEY, JR.

GREEN PUNCH

2 packages lime cool aid
2 quarts water
2 scant cups sugar

1 46-ounce can pineapple juice
1 quart ginger ale

Mix four first ingredients and chill. Add ginger ale at serving time. Serves about 24 4-ounce servings. (I've made this for church. 10 times amount serves 250 people. Cost—approximately $6.50.)

MRS. WALTER SUMMERVILLE

LEMONADE

4 cups water
8 cups sugar
7½ cups lemon juice

2 #2½ cans pineapple
8 oranges, sliced
4 gallons water

Combine 4 cups water and the sugar. Boil for 10 minutes. Cool the syrup. Add lemon juice. Stir in pineapple. Add sliced oranges. Add 4 gallons water. Chill. Serve over ice. Serves 100 people.

MRS. DAVID D. TOWNSEND

PINK PUNCH

2 packages cherry jello
2 cups boiling water
6 cups cold water
1 small can orange juice
concentrate

1 small can lime or lemonade
1 large can pineapple juice
1 quart ginger ale

Combine above ingredients except ginger ale and chill until very cold. Add 1 quart chilled ginger ale.

MRS. WALTER SUMMERVILLE

RASPBERRY SHERBET PUNCH

2 cans (6-ounces each) frozen
pink lemonade
1 quart raspberry sherbet

2 bottles (28-ounces each) chilled
ginger ale

Partially thaw lemonade. Combine all ingredients at serving time in punch bowl. Serves 25 in 4-ounce cups.

MRS. WILLIAM A. WHITE, JR.

RUBY PUNCH

1 package frozen red raspberries
½ cup water
1 6-ounce can frozen orange
juice concentrate

1 6-ounce can frozen pineapple
juice concentrate
3 cups water
1 pint sparkling water or ginger
ale

Thaw raspberries, drain and save juice. Bring berries and ½-cup water to boil in saucepan. Remove from heat and press through fine wire strainer. Add juice to reserved raspberry juice. Add orange and pineapple juice concentrates and 3 cups water. Chill. Just before serving, add sparkling water or ginger ale. Serve in punch bowl or cups garnished with lemon or lime slices. Makes about 2 quarts.

MRS. WILLIAM A. WHITE, JR.

SUMMER DELIGHT

1 large bottle ginger ale
5-6 tablespoons lemon juice

Leaves of 2 or 3 sprigs of mint

Break or crush mint leaves in container. Add lemon juice and ginger ale. Stir until most of the fizz is gone. Strain into pitcher. Pour over ice.

MRS. JOHN TILLETT, JR.

SUMMER PUNCH

3 quarts unsweetened pineapple juice
1 6-ounce can frozen lemon juice

1 6-ounce can frozen orangeade
½ cup sugar
3 quarts ginger ale

Mix punch base and add 1 quart ginger ale to each quart base when ready to serve. Makes 40 5-ounce cups. Note: 1 pint frozen strawberries may be added for color or use ice ring made with ½ slices of lemons and oranges, cherries, pineapple chunks and mint leaves. (If you boil and cool water for ring, it will freeze clear.)

MRS. JULIAN W. CLARKSON

TROPICAL PUNCH

1 large can pineapple juice unsweetened
1 large can frozen orange juice undiluted
Juice of 4 lemons

2 cups sugar
1 large bottle ginger ale
1 large bottle plain soda or 1 large bottle lemon-lime soda

Combine pineapple, orange and lemon juices, mixing well with sugar in large container. This can be made ahead. At serving time, add ginger ale and soda water. Use the lemon-lime for richer flavor. Serves 25-30. (Punch size cups).

MRS. SAMUEL R. SLOAN

FIRESIDE SPICED PUNCH

2¼ cups pineapple juice
1¾ cups water
2 cups cranberry juice
1 tablespoon whole cloves

½ tablespoon whole allspice
3 sticks cinnamon (broken)
¼ teaspoon salt
½ cup brown sugar

Put pineapple juice, water, and cranberry juice in bottom half of 8-cup electric percolator, and the rest of the ingredients in the basket in the top. Perk for 10 minutes or until spices permeate. Serves 8-10. (This is a delicious hot drink for "homey evening by the fire".)

MRS. E. C. GRIFFITH, JR.

SPICED CIDER

2 quarts cider
12 cloves
4 cinnamon sticks

Rind of 2 lemons
2 lemons, sliced thin
¼ teaspoon nutmeg

Put cider, cloves, cinnamon, and the thinly peeled rind of the lemons in saucepan. Add slices of lemon and nutmeg. Cover and bring to a boil. Reduce heat and simmer for 15 minutes. Allow to cool. Strain through muslin. Discard spices. Chill overnight if possible, for flavors to blend. Serve hot or cold. Makes 2 quarts or 10 servings.

MRS. DAVID TOWNSEND

FRENCH TEA

8 cups water
1 cup sugar
4 oranges (juice)

1 lemon (juice)
3 or 4 tea bags

Boil first 4 ingredients all together for 5 minutes. Set off heat. Drop 3 or 4 tea bags in until amber color, then remove. Serves 10. Good hot or iced.

MRS. HUGH CAMPBELL

ICED TEA PUNCH

12 regular tea bags steeped 4
   minutes in 2 quarts water
1 cup sugar

2 trays ice
1 can frozen lemonade
1 can frozen limeade

Combine tea and sugar in water. Add ice trays to chill quickly. Add lemonade and limeade. Chill until serving. Makes 4 quarts.

MRS. JOE ELLIOTT, JR.*

SWEET ICED TEA

6 teaspoons ground tea (not bags)
1 cup boiling water

1 cup sugar
Juice of 3 lemons

Pour boiling water over the tea (earthenware teapot is best) and steep for several minutes. While tea is steeping, pour 1 cup sugar in bottom of ½-gallon jug. Pour the steeped tea through a strainer into jug over sugar. Let sugar dissolve. Fill jug almost to top with cold tap water and add lemon juice last. No water should be added after lemon has gone in. This will keep, refrigerated, for two or three days and unrefrigerated for a while.

MRS. WARREN W. DENBY

SPICED TEA

16 cups water
Rind of 1 lemon
Rind of 1 orange
2 tea bags
2 cups sugar

1 teaspoon whole cloves
1 3-inch cinnamon stick
Juice of 3 lemons
Juice of 3 oranges
1 cup pineapple juice

Boil rinds of 1 lemon and 1 orange in 8 cups of water for 5 minutes. Remove rinds. Add 8 tea bags for 5 minutes. Make syrup by boiling for 10 minutes: 8 cups water, sugar, cloves, cinnamon stick. Strain. Add lemon juice, orange juice, and pineapple juice. Combine with tea mixture. Makes 18 cups.

MRS. DAVID TOWNSEND

ALVENA'S RUSSIAN TEA

2 tablespoons whole cloves
2 tablespoons stick cinnamon
1 cup sugar
8 cups water
6 tea bags

2 lemons
3 oranges
6 ounces pineapple juice
(small can)

Boil cloves, cinnamon, sugar and 2 cups water slowly until syrupy, about 30 minutes. Put 6 tea bags into 6 cups of boiling water and allow to stand until it gets strong. Remove bags and add strained spice mixture, juice of lemons and oranges, and pineapple juice. Serve hot. Makes 8 cups.

MRS. JOE LINEBERGER

INSTANT RUSSIAN TEA

1 1-pound 2-ounce jar Tang
¼ cup instant tea with lemon
1½ cups sugar

1 teaspoon ground cloves
½ teaspoon cinnamon
½ teaspoon allspice

Mix all ingredients well. Store in tight container. To serve, use 2 teaspoonsful to a tea cup of boiling water.

MRS. W. Z. BRADFORD

Spiked Drinks

CHRISTMAS EGG NOG

12 eggs, separated
1 cup sugar
1 quart milk

2 cups bourbon
1 cup rum
1 quart heavy cream, beaten

Beat egg yolks with sugar until very light. Add milk, bourbon and rum. Fold in cream and six egg whites that have been beaten until slightly stiff. Add more bourbon and rum to taste. Makes approximately 4 quarts.

MRS. SAMUEL H. MCDONALD

RUM PUNCH

8 egg yolks
4 cans Carnation milk
½ cup water to each can
4 cups sugar

1 quart rum
1 tablespoon salt
1 teaspoon vanilla
2 tablespoons cornstarch

Beat sugar, yolks, and salt until light. Add milk and water until all used, stirring constantly. Cook in double boiler for 50 minutes. Add cornstarch and cook 10 minutes, stirring all the time. Remove and cool 5 minutes. Add vanilla, stir well, wait 5 minutes. Add rum. Let cool, store in refrigerator. Keeps indefinitely.

MRS. J. PURNELL

PEACH FUZZ

3 large ripe peaches
¾ cup sugar (more or less to taste)

1 small can frozen lemonade concentrate
1¾ lemonade cans of 80-proof vodka or rum

Peel peaches, removing seed and cut in chunks. Put all ingredients in blender and pulverize. This mixture should be kept in freezer and keeps well for months. When ready to mix drinks, mix half peach mixture and half ice cubes in blender and run until blended. Makes about 10 drinks. (This is also delicious made with fresh strawberries.)

MRS. VERNER STANLEY

TAHITIAN RUM PUNCH

1 cup grenadine
1 large can pineapple juice
2 cans frozen orange juice (large cans)
1 cup lemon juice

1 teaspoon nutmeg
Generous dash of bitters
Dark rum
Light rum

Use a one-gallon plastic container and put the above ingredients (except rum) into it, filling to top with water. This fruit punch can be stored in the refrigerator and used only when ready to mix a drink. Add a jigger of dark rum and one of light rum for each drink, or individual desired amount. (This recipe is directly from Nassau and is absolutely delightful for a summer drink.)

MRS. E. C. GRIFFITH, JR.

SPARKLING PUNCH

1 12-ounce bottle ginger ale, chilled
1 tablespoon lemon juice (fresh)
1 orange, sliced in thin pieces

5 cups cranapple juice, chilled
1 fifth sparkling burgundy or 1 fifth pink champagne, chilled

Pour all the ingredients into the punch bowl at serving time. Float the orange slices for looks. Can add few ice cubes to keep it chilled. Serves 25-30 4-ounce cups. Good Christmas holiday punch.

MRS. TERRY YOUNG

CHAMPAGNE PUNCH

1 quart cranberry juice
2 cups lemon juice
1 12-ounce can frozen orange juice
(not diluted)
1 to 1½ cups sugar

1 bottle sauterne, chilled
2 bottles pink champagne
(Taylor's), chilled
2 large bottles ginger ale, chilled

Mix ahead of serving time the juices and sugar. When ready to serve, place block of ice in large punch bowl. (Make a block from large jello molds, placing red and green cherries in the water and molds and freeze.) Mix juices, sauterne, champagne and ginger ale together and serve in punch bowl. Serves about 60-70 punch-sized cups. Alter amounts of champagne, ginger ale and sauterne according to strength of punch desired. This has a very mild flavor and is very pretty.

MRS. TERRY YOUNG

QUEEN'S PUNCH

1 quart brandy
1 cup maraschino cherries
½ cup sugar

Slices of orange and lemon
3 quarts champagne

Soak ingredients in brandy for ½-hour or more. Add champagne when ready to serve.

MRS. DAVID TOWNSEND

FARMER'S BISHOP, A CHRISTMAS PUNCH

6 oranges
Whole cloves
1 quart apple brandy

½ gallon sweet cider
Sugar and spices to taste

Cut oranges in half and stick skins full of whole cloves. Bake in oven until juice begins to rise. Remove to bowl that can be kept hot. Add sugar to taste (this is hard) and pour over them 1 quart apple brandy. Light brandy and, after it has burned a few seconds, extinguish by pouring over the cider. Place bowl over a low heat. Add pinch of cinnamon, whole allspice and nutmeg (go easy on spices). Stir until hot. Keep hot while serving, but *do not boil*. Serves 24.

MRS. DAVID TOWNSEND

NAVY GROG

5 ounces bourbon
2 ounces light rum
1 ounce triple sec
1 ounce Karo syrup

3 ounces lemon juice
2 ounces orange juice
Crushed ice

Blend all ingredients except ice in blender, or mix in large pitcher. Fill 8-ounce glasses to the top with crushed ice. Pour in mixed drink. Add less bourbon if too strong. Fills approximately six 8-ounce glasses.

MRS. BRUCE H. RINEHART

WHISKEY SOUR PUNCH

2 6-ounce cans orange juice
concentrate
2 6-ounce cans lemonade
concentrate
2 tablespoons bitters
4 tablespoons sugar

2 large jars red cherries
3 bottles (12 ounces each) club
soda
1 fifth bourbon
Lemons and oranges sliced

Mix ahead lemonade, orange juice, bitters, sugar and juice from cherries. Chill. Chill soda. Before serving, add a fifth of bourbon to the mix. Stir well. Add chilled soda. Put in large punch bowl. Freeze ice blocks ahead in large jello molds with sliced oranges and lemons in it for color, or slice them for floating in punch. Makes 33 punch cups.

MRS. BRUCE H. RINEHART

THE VELVET HAMMER

4 ounces half and half cream
1 ounce brandy
1 ounce creme de cacao, white

1 ounce creme de cafe, white
¼ ounce grenadine syrup
1 ounce orange curacao, white

Shake well in cracked ice. Strain and serve. Makes enough for 3-4 in small old fashioned or sour glasses.

MR. ALSTON RAMSAY

SYLLABUB I

1 cup sweet wine
1 cup Madeira wine
Nutmeg to taste

1 quart heavy cream
6 tablespoons lemon juice
Sugar to taste

Soak lemon peel in the sweet wine and Madeira until flavor is extracted, then discard peel. Whip cream until it begins to hold its shape. Gradually whisk in the wine, lemon juice, sugar and nutmeg. Heap in glasses and serve. Yields 3 quarts or 12 portions. (This is best 3 to 4 days old, but will keep indefinitely in refrigerator.)

MRS. J. PURNELL

MULLED WINE

1 cup sugar
½ cup water
2 sticks cinnamon
½ lemon, cut in slices
2 dozen cloves

1 cup lemon juice
3 cups sweet juice (orange or
pineapple)
1 quart red wine
Few drops red coloring

Boil the first 5 ingredients for 5 minutes (to make a syrup). Strain syrup. Add the 4 cups of hot fruit juice. Heat, but do not boil, 1 quart of wine. Combine fruit juices and wine and add a few drops of coloring if needed. Keep hot in double boiler. Serve very hot with slices of lemon. Makes 2 quarts.

MRS. F. A. ADKINS

Wine Chart

Course	Wine	How to Serve
Shellfish or	Chablis	Cold
Hors d'oeuvre	Graves	Cold
	Rhine or Moselle	Cold
Entrees	White Wine	Cold
	Claret	Room Temperature
Soup	Sauterne	Cold
	Dry Sherry	Room Temperature
	Madeira	Cool
Roasts	Fine Claret	Room Temperature
Red Meats	Red Burgundy	Room Temperature
	Sparkling Burgundy	Cold
Roasts	White Bordeaux	Cold
White Meats	White Burgundy	Cool
	Champagne	Cold
Fish	White Bordeaux	Cool
	White Burgundy	Cool
	Rhine or Moselle	Cool
Fowl or Game	Fine Claret	Room Temperature
	Red Burgundy	Room Temperature
	Rhone	Room Temperature
Cheese	Fine Claret	Room Temperature
	Red Burgundy	Room Temperature
	Port	Room Temperature
	Old Sherry	Room Temperature
	Full-bodied Madeira	Room Temperature
Dessert	Madeira	Room Temperature
	Rich Old Sherry	Room Temperature
Coffee	Cognac	Room Temperature
	Old Port, Sherry	Room Temperature
	Madeira	Room Temperature
	Liqueur	Room Temperature

Sauces
Pickles and Preserves

Sauces — Sweet

BUTTERSCOTCH SAUCE

1 pound brown sugar
1 14½-ounce can evaporated milk
4 tablespoons butter or margarine

Put all ingredients in saucepan. Cook very slowly until mixture thickens. Serve over ice cream or desserts.

MRS. RICHARD BILGER

BUTTER SAUCE

1 cup sugar
1 egg
2 tablespoons butter
4 tablespoons cream
¼ teaspoon salt
1 teaspoon vanilla

Mix all ingredients except vanilla. Cook slowly, stirring constantly. When sugar is melted, add vanilla and serve on gingerbread or chocolate cake.

MRS. WALTER SCOTT, JR.

COMPANY CHOCOLATE SAUCE

⅞ cup milk
1½ squares Baker's unsweetened chocolate
3 heaping tablespoons sugar
1 teaspoon flour
⅓ cup whipping cream
¾ stick butter
3 heaping tablespoons sugar
1 pinch salt
1 teaspoon vanilla

Melt chocolate in milk. Add first 3 tablespoons of sugar. Stir well. Add flour mixed with cream. Heat on low and let boil slowly until thick. In another pan melt butter and add second 3 tablespoons sugar. Stir until caramelized. Add to chocolate mixture. Add salt and vanilla. Delicious over ice cream, cake or other desserts.

MRS. KENT WALKER

HOT CHOCOLATE SAUCE

6 squares unsweetened chocolate
2 cups sugar
¼ pound butter
1 large can Carnation milk
1 teaspoon vanilla
Dash of salt

Melt chocolate, add sugar, butter and salt. Boil for a few minutes over low heat; add milk gradually and bring back to boil. Stir constantly. Add vanilla. Blend.

MRS. T. BERNARD WRIGHT, JR.
MRS. CAMERON FAISON

EASY HOT FUDGE SAUCE

1 can sweetened condensed milk   2 squares semi-sweet chocolate

Put in double boiler or in pan over very low heat and let cook until chocolate melts and gets creamy. Serve over ice cream, cake, etc. while still hot. (Good over Hot Milk Cake recipe.)

MRS. LEE A. FOLGER III

HOT FUDGE SAUCE (CHEWY)

1 tablespoon butter
1 ounce chocolate
1/3 cup boiling water
1 cup sugar

2 tablespoons corn syrup
1/2 teaspoon vanilla
1/8 teaspoon salt

Melt butter. Add chocolate and stir over low heat until chocolate melts. Add water gradually, stirring constantly. Heat to boiling. Add sugar and syrup, stirring until dissolved. Simmer for 5 minutes. Add vanilla and salt. Serve hot. Good over ice cream or cake. Serves 6 to 8.

MRS. GRIMES THOMAS

MINT FRUIT SAUCE

1/2 cup sugar
1/2 cup water
3 tablespoons chopped mint
leaves

Juice of 1 lemon
Juice of 1 orange
Powdered sugar

Boil 1/2-cup sugar for 5 minutes with 1/2-cup water. Pour over 3 tablespoons of mint leaves. Cool, strain. Add juice of a lemon and an orange. Chill. Cut balls of cantaloupe, melon, and honeydew in cocktail glasses. Pour syrup over, and garnish with powdered sugar and sprig of mint.

MRS. GABE HILL

ORANGE SAUCE

1/3 cup sugar
2 tablespoons cornstarch
Pinch of salt
1 cup orange juice

1 tablespoon grated orange rind
1/3 cup light corn syrup
1 tablespoon butter

Mix all ingredients (except butter) together in a saucepan. Cook over low heat until thick and clear—about 15 minutes. Stir while cooking. Remove from heat and stir in butter. Cool and serve. Good over Cherry Sponge Cake, or any cake. Makes enough sauce to spoon over a whole cake.

MRS. BRUCE H. RINEHART

ZUNICE'S ORANGE-WINE SAUCE

1 small can frozen orange juice
Juice of 2 or 3 fresh oranges
Small amount grated orange rind

½ teaspoon prepared mustard
¼ cup red wine
1 jar currant jelly

Combine in a pan. Simmer over low heat until blended. Serve hot with any kind of poultry, particularly wild game.

MRS. NOEL LEE DUNN

SHERRY PARFAIT TOPPING

1 10-ounce jar currant jelly
2 pounds canned crushed
  pineapple, drained
⅓ cup sherry

3 tablespoons butter
2 tablespoons lemon juice
½ cup orange juice
Pinch of salt

Heat until jelly is almost melted; leave small lumps. Cool. Spoon over ice cream for parfaits.

MRS. JOHN ALEXANDER STEWMAN III

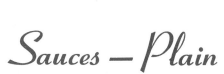

Sauces — Plain

BARBECUE SAUCE (GOOD FOR CHICKEN)

1½ cups tomato juice
2 teaspoons salt
¼ teaspoon black pepper
¼ teaspoon dry mustard
4½ teaspoons Worcestershire

1 bay leaf
1 teaspoon sugar, or more
¾ cup cider vinegar
3 tablespoons butter

Cook ingredients slowly for 10 minutes, adding butter at the end. Pour sauce over meat before cooking.

MRS. WILLIAM F. MEDEARIS, JR.

BARBECUE SAUCE

½ cup catsup
¼ cup water
¼ cup vinegar
¼ cup butter
2 tablespoons brown sugar
2 tablespoons Worcestershire

1 teaspoon Tabasco
1 teaspoon dry mustard
¼ teaspoon black pepper
1½ teaspoons salt
Juice from ¼ lemon
1 onion, diced fine or grated

Heat and stir until boiling. Enough for 2 chickens.

MRS. T. E. HEMBY, JR.

BASTING SAUCE (FOR STEAK OR ROAST)

¾ cup olive oil (or corn oil)
¾ cup dry red wine
1 tablespoon lemon juice
1 clove mashed garlic
⅓ cup finely chopped onion

1 teaspoon oregano
½ teaspoon thyme
1 teaspoon sugar
1 teaspoon salt
Freshly ground pepper

Combine ingredients and let stand at least 1 hour before using. May be kept for several days.

MRS. VERNER STANLEY, JR.

LONDON BROIL STEAK SAUCE

1 garlic clove, sliced (optional)
1 cup oil
½ cup vinegar
1 teaspoon salt

¼ teaspoon black pepper
2 teaspoons dry mustard
2 teaspoons Worcestershire
Dash of Tabasco

Mix well and marinate steak in this for a few hours, after steak has been sprinkled with tenderizer and pierced with a fork. Cook steak on grill about 10 minutes or until desired doneness is obtained.

MRS. R. E. JONES, JR.

MEAT MARINADE

½ cup water
¼ cup lemon juice
¼ cup brown sugar

1 bottle soy sauce
¼ cup bourbon

Mix all the above ingredients. Marinate for 24 hours, turning a few times during the day. Especially good for shoulder roast that can be grilled like steak.

MRS. JAMES S. WILCOX, JR.

TASTY HAM SAUCE

1 jar pineapple preserves
½ jar apple jelly
½ jar Mister Mustard (hot)

½ jar cream horseradish
Worcestershire to taste

Mix all together. Pass as a sauce for ham. Keeps well in refrigerator.

MRS. EDWIN REESE RENCHER, JR.

HOLLANDAISE SAUCE

3 egg yolks
2 tablespoons lemon juice
¼ teaspoon salt

Pinch of pepper
1 stick of butter

Place yolks, juice and seasoning in blender. Cut butter in pieces and heat to foaming hot in saucepan. Put cover on blender and blend egg mixture at top speed for 2 seconds. Uncover (hold towel over top to keep from splattering) and with blender running, start pouring in the hot butter in a *thin stream* of droplets. By the time two-thirds of butter is gone, sauce will be thick. Omit the milky residue at bottom of pan. Blend in more seasoning if desired. If not used immediately, set in tepid (not warm) water. Makes about ¾ cup.

If sauce does not thicken, pour out, and pour back in thin stream at whizzing blender speed. For more sauce: pour sauce out into bowl and beat in additional half-cup melted butter, added in stream of droplets.

MRS. WILLIAM MARCHANT

LEMON BUTTER SAUCE

6 tablespoons butter or
  margarine
½ teaspoon salt

½ teaspoon Tabasco
1 tablespoon lemon juice

Add last 3 ingredients to melted butter and heat a few minutes, then pour over vegetables and serve. Makes about 5 or 6 servings. (This is especially good on French style green beans.)

MRS. THORNWELL G. GUTHERY

MUSTARD SAUCE

¼ pint whipping cream
⅓ cup sugar
2 tablespoons dry English
  mustard

1 egg
1 tablespoon vinegar

Put ingredients in double boiler, in order given. Add vinegar last, stirring vigorously with wire whisk. Great with ham.

MRS. ROBERT LYNN

HOT MUSTARD SAUCE

1 cup dry mustard

1 cup vinegar

Mix, cover, and put aside overnight. The next day add:

1 cup sugar

2 eggs, well beaten

Cook in double boiler until consistency of custard. *Stir constantly over low* heat (about 20 minutes). Permit to cool and refrigerate.

VIRGINIA KILROY

REMOULADE SAUCE FOR BEEF FONDUE

1 cup mayonnaise
¼ cup sour pickles, finely chopped
1 tablespoon capers, drained and chopped

½ to 1 tablespoon mustard
½ to 1 tablespoon parsley
Tarragon to taste

Mix ingredients well and refrigerate before serving. Serves 8.

MRS. WALTER SCOTT

STEAK SAUCE FOR BEEF FONDUE

1 cup sour cream
1 cup chili sauce
1 teaspoon A-1 Sauce

1 teaspoon prepared mustard
½ teaspoon seasoned salt

Combine and mix well all ingredients. Refrigerate at least one hour before using. Serves 8.

MRS. WALTER SCOTT

VINAIGRETTE SAUCE

3 tablespoons melted butter
1 tablespoon tarragon vinegar
2 tablespoons cider vinegar
1 tablespoon chopped parsley

1 tablespoon finely chopped onion
1 teaspoon salt
1 tablespoon sugar
Few grains red pepper

Mix together. (Can be mixed in blender.) Serve hot or cold over asparagus or broccoli. Serves 4.

MRS. THOMAS MASSEY

WHITE SAUCE

	Butter	Flour	Milk	Salt
Thin	1 tablespoon	1 tablespoon	1 cup	¼ teaspoon
Medium	1½-2 tablespoons	2 tablespoons	1 cup	¼ teaspoon
Thick	2-3 tablespoons	3 tablespoons	1 cup	¼ teaspoon
Very Thick	3-4 tablespoons	4 tablespoons	1 cup	¼ teaspoon

Melt butter in saucepan. Add flour and salt and blend until smooth. Gradually add milk, stirring constantly. When comes to a boil, cook 3-5 minutes or until desired thickness.

Variations: Cheese sauce: add ¾ cup American cheese, grated. Stir until melted. Mushroom sauce: Brown ½ cup canned button or sliced mushrooms in the butter before making the sauce.

Preserves and Pickles

FRESH MINT JELLY

1¾ cups mint infusion (made from 1½ cups mint, 2¼ cups water)
2 tablespoons strained lemon juice (1 lemon)

Green food coloring
3½ cups sugar (1½ pounds)
½ bottle Certo fruit pectin
1 box paraffin

First prepare mint infusion: Wash 1½ cups firmly packed mint leaves and stems. Place in large saucepan and crush with masher or glass. Add 2¼ cups water and bring quickly to boil. Remove from heat, cover, and let stand for 10 minutes. Strain. Measure 1¾ cups of the infusion into saucepan. Add lemon juice and a few drops of food coloring. (Don't add too much—just enough for a bright green.)

To the measured juice in a saucepan, add 3½ cups sugar. Mix well. Place over high heat and bring to boil, stirring constantly. At once stir in pectin. Bring to full boil and boil hard for 1 minute, stirring constantly. Remove from heat. Skim off foam with metal spoon and pour quickly into glasses. Have each glass hot and place metal spoon in it so the heat won't break the glass. Cover at once with ⅛-inch hot paraffin. (It takes about 4 squares, melted.) Very easy to make and a nice Christmas gift. Yields about 5 8-ounce jars.

Mrs. Edwin R. Rencher

EMILY DABNEY'S LEMON MARMALADE

3 pounds lemons   3 pounds sugar

1st Day: Slice lemons very thin, pour 4 cups cold water over the sliced lemons, set aside and let stand for one day.

2nd Day: Strain lemons, pour 4 cups of fresh cold water over the lemons, put in pan, bring to a boil, set off stove and let stand for a day.

3rd Day: Use same water the lemons soaked in 2nd day; simmer until tender and strain.

Bring to a boil, 3 pounds sugar in 3 cups of water. When this comes to a boil (or sugar is melted), add lemons and simmer for 50 minutes. Pack in sterilized jars.

Mrs. Douglas Booth

MOTHER'S PEACH PICKLE

1 peck firm peaches
7 pounds sugar
1 pint water

1 pint vinegar
2 dozen whole cloves
Cinnamon sticks to taste

Boil sugar, water, vinegar until rather thick. Add peeled peaches and spices. Boil until peaches can be stuck with a straw. Fill jars with peaches. Boil syrup a little longer. Pour into jars and seal.

MRS. GEORGE IVEY, JR.

PEACH PRESERVES

4 cups peaches, coarsely mashed
5 cups sugar

Paraffin

Peel peaches and quarter, taking out seeds. Combine sugar and peaches in large pan (pressure cooker size). I mash up peaches with my hands. Bring to boil and cook slowly, stirring often. Cook about 30 to 45 minutes until its color turns and begins to jell. Remove from heat. Let stand 5 minutes and skim off foam.

Pour into hot, sterilized jars and cool slightly. Seal, and later freeze or keep in refrigerator. Or melt paraffin and pour over top. Makes 5 or 6 ½-pint jars. If doubling recipe, cook in separate pans. If peaches are very sweet, add equal amounts of peaches and sugar.

MRS. TERRY YOUNG

PEAR PRESERVES

1 pound pears, cored, peeled and
   quartered
¾-1 pound sugar

1 lemon, sliced thin
2 cups water

For one pound of fruit, use 1 pound or ¾ pound sugar. Peel a lemon (leave some white on it) ; slice thin. Use 2 cups of water in kettle or large pot. Put a layer of fruit (with a couple of lemon slices), then a layer of sugar, etc. Do not cover kettle; simmer for 2 hours or until fruit is tender (light caramel or pink color). Do not overcook or preserves will be too hard to chew. Put in sterilized jars and seal.

MRS. ALEX McMILLAN

PEAR CHUTNEY

8 cups diced pears	3 cups sugar
2 cups seeded raisins	1 tablespoon celery seed
½ cup chopped onions	2 tablespoons salt
3 cups vinegar	½ teaspoon cayenne pepper

Cook all this together approximately one hour at medium heat. Stir often. Pour into 3 sterilized pint jars. Seal. (Very good as meat accompaniment or with curry dishes.)

MRS. JOSEPH LINEBERGER

STRAWBERRY PRESERVES

5 cups strawberries	2 tablespoons lemon juice
5 cups sugar	Parrafin

Wash berries. Remove hulls. Place berries in large pan with sugar added. Use one cup of sugar to one cup strawberries for any amount cooked. Mix well. Heat to full rolling boil stirring constantly. Boil for 5 minutes. Remove from heat. Add lemon juice. Pour into a large bowl. Stir frequently, skimming foam from surface. Cover and let stand overnight. Ladle into hot scalded jars. Immediately, cover with thin layer of melted paraffin, then lids and store in freezer. Can freeze them without paraffin if not kept too long.

MRS. TERRY YOUNG

BREAD AND BUTTER PICKLES I

30 cucumbers (1-inch in diameter)	2 teaspoons ground ginger
10 medium-sized onions	4 cups sugar
4 tablespoons salt	1 teaspoon tumeric
5 cups vinegar	2 teaspoons white mustard seed
2 teaspoons celery seed	6 pint jars, sterilized

Slice cucumbers and onions in large bowl and sprinkle with salt. Let stand for 1 hour. Drain in a cheesecloth bag. Make a spiced vinegar (using the next 6 ingredients). Allow to come to a boil, add cucumbers and onions and bring to a boil again. Simmer for 10 minutes. Seal in sterilized jars. Process for 10 minutes at simmering temperature (about 180°). Makes 6 pints.

MRS. VERNER STANLEY

DILL PICKLES

6 pounds cucumbers
1 clove garlic
6 pepper corns
1 clove

4 pinches dillseed
½ gallon vinegar
1 quart water
1 cup salt

Peel and quarter cucumbers. Place cucumbers, garlic, peppercorns, clove and dillseed, evenly divided into five 1-quart jars. Bring to boil: vinegar, water and salt. Pour over cucumbers. Seal and let stand at least 5 days.

MRS. GRIMES THOMAS

PICKLED OKRA

3½ pounds very small okra
1 pint white vinegar
1 quart water
2 teaspoons mustard seed
½ cup salt

3 small hot peppers
10-12 stalks celery with leaves
12 garlic cloves
Fresh dill

Bring brine to a boil. Wash jars and put in one celery stalk, 1 garlic clove and 1 piece fresh dill. Wash okra well and stand upright in jar. Pour brine over and seal. Makes about 10 to 12 half-pint jars.

MRS. FRANK CONNER, JR.

GREEN TOMATO PICKLE

½ peck green tomatoes (thinly sliced)
2 pounds onions (thinly sliced)
5 green peppers (chopped in blender)
8 cloves, whole
⅔ pound brown sugar

¾ ounce celery seed
1 ounce white mustard seed
1 hot red pepper
8 whole allspice
1 cup salt
1 bay leaf
½ gallon vinegar

Put tomatoes, onions and pepper in crock and sprinkle with salt. Let stand overnight. Next morning, drain and cover with cold water for 30 minutes. Drain and pat dry and cover with vinegar. Add sugar, celery seed and mustard seed. Tie pepper pod, allspice, bay leaf, and cloves in cheesecloth and drop in mixture. Cook for 1½ hours, stirring constantly. Remove cheesecloth bag and fill in sterilized jars and seal.

OLD NORTH STATE COOKBOOK

GRANDMOTHER'S TOMATO RELISH

1 dozen large ripe tomatoes
  (skinned)
4 green peppers
6 onions, chopped fine
1 cup sugar
Few white peppercorns
1 teaspoon mustard seed

1 tablespoon cinnamon
1 tablespoon ground ginger
2 tablespoons salt
12 whole cloves
½ teaspoon nutmeg
4 cups vinegar

Boil without lid until reduced to half of original volume. Seal in ½-pint jars while hot. Delicious with string beans.

MRS. GEORGE IVEY, JR.

VEGETABLE RELISH

1 can le Sueur peas
  (approximately 8-ounce can)
1 can shoe peg corn
  (approximately 8-ounce can)
1 can small green beans
  (approximately 8-ounce can)
1 diced red pimento
1 diced green pepper

1 cup finely chopped red onion
1 cup finely chopped celery
1 cup sugar
½ cup oil
1 teaspoon salt
1 teaspoon pepper
¾ cup vinegar

Make a dressing of last 5 ingredients and pour over well-drained vegetables. Chill. Keeps 2 weeks or more in refrigerator. Good with any meat.

MRS. PERRIN Q. HENDERSON

Equivalents and Sizes

WEIGHTS AND MEASURES

Pinch=Less than ¼ teaspoon

1 tablespoon=3 teaspoons (½ ounce)

2 tablespoons=1 ounce (⅛ cup)

1½ ounces (3 tablespoons)=1 jigger

4 tablespoons=¼ cup

5⅓ tablespoons=⅓ cup

8 tablespoons=½ cup

16 tablespoons=1 cup

1 cup=8 ounces (½ pint)

2 cup=1 pint (1 pound)

16 fluid ounces=2 cups (1 pint)

4 cups=1 quart (32 ounces)

2 pints (32 ounces)= 1 quart (2 pounds)

2 quarts=½ gallon

4 quarts=1 gallon (8 pounds)

8 quarts=1 peck (2 gallons)

32 quarts=4 pecks (1 bushel)

CAN SIZES

Can Size	Weight	Cupfuls
6-ounce can	6 ounces	¾ cup
8-ounce can	8 ounces	1 cup
12-ounce can	12 ounces	1½ cups
No. 1 can	11 ounces	1⅓ cups
No. 1½ or 303 can	16 ounces	2 cups
No. 2 can	20 ounces	2½ cups
No. 3 can	33 ounces	4 cups
No. 10 can	106 ounces	13 cups

OVEN TEMPERATURE CHART

Slow Oven	250° to 325°
Moderate Oven	325° to 375°
Hot Oven	400° to 450°
Very Hot Oven	450° to 550°

Equivalents and Sizes

MEAT SERVINGS

1 pound of meat with small amount of bone—serves 3

1 pound of meat with large amount of bone and fat—serves 2

1 pound of boneless meat—serves 4

SUBSTITUTIONS

Baking Powder	1 teaspoon = ¼ teaspoon soda plus ½ teaspoon cream of tartar
Butter	1 cup = ⅞ cup lard, plus salt
Chocolate	1 square = 3 tablespoons cocoa plus 1 teaspoon butter
Cocoa	3 tablespoons = 1 square chocolate, (omit 1 teaspoon butter)
Cornstarch	1 tablespoon = 2 tablespoons flour (for thickening)
Crumbs, Cracker	¾ cup = 1 cup bread crumbs
Flour, All-Purpose, Sifted	1 cup = 1 cup plus 2 tablespoons sifted cake flour
Flour, Cake, Sifted	1 cup = 1 cup minus 2 tablespoons all-purpose flour
Flour, Self-Rising	1 cup all-purpose flour and 1½ teaspoons baking powder
Milk, Fresh	1 cup = ½ cup evaporated milk and ½ cup water
Milk, Fresh	1 cup = 4 tablespoons powdered milk dissolved in 1 cup water
Milk, Sour	1 cup = 1 cup sweet milk plus 1 tablespoon lemon juice or vinegar
Sugar, granulated	1 cup = 1 cup light brown sugar, well-packed
Sugar, granulated	1 cup = 2 cups corn syrup (reduce required liquid)
Sugar, granulated	1 cup = 1½ cups maple syrup (reduce required liquid)

EQUIVALENTS

Beans, green	1 pound	3 cups cut (uncooked)
Beans, dried	1 cup	½ pound
Bread	2 slices	1 cup crumbs
Butter	½ cup (8 tablespoons)	1 stick
Butter, packed solid	2 cups	1 pound
Carrots	7-9 carrots (2 cups cooked)	1 pound
Chocolate	1 square	1 ounce
Chocolate	1 square	3 to 4 tablespoons, grated
Cocoa	4 cups	1 pound
Coffee, ground	5 cups	40-50 servings, 1 pound
Cheese	4-4½ cups	1 pound
Cheese, grated	1 cup	¼ pound
Cheese, cream	3-ounce package	6 tablespoons
Cream, heavy	½ pint	2 cups whipped
Cucumbers	2 6-inch cucumbers	1 pound
Dates, pitted	2 cups	1 pound
Eggs	1	¼ cup
Egg white	1	1½ tablespoons
Egg yolk	1	1 tablespoon
Egg whites	4 to 6	½ cup
Egg yolks	6 to 7	½ cup
Flour, all-purpose, sifted	4 cups	1 pound
Flour, cake flour	4½-5 cups	1 pound
Graham cracker crumbs	11 crackers	1 cup, rolled fine
Lemon	1 juiced	2 to 3 tablespoons
Macaroni	1 cup	2 cups cooked
Meat, cooked and diced	2 cups	1 pound
Meat, crab	2 cups	1 pound
Marshmallows	16	¼ pound
Milk, condensed	1¼ cups	14-ounce can
Milk, evaporated	⅔ cup	6-ounce can
Milk, evaporated	1⅔ cups	14½ ounce can
Noodles	1 cup raw	1½ cups cooked
Nuts, shelled	2 cups coarsely chopped	½ pound
Orange	1 juiced	½ cup or 6 to 8 tablespoons
Peas, in pod	1 pound	1 to 1½ cups shelled or 1 cup cooked
Potatoes, white	1 pound	2 to 5 medium, 2 to 3 cups cooked, mashed
Prunes	1 pound	4 cups cooked
Punch	4 quarts	About 40 punch cups
Raisins, seedless	3 cups	1 pound
Rice, raw	2¼ cups	1 pound
Rice	1 cup	About 3 cups cooked
Saccharin	¼ grain	1 teaspoon sugar
Spinach	1 pound	2 to 2½ quarts raw or 1½ cups cooked
Sucaryl	1 tablet	1 teaspoon sugar
Sugar, granulated	2 cups	1 pound
Sugar, brown (firmly packed)	2¼ cups	1 pound (1 box)
Sugar, confectioners	3 to 3½ cups	1 pound (1 box)
Tea, loose	1 pound	5 cups (about 155 teacup servings)

HANDY KITCHEN METRIC CHART

Measure	Equivalent	Metric (ML)
1 Tbsp.	3 tsp.	14.8 milliliters
2 Tbsp.	1 oz.	29.6 milliliters
1 jigger	1½ oz.	44.4 milliliters
¼ cup	4 Tbsp.	59.2 milliliters
1/3 cup	5 Tbsp. plus 1 tsp.	78.9 milliliters
½ cup	8 Tbsp.	118.4 milliliters
1 cup	16 Tbsp.	236.8 milliliters
1 pint	2 cups	473.6 milliliters
1 quart	4 cups	947.2 milliliters
1 liter	4 cups plus 3½ Tbsp.	1,000.0 milliliters
1 oz. (dry)	2 Tbsp.	28.35 grams
1 pound	16 oz.	453.59 grams
2.21 pounds	35.3 oz.	1.00 kilogram

THE APPROXIMATE CONVERSON FACTORS FOR UNITS OF VOLUME

To Convert from	To	Multiply by
teaspoons (tsp.)	milliliters (ml)	5
tablespoons (Tbsp.)	milliliters (ml)	15
fluid ounces (fl. oz.)	milliliters (ml)	30
cups (c)	liters (l)	0.24
pints (pt)	liters (l)	0.47
quarts (qt)	liters (l)	0.95
gallons (gal)	liters (l)	3.8
cubic feet (ft^3)	cubic meters (m^3)	0.03
cubic yards (yd^3)	cubic meters (m^3)	0.76
milliliters (ml)	fluid ounces (fl oz)	0.03
liters (l)	pints (pt)	2.1
liters (l)	quarts (qt)	1.06
liters (l)	gallons (gal)	0.26
cubic meters (m^3)	cubic feet (ft^3)	35
cubic meters (m^3)	cubic yards (yd^3)	1.3

The Original Cookbook Committee

Mrs. Terry Young—Chairman

Mrs. Walter Summerville, Jr.
Mrs. James H. Glenn, Jr.
Mrs. Joseph K. Hall, III
Mrs. George Ivey, Jr.
Mrs. Erwin Jones
Mrs. Walter Scott, III
Mrs. Moffatt G. Sherard
Mrs. Verner E. Stanley, Jr.

Mrs. Alston Ramsay—Illustrations

Chairmen
Mrs. Joseph K. Hall, III, 1969
Mrs. John L Dabbs, III, 1970
Mrs. Harriman H. Jett, 1971
Mrs. Forrest L. Collier, III, 1972
Mrs. Meredith D. Stoever, 1973
Mrs. Henry L. Smith, II, 1974
Mrs. Allen H. Harris, Jr., 1975
Mrs. Albert L. McAulay, 1976
Mrs. David L. Anderson, III, 1977
Mrs. William B. Brown, Jr. 1978
Mrs. C. Mitchell Andrews, 1979
Mrs. Raymond J. Grodzicki, 1980
Mrs. John J. Davis, 1981
Mrs. Joseph G. Wheeler, 1982
Mrs. Kenneth P. Andresen, 1983
Mrs. Theodore M. DuBose, IV 1984
Mrs. Charles H. Conner, Jr., 1985
Mrs. Graham D. Holding, Jr., 1986
Mrs. William H. Boyd, 1987

30th Anniversary Chairmen
Mary Mac G. Yon, 1998
Leslie S. Graham, 1999

Index

INDEX

INDEX

PICKLES AND PRESERVES

PIES

PORK

SALADS

CONGEALED FRUIT SALADS

FRESH FRUIT SALADS

INDEX

VEAL

VEGETABLES

The Junior League of Charlotte
now has three cookbooks available!

Please contact your favorite bookstore
or the JLC cookbook office for your copy of

Charlotte Cooks Again (1981)

Dining By Fireflies:
Unexpected Pleasures Of The New South (1994)

or

The Charlotte Cookbook (1969)
30th Anniversary Edition (1999)

The Junior League of Charlotte, Inc.
Cookbook Office
1332 Maryland Avenue
Charlotte, North Carolina 28209
704-375-DINE (3463)
800-403-DINE (3463)
fax: 704-375-9730

Visit us on the web @ www.jlcharlotte.org and order
your copy online. Visa, Mastercard accepted.

Notes

Favorite Recipes

Notes

Favorite Recipes

_____

_____

_____

_____

_____

_____

_____

_____

_____

_____

_____

_____

_____

_____

_____

_____

_____

_____

_____

_____

_____

_____

_____

Notes

Favorite Recipes

Notes

Favorite Recipes

Notes

Favorite Recipes